THE CHOSEN ONES

THE

To Laurance
a notable risk-taker
yourself

CHOSEN ONES

SEAN ROSSITER

foreword by RICHARD P. BENTHAM

Sean Rossiter

5 Dec 03

DOUGLAS & MCINTYRE
VANCOUVER/TORONTO/NEW YORK

Douglas & McIntyre
2323 Quebec Street, Suite 201
Vancouver, British Columbia
Canada V5T 4S7
www.douglas-mcintyre.com

National Library of Canada Cataloguing in Publication Data
Rossiter, Sean, 1946–
    The chosen ones

    ISBN 1-55054-930-8 (cloth)
    ISBN 1-55054-993-6 (paper)

    1. Test pilots—Canada—Biography. I. Title.
TL539.R67 2002   629.134′53′0922   C2002-910209-X

Editing by Barbara Pulling
Copy-editing by Robin Van Heck
Cover and text design by Peter Cocking
Cover photographs: Front: Avro Canada's flight test section, mid-1950s.
    Left to right: Chris Pike, Jan Zurakowski, Peter Cope, Stan Haswell, Glen
    Lynes, Mike Cooper-Slipper, Don Rogers. *Avro Canada/courtesy Peter Cope*
    Back: Mike Cooper-Slipper in high-altitude pressure suit climbs into
    CF-100, 1951. *Avro Canada/courtesy Chris Cooper-Slipper*
Typesetting by Rhonda Ganz & Peter Cocking
Printed and bound in Canada by Friesens
Printed on acid-free paper ∞
Distributed in the U.S. by Publishers Group West

Every reasonable care has been taken to trace the ownership of copyrighted
visual material. Information that will enable the publisher to rectify any
reference or credit is welcome.

The publisher gratefully acknowledges the financial support
of the Canada Council for the Arts, the British Columbia Arts Council, and the
Government of Canada through the Book Publishing Industry Development
Program (BPIDP) for our publishing activities.

▼ ▼ ▼

This book is dedicated to the memory of JOHN HIEBERT, flight test observer, killed in the crash of Avro Canada CF-100 prototype 18112, August 23, 1954, at Ajax, Ontario; and of BILL FERDERBER, test pilot, killed in the crash of U.S. Army DHC-3 Otter 53252, February 14, 1956, at Downsview, Ontario.

CONTENTS

FOREWORD

RICHARD P. BENTHAM

IT IS A GREAT PLEASURE to write this foreword to Sean Rossiter's *The Chosen Ones: Test Pilots in Action.* I have known Rossiter personally only a few years but in that time have come to see him not only as a talented writer but also as an insightful and clear-thinking person. This account of Canada's test pilots is in good hands.

The world of test pilots in Canada is, and always has been, a small one—the players are mostly known to one another. Their achievements, however, are large, and, sadly, as elsewhere in the test-pilot world, more than a few have lost their lives. This book tells some of their stories.

There is a sort of hierarchy in the world of test pilots. This hierarchy is not so much about risk and flying ability (these are givens), but more about knowledge, understanding, recognition, and being first.

At the top of the hierarchy is the experimental test pilot, and at the top of that is the holy grail of most test pilots, the first flight of a new aircraft type.

Making the first flight of a new aircraft is the territory of the manufacturer's experimental test pilot. Like being the first on the moon, or the first on Mount Everest, there is a certain test-pilot fulfillment

1

in being the first to take into the air what was in the beginning only a new concept in a designer's mind. There is also recognition when a manufacturer bets the farm, so to speak, that its chosen test pilot will make that first flight safely and deal competently with whatever unforeseen problems may arise. The test pilot chosen for the job is the best. Period.

Given the size of the Canadian aircraft industry over the years, the opportunities for a first flight have been limited. Bob Fowler (the great communicator, the best all-round test pilot I have flown with), Doug Adkins (the best stick and rudder man), Bill Waterton (the most courageous), George Neal and Bill Longhurst are some first-flight pilots I have known personally and admired as indeed being the best.

After the first flight comes the ongoing experimental work of development flight testing, as the aircraft is tested and/or modified to show compliance with civil airworthiness standards or military specifications (milspecs). The experimental test pilots on major programs of development of new aircraft types and major modifications are almost invariably employees of the manufacturers. In Canada, these experimental test pilots are rarely graduates of test-pilot schools. (Jan Zurakowski is the only test-pilot school graduate I know of to do a first flight in Canada—the CF-105.) Rather, they are outstanding pilots well experienced in several kinds of operational flying and have served a demanding apprenticeship flying with the manufacturer.

After the experimental test pilots come military and civil airworthiness test pilots—mostly, but not always, employed by the government. These are almost always graduates of test-pilot schools. They mostly flight test aircraft to determine their compliance with milspecs or civil airworthiness standards. The work is unheralded but can be very challenging and deeply satisfying when done well. Occasionally, these test pilots may do experimental flight testing on certain modifications, or climatic or icing testing. The few private-consultant test pilots in Canada, in determining compliance with standards, regularly carry out experimental flight testing.

Knowledge and understanding of the civil airworthiness standards or milspecs are absolutely essential for all of the above test pilots—manufacturers', military, and civil. Such knowledge and understanding could easily require a postgraduate university engineering course. These test pilots work with these standards on a daily basis and gain a useful familiarity with them only after many years of being in the business.

Last in the test-pilot pecking order comes production flight testing, which involves the first flight of a new aircraft right off the production line. This kind of flight testing is both important and risky, and there is no denying the skill and ability needed to do it well. It is just that production flight testing would be the last choice of most test pilots given the opportunity to choose their line of work.

Finally, the field of research flight testing must be mentioned in any discussion of the world of test pilots. The research business engages a few select test pilots who stand somewhere to the side of this hierarchy—almost in a different world. Led by test pilots with very high academic qualifications, this group is employed mostly by such government organizations as the National Research Council of Canada or the Ames Aeronautical Laboratory of the National Aeronautics and Space Administration in the USA, and they pursue pure research as an esoteric calling. To be sure, ad hoc research flight testing has also been conducted in Canada by both de Havilland and Canadair test pilots on such programs as the PT6-powered STOL Otter at DHC and Canadair's CL-84 tilt-wing Vertical Takeoff and Landing aircraft.

I know of no Canadian test pilot who has been killed doing a first flight, but many have lost their lives in the unrecognized (except in the trade) ongoing flight testing or training. For example, from 1962 to 1965, while I was flying with the Royal Canadian Air Force Central Experimental and Proving Establishment, eight pilots lost their lives.

It behooves any book about test pilots to mention the relationship between the flying side and the technical side of the house. At times, test pilots and (design) engineers have been compared to two scorpions in a bottle. The engineers sometimes look down their noses at the technical and engineering deficiencies of some test pilots, and some test pilots are scornful of the serious lack of practicality exhibited by some engineers. Emotions have been known to run high—to say the least. However, these "Punch and Judy" relationships do not run very deep. Underneath the dustups, there is a profound respect on both sides.

I, for one, owe my life to a technician, Brian Usher, at the Flight Research section of the NRC. Far wiser than I in the business of practicality, he persuaded me to let him install a quick disconnect on a Rube Goldberg device secured to the control wheel of a Found FBA-2C (similar to the Cessna 180). The device, a piece of hardware with large pins and slots, was intended to help me apply step inputs of aileron. I was in a hurry (not a good idea in flight testing) and resented the delay necessary to incorporate the quick disconnect. But I agreed—and that is why I am still here today. On one test flight, low over Quebec's Gatineau Hills, the control wheel locked up with full aileron. I found myself pointed at Mother Earth with all of the flight controls against the stops in an uncontrolled, rapidly rotating form of flight. Just in time, I managed to find Usher's quick disconnect pin and somehow recovered before hitting the ground. A Kodak moment like that makes a lasting impression, and ever after I listened very carefully to any thoughts coming from the technical side of the house. Any experienced test pilot has respect, if not affection, for the engineers.

A book about Canada's test pilots can hope to capture only something of a world which might be described as unspoken and perhaps unknowable. On the dust jacket of James Salter's novel *Cassada*, the world of fighter pilots is described as "a strange camaraderie of loneliness, trust, and alienation." The world of test pilots is not too far from that.

➤ ACKNOWLEDGEMENTS

EVERY NONFICTION BOOK project has godparents, people who take an interest from the beginning and go out of their way to be helpful throughout. The first of these on *The Chosen Ones* was Bob Fowler, "the great communicator," as his colleague Richard P. Bentham calls him, who one day in 1998 produced, from memory, a complete list of Avro, de Havilland, Canadair, and government test pilots, as well as the names of a number of Canadians who have worked as test pilots in the United States. Fowler is one of Canada's pre-eminent test pilots, with the most first flights of new Canadian aircraft prototypes. This book includes half of the 20 test pilots Fowler named: the experimental test pilots at Avro and de Havilland.

This book's other godparent is Richard Bentham, a one-time 409 Squadron CF-100 pilot, Empire Test Pilots' School graduate, government certification and National Research Council test pilot, and aviation historian, who kindly read the manuscript, gave this book its title, wrote its foreword, and was a passionate advocate for Bill Waterton's inclusion in the book. Every book project should lead its author to a Bentham's doorstep.

Thanks, of course, to the test pilots themselves. Seeing yourself through another pair of eyes can be a profound disappointment, one these extraordinary individuals seem to have taken in stride. All but one of the airmen profiled in *The Chosen Ones* hosted me, patiently answered my questions, and provided photographs. The exception was Waterton, who, for his own good reasons, declined to be interviewed but was nevertheless a gracious host during my surprise visit.

Special thanks to Jan and Anna Zurakowski, for documenting Jan's singular career and for the impressions of Spud Potocki (translated from the original Polish). I met the Zurakowskis at Kartuzy Lodge, their resort near Barrys Bay, Ontario. Peter Cope supplied insight into Zurakowski's years in Britain and Zura's invention of the Zurabatic Cartwheel aerial manoeuvre. Chris Cooper-Slipper provided memoirs, timelines, and many photos of his father, Mike. Production test pilots Stan Haswell and the late Chris Pike provided insight into the experimental test pilots they worked with at Avro, as did Mario Pesando's successor as Avro chief flight test engineer, Hugh Young. Don Rogers, who put together Avro's flight test section, was generous with praise for everyone who worked there.

George Neal of de Havilland made two significant contributions. First, he repeated the story of third Caribou prototype CF-LKI's last flight, a rueful task, after my tape recorder failed during the first telling. And it was Neal who insisted on the inclusion of such Canadian flight test pioneers as Leigh Capreol, de Havilland Canada's first test pilot, and Ralph Spradbrow, DHC's wartime Chief Test Pilot (CTP). My brief portraits of them and of the 1928–45 activities of DHC are stitched together from published material and first-hand memories generously provided by Blanche Warren, wife of the late Frank Warren, DHC's first Canadian employee and wartime Mosquito flight test director. I've interviewed Neal and Russ Bannock at least five times apiece, and they keep correcting the same mistakes. They deserve medals.

Anyone who writes about Canada's premier designers and manufacturers of original aircraft, Avro and de Havilland Canada, owes ongoing debts to Greig Stewart, whose award-winning *Shutting down the National Dream* is the definitive account of A.V. Roe Canada's wartime and postwar activities, and to Fred Hotson, whose pair of books on DHC, most recently *De Havilland in Canada,* are milestones among histories of aircraft manufacturers. Larry Milberry, a national treasure, wrote several of the works I relied upon for accurate information, most notably his excellent *The Avro CF-100*. I want also to salute the authors of *Aces High,* whose idea of introducing each WW2 Commonwealth ace with a terse c.v. I borrowed to save words for the narratives of these test pilots' exploits.

Jerry Vernon, president, Vancouver chapter, Canadian Aviation Historical Society, supplied articles from his own files and contacted sources in Britain, notably Michael Oakey, editor of *Aeroplane* magazine, for material I needed on Jimmy Orrell. The CAHS national office rushed back copies of the *Journal* to me. Ted Barris kindly allowed me to use his account of Russ Bannock and Bob Bruce's mission to Bourges Avord from *Behind the Glory*. Bob Bator, a longtime modifier of DH bush planes who retired himself right back into Harbour Air's hangar, gave me his Twin Otter float seminar. Special thanks to Wally Warner, Carlo Marcetti, Bill Hindson, Ab Warren, Hugh Young, and Al MacNutt, the gang at Katz's; Don Stewart; John, Joyce, and Dave Tarvin; and, always, the late Dick Hiscocks. To all of those who helped whose names do not appear here, an extra measure of gratitude.

Most of the subjects of this book live in Toronto, about 2,000 miles uphill from where I live. I want to gratefully acknowledge the hearty hospitality in that neck of the woods from the Hon. J. F. Casey, Suzie Cohen, and family; and from Stephen Bock and Franda Wargo and family.

Publisher Scott McIntyre stuck with this project when it seemed to both of us it might never end. As he did with my books on the Beaver and Otter airplanes, Peter Cocking became an airplane nut himself to design this one. The first advocate for this project at the idea stage, the one who confirmed that its raw manuscript could be made publishable and who painstakingly edited the rewritten manuscript herself, is Barbara Pulling, a recent Canadian book editor of the year. Every writer should be so lucky.

My hero, Bill Gunston, who is well represented in this book's bibliography, once said you publish books only to be told what you left out. For everything I have omitted, let me be all the more thankful to be informed.

SEAN ROSSITER

➤ INTRODUCTION

THE CHOSEN ONES is a book of test pilots' war stories, told, as much as possible, in their own words. All of the experimental test pilots profiled in these pages worked for Avro Canada or de Havilland Canada. All but two were interviewed, some several times. (The two who were unavailable, Bill Waterton and the late Jimmy Orrell, left memoirs of their time at Avro.) My idea was to present the "war stories" of both wartime and peacetime. The surprise for me was that, for the most part, the peacetime exploits are more riveting. That is partly because many of these pilots' adventures in combat have been written about before, whereas their flight test crises became, at most, company lore. Many flight test misfortunes also became military secrets.

When things went wrong for an experimental test pilot, the events became cases for the engineering department to consider. When an elevator fluttered off the third prototype DHC Caribou battlefield transport and test pilots George Neal and Walter Gadzos bailed out, the trail of parts leading to the crash site became evidence in an investigation. When Avro flight test observer Geoff Grossmith took off in an early CF-100 interceptor to find out why an ejection from the aircraft's back seat—the observer's seat—was a near death sentence, he was showing a degree of courage that won him respect from his colleagues but went unnoticed elsewhere.

You could call the Avro and de Havilland test pilots forgotten Canadian heroes. At least, they would be forgotten if they had ever been truly famous. Of their number, only the Polish-born Jan Zurakowski ever had much of a public profile in Canada. That was during the late 1950s, in the surge of national pride that accompanied the flight test program of the Avro Arrow, of which Zurakowski did the first and subsequent early flights. But Zurakowski will always be much better known in Britain, where his contributions during times of war and peace continue to be celebrated.

The code of their generation—"the Greatest Generation"—was to get on with the job at hand and keep quiet about it. They survived the Depression, they beat Hitler, and some of them fought in a Cold War that lasted another 45 years. Ah, but I'm already embarrassing them. These were the guys who didn't tell war stories. Asked why he denies being a fighter ace when an authoritative study ranks him as one, Zurakowski told me he often attacked his adversaries head on because that was the most effective tactic. Moments later you and your adversary were miles apart, Zurakowski summed up. Who could tell what had happened?

On the other hand, what happened was all too clear the time Mike Cooper-Slipper rammed a Dornier bomber on the day of heaviest fighting during the Battle of Britain. He added both the Do 17 and his Hurricane to the British and German loss totals. One bomber for one fighter: a good trade, and a bargain when he survived to fight another day.

Russ Bannock and his navigators flew deep into the Third Reich by night in their Mosquito fighter-bombers to attack returning German night-fighters. Once, after losing an engine to debris from an aircraft he shot down 600 miles east along the Baltic Sea, Bannock and his navigator returned, crippled and visible by the morning's light, the same distance through German-held territory.

Many of the future Avro and de Havilland test pilots were so talented that upon graduation from wartime wings school they were immediately assigned to become flying instructors. As Royal Air Force Wing Commander Jack Meadows gracefully put it once on behalf of those who postponed their hopes to fly in combat on being assigned to instruct, "I trained others to do my fighting for me." Russ Bannock was one of those instructors; he didn't get into action until mid-1944. George Neal's bit for the war effort was unusually versatile. He ended up in New Brunswick flying and maintaining Anson navigation trainers he had assembled at DHC's plant at Downsview earlier in the war. Bill Waterton had 600 students pass through his organization in about two years; he was decorated for his staggering workload, for teaching more than he was asked to.

But the peacetime stories of these pilots are even better. Jan Zurakowski was immortalized when he invented a new aerial manoeuvre, the Zurabatic Cartwheel. The Cartwheel made him better known than flying the Arrow at Mach 1.86, seven years later, would.

Peter Cope, a wartime RAF photo-reconaissance pilot in Mustangs, had also become an armament test pilot during the war. He nearly came to grief when a rocket bounced out of its watery target and struck his Mosquito's wing. Yet three times during his postwar testing of the Avro Canada CF-100's armament systems, explosive devices exploded in the wrong way. Cope almost shot himself down four times.

Bill Waterton's reward for zeal in his instructional duties came after the war: he got to try for the world's absolute speed record in a Gloster Meteor that wouldn't fly straight. He still beat the existing record.

Mike Cooper-Slipper got one of the choicest assignments of all. He was asked to fly an already twitchy Boeing B-47 jet bomber with a huge prototype Orenda Iroquois engine hung on the right side, under the tail. The Iroquois, two of which were to power each Arrow, was so heavy the engineers put four tons of ballast in the nose. But nothing could prevent the B-47 from trying to turn right with the Iroquois shut down or turn left with it lit. One afternoon the Iroquois blew up. It was the first time Cooper-Slipper and his crew had run it at full throttle.

George Neal did the first flights of the single-engine DHC Otter and twin-engine Caribou, qualifying him for the top rung of the flight test ladder: taking an unproven, hand-built prototype into the air for the first time, to see if it flies. But he really showed what kind of test pilot he was just before he bailed out of the third Caribou prototype. Everything in the cockpit was in its place, each item just so, his ball cap tucked into the seat, before he jumped. He was organizing the evidence.

Bob Fowler, a wartime B-25 pilot, joined Neal on a hazardous flight test program that duplicated what had happened in two fatal Otter crashes. Fowler had the propellers of two prototype turbine engines reverse *in the air.* But he will be remembered best for making the first flights of the Turbo Beaver, the Buffalo, the Twin Otter, and the Dash-7 and Dash-8 regional airliners. The first flight of a new type of aircraft is test pilot's heaven. Fowler went there five times.

And Bannock, the long-distance flier, would end up running de Havilland Canada at a critical time in the company's history, the mid-1970s, as DHC stood at the threshold of the regional airliner market. Hired in 1946 as DHC's chief test pilot, Bannock rose to vice-president for sales partly by pioneering a new kind of demonstration in which a DHC aircraft was landed and took off from some impossible place, such as a trout stream in Alaska, a Hudson River dock in New York City, or a parade square near the Pentagon. It always looked like a daredevil stunt. But it was, in fact, a carefully calculated daredevil stunt.

A handful of highly regarded pilots from the Avro and de Havilland flight test staffs have been left out of this book because they were not available to tell their stories. They include Wladyslaw (Spud) Potocki, Jack Fraser Woodman, David Charles Fairbanks, and A. M. (Mick) Saunders.

Spud Potocki (pronounced Po-TOT-ski) was a six-victory Polish RAF ace of WW2 with a personality that could fill the officer's mess. He placed second in his Empire Test Pilots' School No. 10 course and flight tested the Avro Vulcan nuclear bomber before joining Avro Canada at Hawker-Siddeley chairman Sir Roy Dobson's insistence. Potocki flew the CF-105 Arrow more times than anyone else, 33, and faster than anyone else — within a whisker of Mach 2 — at three-quarters throttle. He succeeded Jan Zurakowski as Avro's chief experimental test pilot. With the Arrow cancellation, he joined North American Rockwell, Columbus, Ohio, where he died in 1996.

Jack Woodman, the model for the genial RCAF flight lieutenant in the Canadian Broadcasting Corporation's docudrama *The Arrow,* was the only Canadian-born test pilot to fly the Arrow. An air gunner during WW2, Woodman studied engineering, became a pilot, graduated from the 1952 ETPS No. 11 Course, and became RCAF acceptance pilot at de Havilland. His demonstration of the CF-100 at the 1955 Paris Air Show, which included a spin, led to his appointment as the air force's test pilot on the Arrow, which he flew six times. After the Arrow cancellation, Woodman joined Lockheed in California, where he flew the NF-104A Aerospace Trainer above 118,000 feet, a record for jets. He became Lockheed's chief engineering test pilot in 1968, in charge of flight operations on the F-104 Starfighter, P-3 Orion, and L-1011 airliner projects. He died May 16, 1987, in Palmdale, California.

Dave Fairbanks impressed DHC's Russ Bannock when he showed up at Downsview with a logbook showing 15 victories (including an Arado jet bomber) flying Hawker Tempests, the most of any Tempest pilot—an impressive total in any fighter, but singular with a machine intended for ground attack. Bannock's eyebrows popped when he saw that Fairbanks had *two* bars to his Distinguished Flying Cross. An American, Fairbanks joined the RCAF in 1941 and stayed after the U.S. declared war. He was in the right-hand seat on the Caribou's first flight, but he may have done more for its sales on two global demonstration tours, in 1960–61 and 1964. As a test and demonstration pilot, Bannock considered Fairbanks in a class with Fowler and Neal. He died on the DHC flight line February 20, 1975.

Mick Saunders was a WW2 Typhoon pilot and a postwar Vampire jet pilot in the same Montreal RCAF reserve squadron Fairbanks served with. He was Fowler's favourite co-pilot, netting him the right-hand seat on four DHC first flights: Buffalo, Twin Otter, Dash-7, and Dash-8. Saunders was DHC's director of flight operations from 1983 to 1988. He was killed in the crash of an overhauled Dash-7 in Britain September 3, 1998.

THESE TEST PILOTS, the chosen ones, flew the original aircraft designs produced by Avro and de Havilland during the golden age of flight test in Canada. It was a time when, initially with British support, Canadians built aircraft uniquely suited to the climate, topography, and vastness of their country. Testing them was a special calling. Many of those aircraft sold worldwide, often as a result of dazzling demonstrations by their test pilots, the men who knew them best. Theirs was a brief but intense heyday. Many of their tales appear here for the first time.

A.V. ROE

PART ONE

CANADA

➤ **DON ROGERS:**

JET-AGE PIONEER

CHRONOLOGY: Donald Howard Rogers, b. Hamilton, Ontario, November 26, 1916. Learned to fly Tiger Moths at the Hamilton Aero Club, earning Pilot's Licence 1936 (Commercial Licence 1938, Instructor's Rating 1939). Royal Canadian Air Force instructor course, Camp Borden, September 1939. Instructed RCAF inductees and civilian students at Hamilton Aero Club to October 1940. Assistant chief flying instructor, No. 10 Elementary Flying Training School, Mount Hope, Ontario, to December 1941.

January 1942, transferred to aircraft division of National Steel Car Co. at Malton Airport (today, Toronto International). NSC part of three-company consortium, Federal Aircraft, licence-building Westland Lysanders and Avro Ansons, which Rogers flight tested to April 1943. NSC Malton taken over by the Canadian government, renamed Victory Aircraft, November 5, 1942.

During tooling-up for Avro Lancaster production (April–August 1943), Rogers joined Royal Air Force Ferry Command flight test unit at Dorval, Quebec, tested Lockheed Hudson and Ventura maritime patrol bombers, B-24 Liberator and B-25 Mitchell bombers; delivered a Hudson and B-24 to Britain; spent five days at the A.V. Roe [Avro U.K.] Woodford airfield familiarizing himself with the Lancaster. First Canadian-built Lancaster B.Mk.x

[RAF serial KB700] rolled out at Victory Aircraft August 6, 1943. Rogers did production flight testing on Lancasters to September 1945.

That December Victory Aircraft became Avro Canada Ltd. Rogers became chief test pilot (CTP), flying overhauled and modified Venturas, Mitchells, Douglas Dakotas, and Lancasters for the RCAF, and Hawker Sea Fury carrier fighters for the Royal Canadian Navy.

Avro Canada, strengthened by James C. Floyd from Avro U.K., took up design of 30-seat c.102 jet airliner and CF-100 twin-jet two-seat interceptor. Four years from founding, company had designed and prototyped both aircraft, plus Orenda engine to power CF-100. Rogers was co-pilot to Avro U.K. test pilot Jimmy Orrell (and flight engineer Bill Baker) on Avro Jetliner first flight August 10, 1949. Following November 22, Rogers took Jetliner past 500 mph with Mike Cooper-Slipper as co-pilot, Baker as engineer, and Jim Floyd and Mario Pesando as observers. April 18, 1950, Jetliner flew the first jet airmail, Toronto to New York, Rogers at controls. Flew 440 hours in Jetliner, most of its flight and development testing, until program halted during the Korean War. Orenda jet for the CF-100 first flown July 13, 1950, when two Orendas replaced Lancaster FM209's outboard Merlins (Rogers pilot; Bill Wildfong, Walter Bellian flight engineers). Piloted first flight of the CF-100 Mk.2, 18103 (third prototype and first CF-100 with Orenda powerplants), October 5, 1950. Rogers flew hundreds of hours in each CF-100 variant, including dangerous tests proving the CF-100's anti-icing systems.

In 1958 Rogers was named flight operations manager for Avro as the supersonic CF-105 Arrow project approached first flight. With Arrow cancellation and Avro shutdown 1959, Rogers joined de Havilland of Canada; became test, demonstration, and training pilot on all of DHC's Short Takeoff and Landing (STOL) types. A partial list of places in which he showed what DHC's STOL aircraft could do: Central and South America (Turbo Beaver); Alaska (Caribou); Brazil and Argentina (Buffalo); Morocco–Middle East–India, England-Scandinavia-Greenland-Iceland (Twin Otter). He delivered aircraft to Togo, Chile, Panama, Switzerland, and Nepal, often training the pilots.

Retired from DHC flight operations in 1980 at 63, continuing part-time training of customers' aircrews for seven years, finishing with 12,000 hours on 30 types. Won Canada's foremost aviation award, 1983 Trans-Canada (McKee) Trophy; inducted into Canada's Aviation Hall of Fame 1998.

THERE'S A PHOTOGRAPH in Jim Floyd's book *The Avro Jetliner* that says much about the immediate postwar flight test brotherhood in Canada. Taken in mid-afternoon on a hot, windy August 10, 1949, the photo shows Don Rogers and his two fellow crew members looking relieved and happy, celebrating beside the nose of the Avro Jetliner prototype, the one-hour first flight of which they had completed only minutes before. The Jetliner was the first North American jet-powered airliner ever to fly—and, by two weeks, the second to fly in the world. Now almost forgotten, the Jetliner was one of Canada's great aviation achievements.

The man in the middle is Jimmy Orrell, the veteran test pilot brought in from Avro Canada's English parent company to be captain of the Jetliner's early test flights. No Canadian was considered qualified to fill the pilot's seat, but Orrell was a diplomat; in writing later about the Jetliner's early flights, he emphasized how carefully his Canadian colleagues had monitored the prototype's construction for months before he arrived. In the photo, as if to say the same thing visually, Orrell improvises a one-for-all, all-for-one gesture, his arms crossed so he can shake hands with the men on either side of him: Rogers, the first-flight co-pilot, and flight engineer Bill Baker. From the looks of things, the flight had not been the "piece of cake" Orrell called it back on the ground.

As was the custom, the men had boarded the Jetliner wearing crisp white coveralls and neckties, but they are pictured after the flight in perspiration-soaked, open-collared, creased white shirts. Orrell and Baker have fresh cigarettes clenched between their lips, ready for a celebratory light. The grins on their faces show the joy the men felt in climbing down from the cockpit of what was not just a new aircraft design but a new kind of airplane. The biggest smile of the three belongs to Don Rogers.

Already Avro Canada's chief test pilot (CTP), Rogers was not the most likely candidate to preside over the achievement of more speed and altitude milestones than any other Canadian. He did not have as many flying hours as some others. He hadn't flown as many aircraft types. He had no wartime operational combat experience—the kind of experience that teaches a pilot where an aircraft's real limits are.

And, until that August afternoon, he had never flown a prototype. Unproven prototypes, or research aircraft, are licensed to fly only as experimental aircraft and so are designated with an x appended to their registrations. The test pilots who fly them are an elite within an elite. When Rogers landed in the Jetliner, even though he was in the right-hand seat, he had taken a big step toward becoming an experimental test pilot.

AT A TIME WHEN major newspapers had full-time aviation reporters to note such things, Don Rogers looked the test-pilot part. He was 33 years old in 1949—just old enough to have a decently thick logbook— with penetrating eyes framed by the beginnings of crowsfeet. Those eyes were set off by a neat little Clark Gable moustache, dark, shiny hair that showed care in grooming, and a big, toothy grin.

But Rogers was a test pilot in more than appearance. He behaved strictly in accord with the flight test code. Even today, his voice is steady and even, still the reliable flight instrument it was in those pre-telemetry days when it was the only link between the air and the ground. For the engineers huddled around a radio receiver below, the co-pilot's voice conveyed everything they would know about the flight until the photos of the instrument panel readings were developed.

Rogers also understood that a good test pilot was not only a fully competent flyer but a person driven by a quietly efficient, scientific mind, a dedicated team player with no competing loyalties and a willingness to make whatever personal sacrifices the program called for. Ego was checked in the locker room. No silk-scarf types here.

Rogers had another quality rare among test pilots. "Maybe I'm too easy-going," Rogers would tell this author nearly 50 years later, "but I didn't have any trouble getting along with anyone I've flown or worked with." This was no mean feat. Rogers spent the better part of six months with Howard Hughes at the Hughes base at Culver City, California, trying to sell the Jetliner to Hughes' Trans World Airlines. He even talked the legendary recluse into posing for some snapshots with him in 1952. And he had the essential Canadian quality of being able to fit in with his British or American colleagues. Rogers' easy diplomacy made him the right man in the right place at the right time.

In January 1942, Don Rogers had the singular good fortune to be assigned as part of the war effort to, of all possibilities, a railway-car building concern. National Steel Car's plant at Malton, Ontario, which had started in aviation by building simple Avro Anson fabric-on-wood twin-engine trainers, was taken over by the federal government and renamed Victory Aircraft. The plant assembled 431 four-engine Avro Lancasters, the outstanding bombers of the European war, and Rogers tested them as they came off the line. Impressed by the Malton plant's craftsmanship, Avro bought it after the war. Rogers toiled in the Inspection Department for six months while Avro Canada looked for overhaul work to make ends meet as it designed its postwar jets.

By the end of the 1940s, Avro Canada had designed and built prototypes of the Jetliner and the CF-100, a jet fighter-interceptor optimized for Canadian conditions with a unique combination of near-transcontinental range, twin-engine reliability, working cockpit heaters, state-of-the-art vacuum-tube radar, and heavy armament; it was intended to seek, find, and shoot down the hordes of Russian bombers expected at any moment to blacken the sky over the polar ice cap. The CF-100 was powered by a pair of engines developed and built by an Avro subsidiary, Orenda Engines.

Not long afterward, Avro would be doing preliminary design of the CF-105 Arrow, a fly-by-wire Mach 1.5 fighter painted white to dissipate the frictional heat it generated on the far side of the sound barrier. The Arrow went supersonic going uphill, it could fly itself, and it could track several targets and neutralize them one by one, dictating the terms of engagement from high within the tropopause at the edge of space. The CF-105 was also powered by an Orenda engine, among the most powerful turbojets then being developed in the West.

As unlikely an orchestrator as Don Rogers seemed for a flight test department capable of evaluating and developing such sophisticated hardware, he was aware of his limitations, and he prevailed partly because of that. His strengths were many. He was a quick study; he had great hands as a pilot himself; and he had what it took to assess the flying skills of others. He put together a first-class department, one that got better as the work became more demanding. There were very few combined engine-airframe manufacturers left after the Second World War. Of those, the companies working simultaneously on fighter and airliner prototypes were even fewer in number. Avro Canada was a magnet for wartime pilots who wanted to keep flying.

Rogers' first hire for his flight test section was 26-year-old RAF Squadron Leader Mike Cooper-Slipper, who had arrived in Toronto in November 1947 with letters of recommendation addressed to high-ranking executives at both Avro and de Havilland. There was no flying work available, even for a Battle of Britain ace. But Rogers appreciated Cooper-Slipper's extensive background in flight testing and found him work filing turbine blades for a future jet engine project. Cooper-Slipper would go on to become chief pilot of Orenda Engines. He began his career as an Avro test pilot by test-flying overhauled navy Hawker Sea Furys during the spring of 1949, an enjoyable assignment for a wartime fighter pilot. If the English Jimmy Orrell set the mould for the low-key Avro test-pilot personality, Cooper-Slipper was its embodiment in Canada.

By contrast, another former RAF squadron leader, parachuted in from England for the first flight of the CF-100 fighter in November 1949, ran afoul of the Avro flight-test culture. Bill Waterton was a native Canadian who had finished the war testing captured German aircraft. He became chief test pilot at the British Gloster Aircraft Co., builders of the first and only Allied jet to see war service, the Gloster Meteor. Gloster was part of Hawker-Siddeley, the same aviation conglomerate that owned Avro Canada and its parent company, and Waterton was chosen for his historic task in Canada by Sir Roy Dobson, H-S chairman. He performed some spectacular demonstrations on this side of the ocean in the CF-100, but he became unpopular among his Avro colleagues for what struck them as imprecise testing and a superior manner. Waterton returned to England to test-fly the Gloster Javelin interceptor in February 1951.

Don Rogers hired RCAF Flight Lieutenant Bruce Warren of Nanton, Alberta, to replace Waterton as CF-100 project test pilot. Warren and his twin brother, Douglas, both nicknamed "Duke," had served together on Spitfires with the RAF 66 and 165 Squadrons, fought over Dieppe and the Falaise Gap, and won DFCs. Their CO at both squadrons later wrote, "They had remained together throughout their careers in the service and liked to say that if only one of them had joined up they could have worked alternate weeks." But Bruce was one of two Canadians—the other was Jack Phillips—posted to the Empire Test Pilots' School (ETPS) No. 8 (1949) course at Farnborough. Of 28 personnel on the course, 10 were killed in flying accidents within a few years. Among those 10 was Bruce Warren himself, killed when the second prototype CF-100 did not recover from a vertical dive.

Warren's replacement was Peter Cope, a smooth-flying RAF veteran of P-51B Mustang photo-recon operations over Europe who became an armament test pilot with the RAF and moved on to Armstrong-Whitworth, another part of the Hawker-Siddeley Group. With Armstrongs, Cope tested the early two-seat Meteors. Cope's background made him an ideal pilot to develop the CF-100's heavy rocket armament—dangerous work, even for an experienced pilot.

By 1952, when Jan Zurakowski joined Rogers' staff, the Avro experimental test flight team was almost complete. At the time, Zurakowski was considered possibly the greatest test and demonstration pilot in the world, certified as such by none other than Neville Duke, who for seventeen days in September 1953 was holder of the world's absolute speed record in a specially prepared Hawker Hunter. Zurakowski, Duke said at the time, was "the finest test pilot flying."

Experimental test pilots fly prototypes and test unproven modifications of certified aircraft. But newly built aircraft have to be flight tested too. Production test pilots fly newly assembled examples of aircraft types already certified as airworthy. Between them, Avro production test pilots Chris Pike and Stan Haswell flew all but about 50 of the 692 CF-100s built. They often did what Pike regarded as more thrilling work than the experimental pilots. There could be a lot wrong with a brand-new CF-100, although when one dropped a wing at the stall, for example, that behaviour came as a shock rather than an expectation. Pike had his ailerons lock on one flight due to an extraneous bolt jamming one of them, sending him through roll after roll while he figured out what to do. (He reverted to manual control, fought the jam, and had the bolt fall out.) Once he took off only to discover he had no elevator control. He set the CF-100 down in a farmer's field and became known thereafter around Avro as Ploughman of the Year.

Pike, a native of Sooke, British Columbia, joined Avro in June 1952. He managed just two missions with RCAF 428 Squadron in outdated Wellington bombers before the war ended. Pike was, in common with many test pilots, a victim of his own talent. Despite joining the RCAF in 1942, the moment he turned 18, he did not arrive in England until March 1944, having had to extract himself from an instructor's course to get into combat. Postwar, he spent a year at university before joining the RAF, in which he flew the Avro Lincoln bomber (a development of the Lancaster) for three years. He was posted to a ferry unit, once flying an Auster light airborne observation aircraft, a four-engine Lincoln bomber, and a Meteor jet in a single day. "There were," Pike recalled in 1999 with his characteristic dry humour, "many amusing incidents. It was the most interesting time of my whole flying career." That's saying a lot, considering his adventures over Malton. Pike became Avro chief production pilot a year or two after joining the company.

Experimental test pilots spent most of their time flying straight lines at exact speeds. A production test pilot could get up there and, within certain limitations, wring the airplane out the way any squadron hotshot was likely to. It often took five or six flights to iron out all the snags in a new CF-100. Moreover, Avro's emphasis on catching up to its delivery schedules meant that production pilots often found themselves flying with unproven equipment on assembly-line aircraft. Stan Haswell remembers his first hairy flights as a barely willing passenger in CF-100s fitted with the new Sperry autopilot. If flying in an aircraft controlled by some gismo wasn't experimental test flying, what was?

Haswell had joined the RAF before the war but didn't get himself into a pilot's seat until 1942, flying Dakotas over the hump in Burma and in the Berlin Airlift. He was hired in 1953 by Avro's chief flight test engineer, Mario Pesando, partly for his C-47/DC-3 experience. On Haswell's advice, Avro bought DC-3 CF-DJT as an executive transport, which "turned out to be a pretty darned good DC-3," even if Haswell says so himself. He flew the DC-3 for the company or was Rogers' co-pilot with VIPs aboard. He was also Rogers' co-pilot on later flights in the Jetliner.

Within a month of joining Avro, however, Haswell became Jan Zurakowski's back-seater in the sixth CF-100 built, 18106. His first test flight as pilot came in the thirty-third CF-100, late in 1953. He flew more than 1,500 hours on CF-100s at Avro. "Who got laid off at 40,000 feet?" Haswell once asked an audience of aviation historians. "You're right. It was me." On February 20, 1959, Haswell was aloft in the second-last CF-100 built when the Canadian government announced the Arrow project cancellation shortly after Question Period in the House of Commons, bringing an end to Avro's activities.

That morning, Haswell recalls, he finished testing CF-100 181791 and radioed the mobile test-monitoring truck, saying, "'Tell them to get the next aircraft ready. I'd like to get it done before lunch.'

"'Oh, they're taking it back to the hangar,' the ground answered.

"'What have they found?' I asked. 'What's wrong with it?'

"'Everything' was the reply.

"So I said, 'Well, okay.'

"The truck answered, 'No, Stan. That's it! We've had it. We're all out!'"

"What does a guy do?" Haswell asked in summing up. "Bail out and say that's it? Come and pick up the airplane?"

IT HAS BEEN WRITTEN that the cancellation of the Avro Jetliner was at least as sad as the end of the Arrow program in 1959, if less dramatic. The Jetliner, after all, was a short-to-medium range jet airliner specifically tailored to the intercity routes that typify air travel on the North American continent. It could have introduced the greatest increase in airspeeds of any new transport aircraft type and might have cut travel times by one-third nearly 10 years before jet travel became routine in Canada and the United States. There was interest from the airlines. National Airlines had ordered some. The United States Air Force wanted 20 (although, significantly, National and the USAF wanted theirs powered with American-built Allison engines).

The Jetliner is often said to have been a functional equivalent of the Douglas DC-9, which first flew February 25, 1965. The Jetliner flew 16 years earlier and might have pre-empted the market that has more than 2,000 of the DC-9 and its many derivatives in operation with 70-odd carriers today. Instead, further work on the Jetliner was halted at the order of Canada's industry minister, C. D. Howe, so Avro could concentrate on the CF-100 for the Korean War effort.

Bill Baker, flight engineer on the Jetliner's early flights, writes that its demise, a gradual wind-down as the prototype continued to perform sales demonstration flights and was used as chase and photography aircraft in early CF-100 fighter development flights, "really did not hit me hard till many years later." As he explains in a kind of postscript in *The Avro Jetliner*, "In December 1965 I was hired by the Douglas Company to head up their Canadian operation at Malton in the old Avro plant. My task was to build nearly 25 percent of the structure, wing, empennage [tail group], and floors for all of the new DC-9s sold. The DC-9 was an American solution to the intercity jet specification, essentially the same requirement the Jetliner was designed and built to solve. I was to become a team member in the American jet project 15 years after being a team member on the

Canadian Jetliner project, and both roles in the same plant at Malton. This hurt!"

The Jetliner is often seen to have suffered the penalty of being ahead of its time—40 years ahead of its time, by aviation writer William Mellberg's reckoning. He finds it "ironic that 40 years after the c.102, Canadair is just now introducing a 50-seat intercity airliner— the Regional Jet."

Irony abounds wherever failure touches down. The more glorious the failure, the more ironic. But the demise of the Jetliner, while it may be replete with coincidences—such as the manufacture of DC-9 wings in its empty factory—is much too simple for irony. Accounts of the Jetliner story always express utter mystification that an airliner whose specifications were set at meetings attended by Trans-Canada Air Lines engineering staff was never bought by TCA. But the Jetliner prototype was not the article those meetings produced. The Jetliner TCA was interested in was powered by two Rolls-Royce Avon turbojets. The Avon was an ambitious leap ahead in turbojet engine design. Initiated in 1945, it had a difficult gestation and took until 1953 to approach its intended 10,000-pound thrust level. It became a great engine in such fighters as the Hawker Hunter, English Electric Lightning, and SAAB Draken, but only long after work on the Jetliner was halted. The Jetliner TCA did not buy flew with four 3,000-pound-thrust Rolls-Royce Derwents, developments of the engines that powered the Gloster Meteor. As Avro pointed out, the four Derwents supplied more thrust than two Avons would have at that stage in their development. More important was the fact that no airline flies four-engine equipment when a twin can do the job.

Although Don Rogers happily sat at Jimmy Orrell's right hand on the Jetliner's first flight—and during the second flight, at the end of which Orrell set the prototype down on its belly in the grass beside the Malton runway—he was the Jetliner's foremost advocate, demonstrating its speed and handling qualities throughout the North American continent and showing the way to quieter, vibration-free jet travel from city to city. The Jetliner flew until the fall of 1956.

In that respect, Rogers was a pioneer of jet travel. More than that, he organized and was involved in testing the CF-100, notably flying its critical cold-weather icing tests. The CF-100 is still the only combat aircraft designed and manufactured in Canada. And, by the time the CF-105 Arrow was ready to fly, Rogers had assembled one of the most capable high-performance flight test departments anywhere, to test what may have been the finest interceptor never to go into service.

With the Arrow cancellation, Don Rogers was hired by de Havilland of Canada. The jet jockeys at Avro sometimes wondered what kind of test flying was required for the humble, workaday prop jobs DHC assembled, but Rogers' diplomatic talents fit snugly into DHC's worldwide sales culture. He was instrumental in the success (844 units) of the DHC-6 Twin Otter, which he demonstrated in North Africa, the Middle East, and Scandinavia and in England, where it became a popular commuter aircraft. Rogers often made the vital first impression on the airline's purchasing department and completed the sale by training the pilots. At DHC his career as a test and demonstration pilot was extended by 21 years to February 1980, when he was 63. He continued to train pilots for another seven years. He looks as if he could still do the job today.

JIMMY ORRELL:

FLIGHT TEST

AMBASSADOR

CHRONOLOGY: Capt. J. H. "Jimmy" Orrell, OBE, b. December 1903, likely Liverpool, d. August 3, 1988. Youngest in family of six. Joined RAF as boy mechanic at 16, trained as draftsman at Halton, became drafting instructor, taught at RAF Cadet College. Recommended for sergeant pilot course at No. 5 Flying Training School (FTS), Sealand, March 1926. Soloed first in class after 7 hours dual on Avro 504K (second was Geoff Tyson, future Saro CTP). Posted to 25 Sqn. Hawkinge, Kent, on Gloster Grebes. To Central Flying School, Wittering, for instructor's course; returned as instructor to No. 5 FTS.

Left RAF 1931 to join small airline, worked at A.V. Roe (Avro U.K.) design office briefly, then recruited as line pilot by Imperial Airways. Flew Handley Page H.P.42 biplane airliners (34 passengers to Europe; 24 to Africa and India). With onset of war, Imperial pilots and equipment impressed into National Air Communications Organization: Orrell flew VIPs and troops in and out of France despite Luftwaffe air supremacy, later undertook vital ball-bearing delivery flights to and from Stockholm in unarmed Lockheed Hudson patrol bombers.

Orrell rejoined A.V. Roe as production test pilot 1942. Tested the last twin-engine Manchester bombers before production ended in favour of four-engine Avro Lancaster, one of ww2's most important aircraft. Orrell production tested 900 different Lancasters to 1945.

Attended No. 2 course, Empire Test Pilots' School (ETPS) in 1944–45 with a number of future outstanding test pilots. Was co-pilot with Avro CTP S. A. Thorn on first flight of 12-seat Avro Tudor airliner, June 14, 1945. After death of Thorn in Tudor 2 crash, became Avro U.K. CTP in 1947. Six Tudors modified to take four Rolls-Royce Nenes apiece (Nene was world's first 5,000-pound-thrust turbojet), flew prototype conversion for first time September 6, 1948. Aircraft became Avro Ashton. Following spring, Avro Canada CTP Don Rogers and Canadian Department of Transport chief pilot Des Murphy went to Avro Woodford test centre to fly Ashton with Orrell.

Performed first flight of Avro Shackleton maritime patrol bomber prototype (vw126, March 9, 1949); did further development of the Lancaster and successor Avro Lincoln. Shackleton remained in front-line service into 1980s.

By July 25, 1949, prototype of Avro Canada's Jetliner, CF-EJD-X, similar in layout to Ashton, nearly ready for flight. Orrell travelled to Malton, did first flight (with Rogers as co-pilot, Bill Baker as flight engineer) August 10, 1949. Continued test flight program, including mainwheels-up belly landing of second flight August 16. Orrell returned to Britain October 27. May 1956 awarded Order of British Empire for services to aviation; same year became Avro superintendant of flying, position he held to retirement 1969.

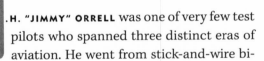

J.H. **"JIMMY" ORRELL** was one of very few test
pilots who spanned three distinct eras of
aviation. He went from stick-and-wire bi-
planes to piston-engine all-metal monoplanes to jets—all in the 10 or
so years of frenzied progress in aircraft design from the late 1930s to
1949. He seemed to become a more capable pilot as aircraft improved.
Many pilots were unable to adapt to the changeover from piston
power to jets, but Orrell took it in stride, going in midlife from outstanding pilot to test pilot able to handle difficult-to-fly aircraft to pioneer of the jet age.

Orrell was a small man with a gracious manner and a generosity
of spirit that seemed to flow from his vast experience as a pilot.
He struck those who met him as modesty personified—the perfect
gentleman. He was, in other words, the ideal British flight test ambassador to come to Canada and get the Avro c.102 Jetliner off to
a good start.

We know very little about Orrell's early life. Being accepted as a
non-commissioned sergeant pilot in 1926 by the Royal Air Force, at a

time when the RAF was one of the few flying arms that did not insist on university degrees for its aircrew recruits, was one example of the good fortune conspicuous talent often attracts. Orrell seems to have had credentials as both a pilot and an engineer, a valuable background for a test pilot. He left the RAF after five years and added to his engineering expertise in the A.V. Roe design office at Manchester.

Soon after, Orrell was tapped for one of the more romantic assignments of aviation's golden age: flying Handley Page H.P.42 biplane airliners for Imperial Airways to the far corners of the empire. The H.P.42 was a stately aerial clipper ship with a thicket of struts and rigging wires and four engines that looked almost randomly placed along the upper and lower wings. The contraption ended with a five-piece tail unit consisting of a biplane horizontal tail enclosing three fins. The whole thing cruised at 100 mph. The drag induced by this multitude of flying surfaces gave the H.P.42 what was called its built-in headwind. The H.P.42s became renowned for their safety. They were so slow and flew such long routes, landing at dusk for overnights in hotels, that being captain required social skills in addition to a steady hand on the controls.

"In the 1930s we were very decent to our customers," Orrell explained to Don Middleton, author of *Test Pilots: The Story of British Test Flying, 1903–1984.* "The captain was expected to take a keen personal interest in the welfare of his passengers and he always had a dinner jacket in his luggage. Navigational decisions were made upon the principle that the mail may be lost but not delayed; the passengers may be delayed but not lost!"

Orrell didn't lose any VIPs, either, when he flew unarmed airliners in and out of France at the time of Dunkirk, despite German control of the skies over the continent. Soon after, he flew the famous ball-bearing runs between England and Stockholm in Lockheed Hudsons, fast patrol bombers that could do 246 mph, "running the gauntlet of the Luftwaffe on every flight," as Middleton puts it.

In 1942 Orrell rejoined Avro as a test pilot, flying late-production twin-engine Manchester bombers as they came off the line. These were failures because of their engines. Re-engined with four Rolls-Royce Merlins, the same airframe became the Lancaster, the outstanding payload-bearing bomber of the European war. Orrell handled the first flights of many of the 3,670 Lancasters built by Avro (about half the total number built).

One of three company test pilots who attended the No. 2 course of the newly created Empire Test Pilots' School (ETPS) at Boscombe Down, England, in 1944–45, Orrell was more faculty than student. Also attending was test pilot Ken Waller of Miles Aircraft, who flew a de Havilland Comet racer in the historic 1934 MacRobertson London-Melbourne race. Other members of the course included Mike Lithgow (a future world airspeed record holder: 737 mph, September 24, 1953, in a Supermarine Swift; killed during 1963 in the British Aircraft Corporation 1-11 jet airliner prototype) and Jan Zurakowski, the Polish fighter pilot who had risen to squadron leader in the Royal Air Force during the war and was already well known as a demonstration pilot.

"I was sent on No. 2 Course," Orrell related to the authors of *Learn to Test, Test to Learn,* a history of ETPS, "and I must say I had an enjoyable year there because my experience already in test flying put me in a different category from the other people. I found myself, when it came to the Lancaster, flying as the tutor rather than one of the students.

"An amusing incident took place with Mike Lithgow ... when we first reported. It was suggested that Lithgow might come with me in an Oxford [a small twin-engine trainer] because he hadn't been in a twin aircraft and flying around I was letting him have a bash in it and then it came to the landing, and the engines wouldn't play ball— wouldn't drag us into the airfield, so I landed it in a ploughed field just before the boundary.

"As we were coming in Lithgow was about to raise the undercarriage, which was the Service's requirement when force landing—I slapped his hand and said 'Don't do that'—[we] landed in the ploughed field and kept the aircraft in one piece, much to Lithgow's surprise.

"The [ETPS] commandant at that time was [Group Captain J. F. X.] McKenna and he said, 'Thank you very much, Jimmy, for not breaking our airplane on the first day of flying—we can recover it from the ploughed field.'"

There was a good reason for the RAF requirement to land aircraft in ploughed fields wheels-up. Doing so caused less damage. It took a superior airman to both put an airplane down on such a field on its landing gear, breaking the rules but causing no damage, *and* get a pat on the back from the CO.

Soon after, Orrell made one of the most important first flights of his career—in an airplane that was an abject failure. He was co-pilot to Avro chief test pilot S. A. Thorn in the Avro Tudor 12-seat airliner prototype June 14, 1945. The flight revealed an almost unusable aircraft: it was unstable in pitch and yaw and bounced badly on landing.

The Tudor 2 was Avro's response to demands from its customer, British Overseas Airways Corporation, for 346 modifications and alterations to the Tudor. The Tudor 2 first flew in March 1946 and crashed August 23, 1947, killing Thorn and Avro chief engineer Roy Chadwick (designer of the Lancaster). The reported cause was aileron actuation cables that were incorrectly wound, which reversed their effect—an appalling statement about workmanship in Avro's experimental hangar at the time. Orrell succeeded Thorn as Avro CTP.

A silver lining in the Tudor fiasco was the British Ministry of Supply's order for six Tudor airframes to be modified to take four Rolls-Royce Nene jet engines each. The Nene was one of the great early turbojets, but it was not finding applications in Britain. Essentially a jet-engine testbed, the aircraft was designated the Tudor Mk.8 and later renamed the Avro Ashton. The prototype conversion, VX195, first flew in Orrell's hands September 6, 1948, making it the world's first four-jet airliner, and Orrell the second pilot of a jet-propelled civil transport.

"Jimmy Orrell recalled the fascination of the first [jet] flights," Middleton writes. "Takeoff procedures were quite different, altitude and speed were vastly increased, whilst the absence of propeller drag required a complete review of landing procedures ... Once airborne, [Orrell] realized that he had entered a different era of aviation, 'The smoothness and quietness of the flight made it so different and pleasant.'"

The following spring, Avro Canada chief test pilot Don Rogers and Des Murphy, the Canadian Department of Transport (DOT) chief test pilot, arrived in England to be initiated into the multi-jet fraternity. Both flew the Ashton with Orrell. Rogers added further jet time to his log by flying the RAF's Gloster Meteor, still one of the faster airplanes in the world at the time, powered by two Rolls-Royce Derwent engines. Back in Canada, four Derwents were being installed in the Avro Canada C.102 Jetliner prototype, CF-EJD-X.

BY JULY 25, 1949, the Jetliner appeared ready for rollout at Malton. It was pretty much complete. The Avro engineers were aware they were in a race to get the first jet-powered transport into the air. The airplane *had* emerged on June 24 for its first engine tests. Designer Jim Floyd and the flight test engineering group under the brilliant Mario Pesando were working suicidal hours in search of the dreaded *unk-unks*—unknown unknowns—that lurk within new and untested machines. In their zeal to uncover these question marks, they ran an engine test too long, causing the nacelle skins to collapse. Floyd found Rolls-Royce technical representative Harry Halstead working on one of the Derwents at 3:30 on a Sunday morning. Despite the all-out effort, the de Havilland Comet became the world's first jet-powered airliner to fly on July 27. The Jetliner finally rolled out of the Avro Canada hangar into the bright sunshine August 8, when runway tests began.

One farcical handicap Avro's engineers faced during those weeks was the program of runway repaving underway at Malton, courtesy of Canada's DOT. Even with the brevity of Canada's road-paving season, it seems incredible that Avro's landlord had no idea an important prototype was poised to fly, its debut held up as asphalt trucks and steam rollers inched their way over all but Malton's shortest runway, the NE/SW one.

By July, Rogers and flight test engineer Bill Baker had been monitoring construction of the first Jetliner for some time. In a typically graceful message to the workers who had built the Jetliner, Orrell credited Rogers and Baker with, as he phrased it, "watching the aircraft grow, learning all about it and making sure that they knew their way around, just as you do in your own home with the lights on or off. That is a necessary factor for maximum safety of a prototype."

"Likewise," Orrell wrote, "when I arrived here, I wanted to know a great deal about the design factors, estimated control forces, performance, takeoff and landing speeds, controls, hydraulic and electrical systems; a thousand and one things. Don't think I wanted to know the details, I ain't all that clever, just the basic principles were a necessity. You see, a test-pilot is a most inquisitive animal; a necessary quality if he wishes to do justice to the aircraft and become a useful member of the design and experimental team.

"That is really the beginning of the work, and quite a few technical brains have to translate their section of the work into suitable 'baby talk' so that we test-pilots get the idea.

"When the aircraft was handed over for the taxiing tests a general program of qualification was drawn up, but limited runway length and hot weather curtailed the tests."

Orrell was being cautious. Like most test pilots of the immediate postwar period, Orrell had no simulators to preview the Jetliner prototype's flight characteristics. He and Rogers inched their way into the air over three days of working up to takeoff speed, doing short hops, developing some feel for the controls, touching down, and braking hard, all on the shortest runway at Malton. The high summer temperatures robbed the engines of power, and keeping the Jetliner from running off the end of the runway was using up tires. On one touchdown, all four main wheel tires blew. Despite the shredded rubber, Orrell kept the Jetliner safely on the runway centre-line.

"Nevertheless," he wrote shortly after the first flight, "we got a fair amount of information and proved a few points, such as burst tyres were not such a disastrous thing with the short-legged tricycle undercarriage. In each case the aircraft was kept straight on the runway without damage occurring.

"Having proved all that was possible, and feeling reasonably satisfied with the aircraft and controls, eventually one has to face up to the fact that the aircraft is expected to fly and to make that long waited statement, 'OK, we are ready for flight.'

"At this point the crew must be a completely co-operative team—each member must know exactly what the skipper intends to do and that if he departs from a preconceived plan, that there is a darned good reason for it. The talks before flight cover all possibilities, each knows his duties and is prepared to act cooly, without fuss or confusion."

Despite Jimmy Orrell's trademark cool, tires remained a headache. Wednesday morning, August 10, arrived sunny and hot, with a stiff crosswind off Lake Ontario blowing over Toronto's downtown, through then-suburban Weston, over farm fields and out to Malton, northwest of the city. The temperature on the Avro tarmac was 113°F. The Jetliner, in Orrell's gentle hands, made three runway hops, as it had been doing under somewhat more favourable conditions for a couple of days. On the third hop that day, the main landing gear tires blew out again.

Orrell decided that, in view of the limited life of tires on the Jet-liner—two of them per landing gear strut, destructing with the air-craft lightly loaded—he would take advantage of the new ones being installed as the flight test crew ate their sandwiches and keep going next time instead of braking. It happened at 15:25 Eastern Daylight Saving time.

"Despite a small gale blowing with a stiff crosswind on the only available runway, the next time they went down the runway they just kept on going, rose into the air after a relatively short run and climbed away to about 500 ft., where Jimmy tried out the controls," Jetliner chief design engineer Jim Floyd recalled.

From Orrell's point of view, the liftoff was uneventful: "Clearance from the control tower—open up the throttles, all engines OK, the air-craft starts to move forward, then runs, then rushes with a smooth acceleration. The elevator becomes effective and the runway is run-ning out, she is airborne, the rudder is showing up, the undercarriage is going up, how are the ailerons? Yes, they are dandy. The under-carriage is locked up, get the throttles back to climbing power, flaps up please [to co-pilot Rogers]. That took a mighty full three or four minutes. Now we can settle down and check the various controls and services. Bill Baker reports everything in his department working like a charm. Don Rogers has been radioing all the procedure to the ground station where a tape recorder is running; he now looks around and reports everything OK in his sector."

Then Jimmy Orrell, the flight test ambassador from Manchester, did something seldom seen in the annals of first flights. Floyd describes in his book how Orrell buzzed the people who had built the airplane, those whose hopes and dreams he held in his hands. "He did a circuit of the field and then asked for clearance to bring her over the spot where the engineers and ground crew were standing to let us take a look at the aircraft in the air. He then climbed away to about 8,000 ft., and after a few minutes at that altitude reported that everything felt fine and that he was going to carry out some scheduled tests at higher altitude."

Back to Orrell's account of the Jetliner aloft: "We climb away to the clouds to carry out our first real check on the controls and to find out how she behaves over a range of speeds. What will be the best approach speed and angle, how do the controls operate with undercarriage and flaps down? Are all the services still OK?

"Don Rogers gives a running commentary on all the tests as they are made, the tape recorder is taking the notes, the people on the ground take mental notes, all is going well . . .

"It is rough below cloud base and the control tower report a crosswind of 40 degrees [and] about 35 knots on the duty runway. This raises the query, is rudder control sufficient at the landing speed to counteract weathercocking? [This is the tendency for an airplane to fly directly into the wind, rather than landing down the centre-line of the runway.] We must be prepared. A circuit of the aerodrome in the bumpy conditions and permission to land is given."

In the cockpit, the sweat-soaked Rogers, Baker and Orrell were on the verge of the most critical task of the flight: bringing the prototype down in one piece, in a 35-mph crosswind, with tires more than likely to blow out.

Orrell's thoughts at that point were serene and near-poetic. "A fairly long, steady approach with undercarriage and flap down to decrease the speed and obtain a good angle of approach. It is bumpy, but the aircraft behaves well. Now wash-out the drift effect of crosswind. We are getting near, can we cut the engines? Yes—now. Hold her off, steady, yes, she's touched, keep her straight, hold her, hold her—the nosewheel touches—watch the crosswind, turning a bit, left rudder, a little left brake, again, she's stopping, stopping, nicely girl, there you are beauty, and now back to the stable."

"The first flight of North America's first jet transport was over," Jim Floyd sums up in his book. "At the post-flight debriefing Jimmy Orrell described the flight as 'a piece of cake' and said there were no snags worth reporting. 'She was,' he said, 'the perfect lady.'"

"Well," Orrell added later, "she *was* the perfect lady and gave us a very fine flight. Smooth—as smooth as a surface plate [an aircraft skin panel]. Noise—we could talk to each other in ordinary voices, used the loudspeaker with the volume turned down instead of earphones. The controls and services operated just as they should. On the first flight we could not answer all the questions, as you can well imagine, we were fully occupied doing what we did in one hour.

"What was our general opinion? We were mighty happy with our experience and ready to continue with the schedule of tests that are necessary for a prototype."

Since most Avro employees were on vacation during the first Jetliner flight, all those at work on August 16 were invited to leave their desks and benches and assemble at the boundary fence facing the airport to watch the second flight. As Floyd recalls, they saw more than they had bargained for.

"After almost one hour of testing in the air, during which time the aircraft was put through stall tests and other engineering procedures, Jimmy Orrell selected undercarriage down, but there was no response and the landing gear stayed up. After several tries to get the gear down by the normal selection control, the next step was to try the emergency procedures, for which there were three separate and independent systems, but nothing worked. After long conferences with us on the ground, Jimmy decided to carry out a belly landing with the nose gear down, the main gear up and no flaps, due to the loss of hydraulic power during the abortive emergency procedures."

The Jetliner was an irreplaceable hand-built prototype. There was no second prototype Jetliner. No spare. This moment was the reason Jimmy Orrell had been imported to do the Jetliner's early testing. The entire program was on the line. Few pilots would have landed main gear up, nosewheel down, but that was a calculated risk. "It has been suggested to me that this was the day on which my hair started to turn white," Jim Floyd writes, "and I believe it!"

Orrell, faced with this dire emergency, had the presence of mind to kid the Jetliner's designer, who was distraught after having convened a meeting of his engineering staff that did not result in a solution to the test crew's fix. Floyd asked the controller in the Malton tower for a last word with the pilot. The controller gave Floyd the microphone. "All right, Jim," Orrell deadpanned, "let's get going. Our Father, which art in heaven . . . "

The test pilot then took responsibility by saying, "Don't worry, you have all done your best. It is up to me now. I will put it down on the grass alongside the runway—I hope." Orrell chose to set the Jetliner down alongside Malton's east-west runway at the north end of the airport. Using the grass was a bright idea, one that might not have occurred to a pilot who hadn't flown airliners from grass fields in Africa during the 1930s. Still, it took four attempts to get the Jetliner down just right.

The prototype's watching builders held their breath each time. With its low wings, the Jetliner tended to float in ground effect, the dense layer of air blanketing the ground. Orrell minimized the float by leaving the Jetliner's flaps up, losing lift at the cost of a hotter, faster landing. He bled off speed by fishtailing over the runway threshold. If luck is the residue of preparation, the smooth ride the gear-up Jetliner got, despite the crosswinds, slithering through the grass nose up, was the reward for Orrell's diligence in the air, where he had some measure of control.

As popular as Jimmy Orrell and his charming wife, Nan, made themselves during their three-month stay, his masterful belly landing of the Jetliner was his defining moment in Canada.

"Jimmy landed the aircraft safely in that condition and the damage to the aircraft was minimal," writes Jim Floyd. "While hair-raising at the time, the episode served to highlight the inherent safety of an aircraft with no propellers to get in the way in an emergency such as this, and at least we had one test under our belt that no manufacturer would dare to carry out at that stage in the life of a prototype aircraft unless by accident ...

"Examination of the aircraft after the belly-landing revealed that the use of a liquid-spring oleo shock absorber on the main leg of the undercarriage, coupled with the stall tests carried out on that flight, resulting in severe shaking of the aircraft, had prevented the uplocks on the main gear from releasing either normally or with emergency systems. The corrective design solution was simple, but the price paid in nervous energy by the crew and ourselves was very high."

Not just nervous energy, either. Flight engineer Bill Baker, a tough, wiry man, later discovered he had broken some ribs as he strained to release the landing-gear locks by hand with the emergency cable. Broken ribs are painful. Every breath is agony. Yet Baker was sufficiently wound up that he didn't realize the damage he had suffered until later.

To Don Rogers, Jimmy Orrell seemed no different in the midst of this crisis than in any routine situation. "He was an outstanding pilot and a most agreeable person to work with, to fly with and to be with. He was very smooth, very cool, calm and collected, an excellent pilot. [When the Jetliner landing gear wouldn't come down] he was absolutely 100 percent cool about it."

The Jetliner was repaired and its landing gear modified. Its third flight took place September 20, little more than a month after what might have been a tragedy.

"The next few weeks saw an intensive program of flight tests aimed at obtaining data for Engineering as part of the preparation for certification, which we hoped to obtain around mid-1950," Floyd's book relates.

"Investigations were made on fuel flow at various speeds, aircraft stability power-on and power-off, the stall regime at various weights, control response and control forces throughout the flight envelope, engine cuts at all altitudes and speeds, and checks on aircraft drag, including the drag with flaps and undercarriage down. The aircraft was later fitted with large water-ballast tanks so that we could load it to a representative full-passenger weight and also transfer water from forward tanks to aft tanks to represent various positions of the pay-load centre of gravity. Two tables were installed for engineering ob-servers who were taking test readings and on which appropriate test gear was mounted. A few passenger chairs were later installed to take other personnel on the test flights."

Aside from the direct benefits of these tests in moving the Jetliner toward certification, Don Rogers and Bill Baker were being trained to become the most highly qualified high-performance flight test crew-men in the country. Not only did Jimmy Orrell show them by example how this difficult task was done and explain it in writing for anyone at Avro who cared to know, he was happy to show off the airplane to anyone who wanted to see it fly. Moreover, he tutored the pilot who would join Rogers and Baker in the Jetliner cockpit.

On October 22, Orrell demonstrated the Jetliner at Malton as the highlight of a gala day celebration for Avro employees of the Jetliner's success so far. Two days later he checked out Battle of Britain Spitfire ace Mike Cooper-Slipper on the prototype. Working with him made Cooper-Slipper a lifelong admirer of Orrell's personality and skills: "He was a role model. He was a very quiet sort of a man who did everything gently. What did I learn from him? How to behave as an experimental test pilot. He did everything he had to do, and he didn't do anything he didn't have to do—any throwing the airplane around or aerobatics or anything. I had absolute confidence in him."

Jimmy Orrell returned to England late in October, having flown the Jetliner 16 times. For those and his many other services, he was enrolled in the Order of the British Empire.

3

> ## MIKE COOPER-SLIPPER:

IROQUOIS PILOT

CHRONOLOGY: Sqn. Leader Thomas Paul Michael Cooper-Slipper, Royal Air Force DFC (ret'd), b. January 11, 1921, at Kinver, Staffs. Joined RAF, began flying training in October 1938, graduated second in class May 1939 and given choice of aircraft to fly. Joined 74 Sqn. on Spitfires September 1939 but quickly transferred to Ferry Pool, Bristol, exposing him to many different types. December 1939 to 11 Group Pool, St. Athan (again second in class), chose Hurricanes, posted to 605 Sqn. February 1940. Saw action over Dunkirk, then Battle of Britain; rammed a Do 17 September 15, destroying both it and his Hurricane L2012; awarded DFC November 26, 1940, citation noting 7 enemy aircraft downed, 3 damaged.

November 1940 rested, posted to instructor's course, February 1941 to Naval Flying School as instructor. July to No. 10 (Night Fighter) OTU East Fortune; joined 96 Sqn. on Defiants that September, then made brief return to 74 Sqn. as flight commander but quickly moved to 135 Sqn., married Margaret Mary (Rita) Brown November 5, left November 10 for South Africa but diverted to Singapore with pilots of 3 other units.

These personnel formed into provisional 232 Sqn.; Cooper-Slipper commanded C Flight at Kallang. January 1942 shot down two bombers; February led survivors to Palembang, Sumatra. Flew two sorties during Japanese invasion of island: strafed barges on first, shot down 3 bombers on second. Captured during paratroop attack on Palembang, escaped to Java, took hospital ship to Ceylon, then to Egypt via India and South Africa, arriving October. Became CO Special Performance Flight at Aboukir, Egypt, and CTP at 103 Maintenance Unit (MU) at Helopolis, flying Spitfires modified to intercept high-flying Ju 86P and Ju 188 recon aircraft, one of which he damaged, injuring himself.

Limited to low-level flying, joined 267 Sqn. November 1943 on Dakotas. February 1944 posted to Middle East Communications Sqn. Returned to test flying at MU Helopolis May 1944, then to Kabrit, Egypt. November returned to U.K., became chief test pilot at MU Litchfield February 1945, at Cosford January 1946. Left RAF June 1946. Wartime score calculated by *Aces High:* estimated 8–10 victories, 2–4 shared destroyed (total 12), 4 damaged.

Emigrated to Canada November 1947. Became Avro Canada test pilot September 1948. Production tested Sea Furys, Lancasters, B-25s. Flew B-25 chase on Jetliner first flight August 10, 1949; checked out on Jetliner October 24; co-pilot with Don Rogers on first Jetliner 500-mph flight, November 22. Flew Lancaster testbed with Orenda 11 turbojets after July 1950. Was third pilot to fly CF-100. Raced English sportscars until forbidden to do so by Avro.

June 1955 became chief test pilot, Orenda Engines, flying B-47 Orenda PS-13 Iroquois testbed. First flight with Iroquois November 13, 1957; first flight with Iroquois lit, date unknown. More than 125 hours flown on Iroquois tests in B-47. Was pre-flighting Orenda B-47 February 20, 1959, at 3:00 P.M. EST when CF-105 Arrow cancelled. Was to pilot RL 206, next prototype on production line, scheduled to be first Arrow to fly with Orenda engines.

Mike Cooper-Slipper was inducted into Canada's Aviation Hall of Fame June 7, 2003, at Halifax.

▼ ▼ ▼

EVEN AMONG ROYAL AIR FORCE WW2 ace Tom Cooper-Slipper's memorable wartime exploits, his ramming of a Dornier bomber stands out. It happened on September 15, 1940, and was the eighth of Cooper-Slipper's dozen victories. Eight days before, Hermann Goering had shifted the Luftwaffe's tactical objective from RAF airfields to London. The Blitz was on; 448 civilians were killed September 7. Losses in the air on both sides peaked at 66 aircraft that day, subsided to single-digit figures for some days afterward, and then suddenly ballooned to a total of 83 the day Cooper-Slipper rammed the Dornier. Cooper-Slipper added to both sides' scores that fateful day, widely regarded as the Battle of Britain's turning point. He contributed one Hurricane to the RAF losses of 27 and one Dornier to the Luftwaffe's 56 aircraft downed.

"The sky was black with [the Dorniers]," Cooper-Slipper recalls. Author Len Deighton records that the first wave's main formation approaching London just before noon that day consisted of 100 Do 17s— not a large number compared with later Allied thousand-bomber raids, but enough to make a lasting impression. Cooper-Slipper selected his adversary over South Dungeness and placed himself just behind and below the Dornier's tail. Like many aces, Cooper-Slipper had his eight machine guns harmonized to converge at a close-in range where he could hardly miss. But he was almost out of ammunition.

Worse, the gunner in the Do 17's underfuselage cupola was very accurate. He was scoring hits on Cooper-Slipper's Hurricane, L2012, shooting away, among other things, the British ace's aileron controls. Cooper-Slipper pulled up the Hurricane's nose, partly for protection behind the engine, and attempted to sideslip leftward across and above the bomber, hoping for a burst at it. Few pilots would have tried such a stunt from so close. His left wing dropped. It struck the Dornier's left wing directly behind its engine.

"I remember various things, like being in an inverted spin, and the undercarriage coming up beside me [seen through what remained of the upper surface of the wing]. My nails were all badly torn, so I had quite a job getting out," Cooper-Slipper says. He assumes he banged his head on the Hurricane's canopy, judging by the colossal headache he had when he resumed consciousness. "I don't remember pulling the ripcord or anything. I came to at 20,000 feet, floating under my parachute."

The RAF knew what it had in Tom Cooper-Slipper. He was the proverbial son of a vicar with a wild streak, racing motorcycles at 14, joining up to do his bit at 19, turning out to be a natural pilot. At each stage of flying training, he finished near the top of his class and was offered postings to fly whatever aircraft he wanted—a rare privilege. He was moved quickly from unit to unit, ferrying various single- and twin-engine types from aircraft pools to squadrons, getting introduced to a wide variety of RAF equipment. He flew both Spitfires and Hurricanes in combat. He became a flying instructor with the Royal Navy's Fleet Air Arm, exposing him to yet more different types of aircraft. By 21 he was a front-line squadron section leader. Cooper-Slipper was given the RAF's enriched diet, and he ate it up. He found he had that ace factor: the ability to see everything around him and the confidence that, in combat, things would slow down until the enemy on his tail became easy to outfly.

Shipped to the Pacific after Pearl Harbor, Cooper-Slipper found himself fighting a war straight out of a *Boy's Own* annual. He shot down five Japanese bombers during two of the very few sorties his squadron was able to manage, but the action was mainly on the ground. "In a slit trench in Singapore he got a good look at courage," June Callwood wrote in a 1958 *Maclean's* magazine profile, "watching a handful of survivors of a Highland regiment lacerated by Japanese machine-gun fire rise and march, in formal parade order, across a causeway through cross fire that missed every man."

Cooper-Slipper's war continued on Sumatra after the fall of Singapore. He was captured by Japanese paratroopers at Palembang, escaped to Java, and made his way around Africa to Egypt, where he arrived in October 1942. It was there that Cooper-Slipper became a test pilot. He became co of the Special Performance Flight and chief test pilot of the Maintenance Unit (MU) at Aboukir, Egypt, where he test-flew, as he put it, "anything odd that had to be done with a Spitfire or Hurricane."

One of 103 MU's tasks was figuring out how to deal with high-flying German Ju 86P and Ju 188 recon aircraft. The MU pressurized the cockpits of Spitfires and extended their wingtips for better high-altitude performance. Cooper-Slipper tried out the modifications, damaging a Ju 188 during 1943 for his final claim, but injured himself in his zeal to engage the peeping toms. Later in the war he was posted to a succession of RAF Maintenance Units in the United Kingdom, where he flew repaired and modified Hawker Typhoons and Tempests, becoming chief test pilot at Cosford in January 1946. He resigned from the RAF that June. Why? "I was fed up with England."

Cooper-Slipper was in Birmingham after the war ended and one day found himself staring at a poster depicting Lake Louise, Alberta. As he tells it, the copy under the photograph of Lake Louise's spectacular mountain backdrop read, "Come to sunny Ontario." He and his wife, Rita, thought that looked good.

When the Cooper-Slippers arrived in sunny Ontario in November 1947—puzzled to find no Lake Louise in Canada's central province—Tom was, in all likelihood, the most experienced test pilot in the country. He came to Canada as well equipped as any immigrant: with £50 in his pocket, time flying most of the Royal Air Force's front-line fighters in his logbook, and letters of recommendation to the top men at de Havilland Canada and Avro Canada. To commemorate the change in his life, he changed his identity, selecting another of the three names he was christened with, and introduced himself from then on as Mike Cooper-Slipper.

He visited Avro first. Being located at Malton, Avro was easier to find. Don Rogers was handling the test flying of Lancasters, B-25 Mitchells, Venturas, and Dakotas, all modified for peacetime roles. But there was more exciting test flying on the horizon. Avro's engineers were working on two new jets, the XC-100 fighter (to be powered by an engine from Orenda Engines, Avro's gas turbine engine division) and the C.102 Jetliner.

To keep him busy until those paper airplanes flew, Cooper-Slipper was put to work first pushing a broom, then filing turbine blades (at $2.50 an hour, good money then) for a future jet engine known as the Chinook. He started flying again in September 1948, testing Lancasters converted for search and rescue and B-25s converted to VIP transports and navigation trainers.

His late-war experiences flight testing Typhoons and Tempests came in handy the following spring, when six Hawker Sea Furys that Avro Canada had overhauled for the Royal Canadian Navy needed testing. The Sea Furys were navalized Tempests, representing the peak of British piston-engine fighter development. Don Rogers flew the overhauled aircraft from Halifax to Malton, and Cooper-Slipper got to return them while Rogers learned to fly jets at Avro U.K.

That summer Cooper-Slipper was flying chase for the Jetliner's first flight August 10, 1949, in a B-25. A photograph of him posing before one of the Mitchell's engines shows a North American–looking flyboy in a straw cowboy hat, having the time of his life. He was present in the Jetliner cockpit on its fourth flight and was checked out on the Jetliner by Jimmy Orrell October 24, which made Cooper-Slipper an experimental test pilot. Once Orrell returned to the United Kingdom, either Cooper-Slipper or Rogers was captain on all Jetliner flights. They were flying the commercial transport of the future. His recent summary of the Jetliner's flying qualities was typically terse: "It was a very nice aeroplane. It had no bad habits. It just flew. It was my first jet. Very quiet. Very gentlemanly. Everything happened quite slowly. Of course, it was a fairly big jet. No bumps."

On November 22 Rogers and Cooper-Slipper took the Jetliner past 500 mph, or about Mach .73. The idea was to be able to set the Jetliner's cruising speed in the high 400-mph range, far in excess of the fastest piston-engine airliners. Cooper-Slipper says he had no concerns about these speed runs. "It used to howl and wail at Mach .75 or somewhere about there. There was an intake under the cockpit. I forget what it was for. But it made all the noise. The engines, you couldn't really hear them; they were pretty quiet. The tailpipes were well behind."

THE TEMPORARY WORK Mike Cooper-Slipper had been given filing turbine blades in 1948 was prophetic. He would spend much of his Avro Canada career as chief test pilot of the company's Orenda Engines subsidiary. Orenda grew out of a wartime program, Turbo Research, to develop Canadian jet engines.

Engines have to be flight tested, just as aircraft do. Mike Cooper-Slipper and his crews did the specialized and dangerous work of starting new jet engines in the air and flying them on aircraft called testbeds that were sometimes crudely modified to carry those engines aloft. Cooper-Slipper would often have doubts about both the lashed-up testbeds and the engines, and he had problems with the young engineers he worked with. But he quietly got on with the work.

A Lancaster, FM209, was modified by having its outer Packard-Merlin piston engines replaced by Orenda 11s, making it a testbed for prototypes of the engines intended to power the new Avro interceptor, the CF-100. The Lancaster first flew in that form in early July 1950, and then with the Orendas lit July 13, with Don Rogers at the controls. Flying on its jets alone, with the inboard Merlins' props feathered (blades in line with the slipstream), the Orenda Lancaster testbed was as fast as a stock four-engine Lancaster bomber.

Aviation historian Larry Milberry tells the story of how Cooper-Slipper was demonstrating the Orenda Lancaster on jets alone at an airshow at Malton when he called to the engineer to restart the Merlins.

"Something went afoul in the shuffle," Milberry writes, "and, instead of getting back to four engines, Cooper-Slipper had a chance to fly the Lanc with no engines. The jets were accidentally shut down and the plane was momentarily a glider. Quick work got the jets going again and the day was saved, though not before some of the local residents got a very close look at an airborne Lancaster!

"On the odd weekend the Orenda Lanc was used for a bit of joyriding over nearby New York State. The plane would be taken across Lake Ontario very low and would then pop up to appear on U.S. Air Force radar scopes. The P-47 Thunderbolts based with the Air National Guard at Niagara Falls would be scrambled against the radar blip, but were never able to catch the fast-climbing, jet-propelled Lancaster."

As thrilling as the Orenda Lancaster could be, the ww2 bomber's flying qualities evoked nothing but praise from its pilots. The Lancaster was, in that sense, an ideal engine testbed, able to fly safely on either its jets, its piston engines, or both. The historic FM209 was lost March 22, 1955, in an overnight fire that destroyed Avro's wartime wooden flight test hangar.

Cooper-Slipper also flew the Orenda 11 engine in both of the fighters it was installed in, the CF-100 interceptor and the Canadair Sabre, a development of North American's great F-86. He was an early pilot of the Orenda-powered Sabres, one of which failed to relight in the air north of Toronto, as Avro production test pilot Stan Haswell recalled in later years. The Ontario Provincial Police blocked both north- and southbound traffic on Highway 400 for an impromptu runway, but Cooper-Slipper, lined up with the highway, recovered power at about 2,000 feet. Haswell figures the OPP are still looking for Cooper-Slipper, "maybe for low flying!"

Cooper-Slipper was only the third pilot to fly the CF-100. During 1954–55, he flew a program intended to boost the Orenda 11's power to 8,250 pounds of static thrust by the addition of an afterburner unit. The proposed higher-thrust Orenda 11R (R for reheat, the British term for afterburning) would power a proposed CF-100 Mk.6 that would intercept high-altitude targets with radar-guided Sparrow 2 air-to-air missiles at altitudes up to 60,000 feet. But design of the CF-105 Arrow supersonic interceptor was well underway by then, so the RCAF's interest in a hotrod CF-100 was nil. The CF-100 Mk.6 was never built. In those heady times, it would never have occurred to anyone at Avro or in the RCAF that the CF-105 would not be forthcoming.

IT WAS THE ORENDA PS-13 Iroquois engine, developed to power the CF-105, that provided Cooper-Slipper with his most exciting moments as a test pilot. Work began on this 19,250-pound-thrust (27,000 pounds with afterburner) engine in 1953. It was lit for the first time December 15, 1954, passed its 50-hour preflight rating test June 24, 1956, and produced 18,750 pounds dry (non-afterburning) thrust during its 100-hour test July 27, 1957. Aviation historian Bill Gunston has called the Iroquois "perhaps the greatest turbojet of the 1950s" outside of the Soviet Union. It was named for the most warlike of central Canadian aboriginals.

Cooper-Slipper was promoted to Orenda CTP in June 1955. That fall he, fellow test pilot Len Hobbs, and flight engineer John McLachlan attended a U.S. Air Force course at McConnell Air Force Base to be checked out on the jet bomber that was then the backbone of the USAF Strategic Air Command's nuclear deterrent. This was the swept-wing, six-engine Boeing B-47 Stratojet. McConnell AFB is not far from the Wichita, Kansas, plant that built enough B-47s to equip 28 Strategic Air Command Bombardment Wings with 45 combat-ready aircraft apiece, plus 300 recon models and electronic intelligence spyplanes—more than 1,400 B-47s in total. One of those Stratojets would take the Iroquois aloft for the first time.

Great Cold Warrior that it was, prototype of the big multi-engine swept-wing jet that it was, the B-47 was not an ideal engine testbed. Cooper-Slipper's piloting skills would have been fully occupied flying a stock B-47. Near the ground—either trying to leave it or approaching it—the B-47 was a dog. Even with six engines, it was underpowered. It often needed the help of jettisonable rocket packs to get itself aloft. Landing was worse.

"It was relatively difficult to land," wrote one former B-47 pilot, "terribly unforgiving of mistakes or inattention, subject to control reversal at high speeds, and suffered from horrible roll-due-to-yaw characteristics. Crosswind landings and takeoffs were sporty, and in-flight discrepancies were the rule rather than the exception. All in all, the B-47 was a very demanding machine for its three-man crew."

The B-47 was especially sensitive to variations in pitch. It lacked longitudinal stability; that is, it tended to diverge in pitch. Keeping the B-47 at the proper attitude meant flying by the numbers (within a narrow range of speeds) anywhere near the ground. It had bicycle landing gear: two trucks, each with paired wheels, arranged in tandem, with light outrigger landing gear at the inner engine nacelles. The B-47 had to be touched down barely nose-high, on the rear pair of wheels.

Orenda proposed to use this twitchy craft as the testbed for its huge Iroquois engine. They would take the Iroquois, a two-and-a-half-ton, 30-foot-long powerplant that could generate as much thrust as four of the B-47's six engines combined, enclose it in a six-foot-diameter nacelle, and hang it under the bomber's right tailplane, of all places. Adding a large object on one side—the right, or starboard, side—made the B-47 want to turn right because of the installation's drag with the Iroquois unlit, then go left when it was ignited. The B-47, even with its yaw damper and without a huge seventh engine on one side, liked to start rolling into unintended turns as its nose hunted left and right.

The RCAF borrowed B-47 51-2051, the only aircraft of its type ever to wear non-U.S. markings. Canadair at Montreal did the conversion work over several months of 1956 and 1957, calling the project the CL-52. The test-engine installation on Baker-Forty-Seven x-Zero-Five-Nine, as that particular B-47 was referred to, was, for some reason, toed outward rather than inward. This added to both drag with the engine unlit and the power-on yaw problem by increasing the leftward tendency with the engine lit. Moreover, Canadair needed to put four tons of ballast in the B-47's nose to balance out the engine installation, thus making the bomber more reluctant than ever to take to the air. The Orenda itself exacerbated the landing problem; once the B-47 was close enough to the ground, it became an airfoil that tended to raise the tail.

After all those modifications that made a tricky airplane trickier, they would ask Mike Cooper-Slipper to fly the damn thing. What a compliment.

AT THEIR B-47 CONVERSION course at McConnell AFB, Cooper-Slipper and his crew had encountered an American pilot who simply could not believe what the Orenda crew were setting out to do.

"Do you mean," asked the Texan, "that you little old Canadians have got the biggest engine in the world? And you're going to put it in the tail of a B-47? Man, you're crazier than we are."

In time, Cooper-Slipper came to agree. As he explained to author Greig Stewart, "The B-47 just wasn't the right airplane for the job. The other big mistake was the engine nacelle pointed outboard five degrees, which affected running, so you had to keep two [of the B-47's left wing-mounted] engines at full power to counteract this. You couldn't bring the Iroquois and the two B-47 engines to full power." Not if you wanted to fly straight ahead. Controlling the Orenda B-47 was a balancing act, even in what might be called normal flight. With an engine as powerful as four of its own six engines hung on one side of the B-47, the smaller engines podded under the wing had to be managed to offset the Iroquois when it was running.

"When the B-47 was in flight, one of the B-47's [port] engines had to be kept running at full power to offset the assymetric thrust of the Iroquois and another to keep the hydraulic [and] electric services etc., running, but progressively the balance of the engines could be closed down," the authors of the 1980 book *Avro Arrow* report. "It was not possible to open up all seven engines to full power."

Did the Orenda B-47 ever run on the Iroquois alone? Once, say Ron Pickler and Larry Milberry, authors of an account of Canadair's CL-52/B-47 conversion. "In subsequent test flights, the B-47 pilot was able on one occasion to shut down his six regular engines and fly on the single Iroquois." They do not say how Cooper-Slipper kept the testbed flying where he wanted it to go.

With the B-47's lopsided thrust evened out, though, "the acceleration was nothing short of fantastic. It could go from idle to full thrust in 2.8 seconds and if you selected idle to afterburner, then it would go up to full thrust; the afterburner would light; the final nozzle would arrange itself and stabilize 4–5 seconds from initial throttle opening," write the authors of *Avro Arrow*. They further exult: "Remember! The engine was still being developed!"

That was all too true. The Iroquois could not be brought to full power at that stage without risking an explosion. The Iroquois had exploded "more than once" in its test cell, according to Burt Avery, Orenda deputy chief engineer. The engine test cell at Orenda was henceforth sheathed in sheet steel. Explosions were "to be expected" in the development of a new jet engine, especially one that was such a leap past Orenda's previous models. But it was not possible to sheath the Iroquois in sheet steel on the B-47.

"He [Avery] was as certain as an engineer can be that the Iroquois in the B-47 would not explode, but he nevertheless was uneasy," June Callwood wrote in her *Maclean's* article. "'What's there to worry about?' co-pilot Hobbs rationalized the day before [the first flight with the Iroquois lit]. 'The worst thing that can happen is an explosion that blows off the tail. Right? Well, we've got ejection seats and we'll have plenty of altitude. Just a bit chilly on the way down, that's all.'"

Cooper-Slipper had his own misgivings. He was beginning to develop a distrust of some of the many young engineers hired for the project. "[Engine] testing at Orenda was not a very happy experience," he remembers. "They had hired a lot of engineers from the University of Toronto. They had to be right. So it was unhappy."

Those young engineers, working on an engine project at the leading edge of the metallurgical and turbine state of the art, were under pressure because of an unrealistic deadline that had them a year behind schedule before the engine flew. Finally, on July 27, 1957, the Orenda Iroquois passed its first 100-hour endurance test on the ground at close to its designed peak power, 18,750 pounds dry thrust. On the first of November it was demonstrated for government officials at its full 19,000-pound thrust. Twelve days later, at five minutes past noon, Cooper-Slipper, Hobbs, and McLachlan took off in the seven-engine B-47.

"The time was reached when the Iroquois had to be flown," Callwood wrote. "The government was impatient ... [and] one of the payments on the RCAF contract was hanging on the event. The company itself was suffering from a mass case of nerves. Tempers were waspish and irritation became almost constant."

Recalled Boeing historian Peter M. Bowers: "In the following weeks over 125 hours of air flight testing was carried out, supplementing the thousands [of hours] of ground running, and the Iroquois tested to the full altitude limits of the six-jet-engined B-47 [service ceiling, B-47E, 40,500 feet]."

It was regrettable that the engine, intended for an interceptor that would fly and fight at well above 40,000 feet, could not be tested above that altitude on a B-47. Of those flight test hours, 31 were flown with the Iroquois lit.

Cooper-Slipper, his crew, and the Orenda B-47 were over Barrie, Ontario, at low altitude and climbing, when the PS-13 was opened up for the first time to full throttle.

"Suddenly there was an enormous bang and the whole aircraft shook, followed by a deadly silence. The pilot's position was a long way from the Iroquois but dust flew up into the cockpit. The Iroquois was immediately shut down and its fire extinguishers pulled. The vibration diminished as the engine came to a stop," is how the authors of *Avro Arrow* describe the event.

One of the turbine blades in the PS-13 had detached itself, instantly shredding nearby components to shards of steel and titanium that were flung by centrifugal forces out through the Orenda's shell and its nacelle. They sliced through the B-47's tail, creating dozens of holes but miraculously leaving it attached to the rest of the B-47.

The engine oil ignited, causing a fire that the first fire extinguisher failed to put out. The second worked. The pilot of the CF-100 chase plane pulled in close to the B-47's five o'clock, took a look, and reported that, while there was plenty of smoke, there seemed to be no fire. The explosion and subsequent recovery "popped rivets all over the aeroplane," Cooper-Slipper recalls.

His first reaction was to stop the B-47 from rolling to the right with the loss of power on that side. Cooper-Slipper, Hobbs, and McLachlan felt lucky to be alive. They still faced the question of whether X-Zero-Five-Nine would shed its perforated and weakened tail when they streamed its braking parachute on the ground. But they were happy to be in a position to wonder what would happen back at Malton, knowing they had a chance to get there.

FLYING THE IROQUOIS and having it explode the first time it was run in the air at full throttle is a noteworthy, if largely forgotten, Canadian aviation achievement. Test pilots prevent loss of life by provoking unproven machinery to the breaking point. Usually they take those risks so others can benefit. In this case, Cooper-Slipper, having survived the Orenda explosion on the B-47, was expected to risk going back into the air with *two* Iroquois engines—in a CF-105— at some point in 1959.

The first five Arrow prototypes were powered by American Pratt & Whitney J75s. A pair of Iroquois were about to be installed in the sixth Arrow built, RL 206, on Friday, February 20, 1959. Though not quite ready, two engines had been test-fitted. That morning new, stronger turbine blades that would have made the Iroquois more reliable were delivered to Orenda. Arrow RL 206 was to be Mike Cooper-Slipper's bird. At three that afternoon, Cooper-Slipper, doing the seven-hour preflight check on the B-47 required before every flight, was told, as he recently recalled the moment, "Stop, no more work, finished." The Arrow program had been cancelled.

While he clearly feels disappointed to this day at not having flown the Arrow, Cooper-Slipper says he would have had serious misgivings about flying RL 206 with two Iroquois engines. "The thing with the Iroquois is that it wasn't a good engine. They had oil problems, a weird new oil system . . . I don't think it would have worked," he told author Greig Stewart.

"The engine just wasn't ready, and my reports said it wasn't ready. There was about a year's gap [before the engine would be] ready to put in the Arrows . . . It was rushed, it was a mad scramble . . . We just didn't do enough flight-testing . . . It would have been a catastrophe if the Arrow had flown with the Iroquois in it when it was supposed to."

A might-have-been catastrophe for Canada. But also a catastrophe in the making for Mike Cooper-Slipper. He never flew as a pilot again.

4

> **BILL WATERTON:**

FIRST TO FLY

THE CF–100

CHRONOLOGY: Sqn. Leader William Arthur Waterton, Air Force Cross and bar, George Medal, (RAF ret'd), b. Edmonton, Alberta, March 18, 1916, son of police chief at Camrose. Attended Royal Military College, Kingston, mid-1930s, commissioned in Alberta Dragoons, 1937. Worked as youth fitness instructor. Applied to RAF in Canada, 1938. Travelled to England as civilian; learned to fly Hanworth, Middlesex, summer 1939, joined RAF June 10, 1939.

Joined 242 (Canadian) Sqn. November 20, 1939, flew operationally in Battle of France to May 25, 1940, when crash-landed Hurricane in England with severe head injuries, so cause unknown. Posted to No. 6 OTU from August 1940, became flying instructor; then to No. 39 Service Flying Training School; had 600 students pass safely through his hands. Awarded Air Force Cross, 1942 "for exceptional devotion to duty": 900 flying hours as instructor and 100 in one month "although not required to do so." Postings during 1943–44: Empire Central Flying School; No. 53 OTU (Spitfires); Sub-Statospheric Sqn. (Spitfire VIIs used to intercept high-flying intruders). May 1944 to Air Fighting Development Unit (AFDU), Wittering, evaluating British, German, U.S. fighters. Moved with AFDU to Tangmere February 1945 to compare Gloster Meteor jets with German Me 262s. Immediate postwar, as Sqn. Leader to Central Fighter Establishment, West Raynham.

June 14, 1946, RAF High Speed Flight formed at Tangmere under G/C Teddy Donaldson with Waterton and Neville Duke (then at Empire Test Pilots' School) for world airspeed record attempt in Meteors. September 7, Donaldson set new record of 616 mph; Waterton did 614 mph; awarded bar to his AFC June 12, 1947.

October 21, 1946, joined Gloster Aircraft Co., manufacturer of Meteor, as test pilot. January 15, 1947, flew low-level beatup of Champs Élysées, Paris. Next day set new Paris-London speed record. Became Gloster CTP February 1947. Later same year 100 Meteor 4s sold to Argentina; Waterton trained a dozen pilots. October 1949 delivered 14 Meteors (2 of them two-seaters) to Egypt.

Summoned from Egypt to test Avro Canada CF-100. January 19, 1950, first flight CF-100 prototype 18101, Malton; landing gear did not retract. Third flight, January 31, did mild beatup of Malton to salute visiting Hawker-Siddeley chairman Sir Roy Dobson; wing-root fairings cracked from spar flexing. Cracked again at Canadian National Exhibition airshow, September 1950. February 7, 1951, returned U.K. for Gloster Javelin testing.

November 26, 1951, first flight of Javelin: Waterton noted buffet at tail at only 200 mph. June 2, 1952 flew modified Javelin; elevators broke off and aircraft exploded, burned, on landing. Awarded George Medal July 29, 1952. Javelins not delivered to RAF squadrons until February 1956.

Worked on Fleet Street as aviation correspondent. Wrote, with Timothy Hewat, *The Comet Riddle* (London: Frederick Muller, 1955), the story of the world's first jetliner, its crashes, and lessons for future. Following year published autobiography, *The Quick and the Dead* (London: Frederick Muller, 1956).

∨ ∨ ∨

THE BRITISH TWIN-JET GLOSTER METEOR was still the fastest airplane in the world in early 1947. As a reigning world champion, the record-setting Meteor became a priceless global sales tool for its manufacturer, the Gloster Aircraft Company (GAC). With the end of the war, Gloster, whose main product before WW2 had been a two-gun biplane, found itself marketing the only fully combat-tested jet fighter in production in the world. The world-record holder, RAF serial EE549, and a current production Meteor 4 were stars at the annual Paris aero exhibition in December 1947.

The following month, Canadian-born ex-RAF Squadron Leader Bill Waterton, by then a test pilot with Gloster, was assigned to retrieve EE549 from Paris. As he explained in his 1956 autobiography *The Quick and the Dead,* he had been asked by Gloster's general manager "to try for the Paris-to-London record" on the way home. But first, Gloster's French agent, "a tough, ex-Maquis boy," arranged for one final low-level fly-past over the centre of Paris.

"Paris, it appeared, was seized by that crazy fever for lunatic spectacle peculiar to the French," Waterton reminisced, "and [due to headlines about *le Meteor, l'avion plus vite du monde*] the street would consequently be packed with intrepid Parisians anxious to be scared out of their wits." Not just any Paris boulevard, either. The Champs Élysées. At 50 feet. At 600 mph plus.

The one-man airshow was scheduled for noon. Waterton's reconnaissance that morning of January 15, 1947, was intense, if rushed. Nothing could fully prepare him to fly inverted between buildings at the speeds the Meteor was capable of after swooping down over the Arc de Triomph. "The slightest error there could mean the slaughter of spectators as the Meteor fell among them. Timing and precision were essential . . . At over 600 miles per hour such flying did not allow for even an infinitesimal margin for error."

Waterton did fast and slow passes along the Champs Élysées in both directions, inverted and right-side-up, punctuated with upward rolls, inverted climbs, and tight, multi-G aileron turns. Then he came to the Eiffel Tower.

"It was a strange and wonderful experience to fly round the great structure looking up at the people on the galleries who were waving to me. But with an icy stab of fear I suddenly saw the sloping, almost invisible steel cables which guy the great tower. In dropping my height to fly around the tower, I had missed one by no more than twelve feet. A bit closer and the steel rope would have sheared off a wing as easily as a hot knife slices butter.

"I left the tower in a hurry, sweating freely. I flew upside down from west to east along the Champs Élysées, and made an inverted climb over La Concorde. I dived in at speed from the east, and disappeared from view in a series of climbing rolls into the western sky. The show was over."

The following day Waterton set a new Paris-to-London speed record, 208 miles at 618.4 mph—faster, Waterton cannot help pointing out in his book, "than the world's absolute speed record" set by the commanding officer of the RAF's High Speed Flight the previous autumn in the same Meteor. (Waterton was part of that record-setting effort, but his Meteor, EE550, did not handle as well as EE549, costing him speed.) Flying at close to the airframe limit of the Meteor, a wartime design, involved the aircraft "kicking, bucking and bouncing with twitching wings as the hard, compressed air slapped at her with sledgehammer blows. The engines shrieked as we climbed up and away towards the channel."

The trip took him 20 minutes, 11 seconds, Le Bourget to Croydon. His main worry was having enough fuel to make Farnborough, the U.K.'s centre of experimental flight, where—imagine this—he was to clear customs. "It would be a bit of an anti-climax," he thought, "to prang through lack of juice."

Waterton figures he reached 625 mph at one point. He did it wearing the chalk-stripe suit, "never a Saville Row creation at its best," that became his civvy-street outfit when he left the RAF. Later that day Gloster's general manager shook Waterton's hand and, as the pilot recalled, actually said, "Jolly good show, Waterton."

BILL WATERTON WAS the first Canadian-born test pilot of international note. His first flight in the prototype Avro Canada CF-100 interceptor by itself makes him a pioneer of high-performance flight in Canada. His stewardship of the CF-100's early flight test and demonstration program lasted about 14 months—not long enough, or far too long, depending on your point of view—from December 1949 to early February 1951. But his contribution to the early stages of jet fighter development was much greater than that.

The Meteor was the first operational Allied jet fighter of WW2; just before the war ended, Waterton flew it with an RAF unit that evolved tactics to fully exploit the new jet's performance in combat. He subsequently flew a Meteor with the RAF's High Speed Flight. By early 1947 Waterton had become CTP with Gloster, the Meteor's builder.

Waterton's experiences during the war and with the RAF and the British aviation industry made him an entirely logical choice to do the early CF-100 testing. In his own estimation, by the winter of 1948–49, he was "by far the most experienced jet pilot in the [Hawker-Siddeley] Group at the time. I had flown hundreds and hundreds of hours in jets, single and twin engined, and knew the Rolls-Royce Avon engines fitted initially in the CF-100 . . . An additional factor may well have been a political one: to boost national pride by enabling the Group to say that Canada's first completely home-produced fighter was initially flown by a Canadian-born pilot. Avro Canada's own chief test pilot, Don Rogers, was an exceptionally fine flyer, but he then lacked experimental and jet experience."

Even now, in his eighties, crippled by gout and sometimes using a crutch to get around, Waterton has a powerful presence, an erect military bearing, and a decisiveness that must partly account for his rapid rise through the wartime ranks of the RAF. The dramatically upswept moustache that was his trademark is still there, almost as common in the wartime RAF as sheepskin Irvin jackets. He looked like a squadron leader and test pilot, and he behaved like one. "He rubbed some people the wrong way because of his rather, maybe, overbearing attitude in some ways," Waterton's nominal boss at Avro Canada, Don Rogers, recalls, emphasizing that he got along fine with Waterton. "He bothered the engineers and the design people. He was a very competent pilot, no question about that." Waterton's colleagues in Canada were not so diplomatic. "He acted as if he was a white knight," Mike Cooper-Slipper thought, "here to show the Canadians how to fly their own plane."

Those, more or less, were Waterton's orders. Sir Roy Dobson encountered Waterton at a company party at the Dorchester Hotel in London during the winter of 1948–49. Dobson had joined A.V. Roe in Manchester as a draftsman in 1914 and by the end of WW2 was running not only Avro U.K. but Hawker-Siddeley, the conglomerate of which Avro was a part. Gloster had become part of Hawker-Siddeley during the early 1930s. Dobson asked Waterton, "Going to Canada to fly that new fighter for us, Bill?"

Waterton replied: "I guess I'm as big a sucker as the next one."

"Dobson laughed," Waterton recalled in his account of the offhand exchange over drinks. "Big sucker," Dobson replied. "That's a good one!"

Dobson laughed again and moved on.

Sir Roy, who had admired the craftsmanship that went into Canadian-built Avro Lancasters during the war and the numbers of them turned out at Malton, had one final brief for Waterton, either at the Dorchester or some time before he went to Canada: "He told me that the Canadians were keen, eager to get on with it, and the most ignorant lot you'll find anywhere."

For his own part, Waterton acknowledged in his book that "I was never blessed with a great deal of tact—too much Irish blood, perhaps." But he *was* tactful during his time flying the CF-100 prototypes, praising the aircraft and its engineers. Like all new designs, the CF-100 had problems. Its wing spar flexed under moderate manoeuvres, cracking the wing root fairing. But some criticize Waterton for not having been critical enough of the CF-100.

Waterton, one of the highest-time jet pilots anywhere in 1949, arrived in Canada that December to check himself out on the CF-100 prototype, RCAF 18101. It was the first time he had been back to his native country since ferrying a Douglas Boston bomber from Dorval, Quebec, to Prestwick, Scotland, in March 1943. He had been in Egypt since October 1949, delivering a dozen Meteor 4s and a couple of Meteor 7 trainers by way of Italy, when the urgent call came. He did wonder what the rush was.

"I liked the new plane—although she was by no means ready for me, despite the frantic cables to Egypt and the hurry to get me across the Atlantic," he writes in his autobiography.

"I spent a busy day acquainting myself with the Avro setup and the people with whom I would be working. The Canadians were a refreshing bunch. By English standards they were inclined to be brash, crude and showy—but what a spirit of bustling enthusiasm they showed. They wanted to get things done."

The big rush to get him to Canada, Waterton figured, was as political as his assignment. "The atmosphere was tense," he writes in his autobiography, "not only at Avro's, but throughout the country. Most of the money financing the fighter came from public funds, and since the North American taxpayers are quick to raise hell, the enterprise had become the centre of a bitter political squabble. Canada had built fighters before, but she hadn't designed and built them, and many people felt that she should stick to the old policy of building proven planes under British and American licence . . .

"As is so often the case in Canada . . . a large section of the population lacked confidence in their country's ability—and, of course, certain British and American manufacturers did not want to see their Canadian market disappear . . . But none of the existing designs quite filled Canada's particular requirements: extremely long range, a good takeoff, and high rate of climb. The British had the latter, but not the range. The Americans lacked climb performance, and required huge, costly aerodromes—not currently available or immediately practicable in Canada with its ... population of some 14 million. The [Royal] Canadian Air Force wanted their own, specifically designed, aircraft. Further, they were anxious to build up their own aircraft industry in order to make themselves independent, in part, of Britain and America ... There was pressure to get the aircraft in the air before the end of 1949, but it could not be done. Faces dropped, and morale was low. When I saw the aircraft at the beginning of December, I doubted whether she'd be ready in four months. But this was Toronto, not Gloucestershire, and on the evening of January 17, 1950, I commenced taxiing trials."

These early ground runs revealed minor flaws in the CF-100's controls—more matters of preference than function. Waterton was very happy with Avro's responses to his concerns. "I formed a deep respect for Avro Canada's aerodynamicist [Jim Chamberlin]. Unlike some others of the breed, he would tell me what I could expect from the plane—and was invariably right ... Everything had been [wind] tunnel tested: even the wingtip tanks. Such thoroughness was an eye-opener, and gave me great peace of mind ...

"I ground ran the CF-100's engines, worked her hydraulics, and called for one or two changes in cockpit layout. To my delight—and in direct contrast to past experience—the alterations were made expeditiously and without argument."

Waterton had the fighter's rudder pedals (which incorporated the wheel brakes) beefed up to accommodate clumsy feet and asked to have their operation require more force "to avoid over-braking." Finding the nosewheel over-sensitive as well, he had its steering inputs disconnected. "Despite the snow on the runway," he writes, "the CF-100 was at least the equal of the Meteor in ground handling, and that was good enough for me ... The taxiing trials on 18101 went off better than those of any prototype I handled." At near takeoff speed he found he could place the nose where he wanted it. The elevators were "O.K." The rudder was "satisfactory" and the ailerons responsive. "All in all 18101 seemed an excellent job of work ...

"I had no personal doubts about the CF-100's success. She looked right and seemed right . . . She was a big plane, her twin engines close to the fuselage—exactly as I had wanted Gloster's to do with the Meteor. With her black paint, white markings and tall, stalky undercarriage, the CF-100 had a decidedly Germanic appearance."

"JANUARY 19"—two days after ground tests started—"was cold and bright, the wind blowing almost straight down the runway: ideal conditions for a maiden flight," in Waterton's judgement. "The hangar was an agitated, nervous, excited, confident confusion of activity as final inspections and checks were made."

That morning Bill Waterton made one of the diplomatic blunders that marked important moments in his career. Informed that a planeload of air force brass and government "bigwigs" were scheduled to arrive from Ottawa and lunch before the big event, Waterton dodged them by doing a weather and runway recon in an Avro Anson utility transport. He excused himself for not joining them to eat because he had not been officially invited to the glittering lunch. By the time the brass were finished, Waterton was in 18101's cockpit, doing double cockpit checks, an engine runup, and a brake-holding power test. Later, he would find out that he was seen to have snubbed the RCAF's procurement and staff people and the national defence hierarchy, the very men whose careers rode on the airplane that would soon represent more than half the Canadian defence department's budget. He could always argue that he had more pressing matters on his mind.

"I was carrying half fuel, the plane was light, and in the low temperature the [Rolls-Royce] Avon engines [that powered the first two prototypes] behaved superbly," Waterton recalls in *The Quick and the Dead*. "Acceleration was tremendous, and in less than 500 yards we lifted cleanly from the runway. I throttled back, and at 140 knots climbed to 500 feet."

Then Waterton tried to retract the landing gear. He pushed the UP button, but it would not fully depress. He pushed again, harder. But he did not push hard enough to override the UP selector, knowing to do so would not only be "to ignore that something was wrong" but likely result in a wheels-up landing before his blue-ribbon audience.

Waterton says he decided to leave the gear down and fly slowly. He minimizes this snag in his book, saying that "as on all my first flights in prototypes, part of the machinery had gone wrong." He flew 18101 for 40 minutes at altitudes to 5,000 feet, at 180 knots (207 mph), testing controls, turning the aircraft, "and getting the 'feel' of the aircraft's general flying qualities. There was nothing to worry about: she seemed a sound design . . .

"When I had used two-thirds of my fuel I came in on a straight approach. The plane was steady as a rock, and touched down at about 100 miles an hour within the first 150 yards of runway. We stopped with smooth ease within 600 yards of the start of the runway. For a first flight I was well satisfied. The CF-100 proved pleasant to fly, and takeoff and landing were easy."

His overall satisfaction with the CF-100 notwithstanding, Waterton goes on in his memoir to further insult the blue-ribbon crowd he had snubbed before the flight, describing them as "always rather pathetic at such times: looking at you with spaniel eyes, pleading to be told the best, terrified they'll hear the worst. For once I was able to be cautiously optimistic."

The second flight of the all-black prototype, with its white fuselage lightning bolt and code letters FB D, took place six days later, on January 25. The flight was an exploration of 18101's low-speed handling and stall behaviour. The third outing would be a demonstration for Sir Roy Dobson, who was curious to see what the CF-100 would do.

"I did a mild beat-up," is how Waterton describes his second flight in 18101 in his book. "Nothing elaborate: just high and low speed flying, with rolls and tight turns. Previously I had reached 430 knots [494 mph] at 12,000 feet—beyond the point at which a Meteor ran into compressibility trouble. There was no sign of compressibility— but the elevator trim control started to seize-up. It seemed there was a distortion somewhere in the back end, and it put an end to ideas of going any faster until investigations were made. When I landed after the beat-up we discovered that the wing-root fairings were torn and twisted. This was disturbing, for it meant, quite simply, that the wings were bending and twisting far more than they should have done. And this was happening during only mild manoeuvres—a fraction of the treatment an operational fighter would have to put up with."

THE ORIGINS OF THE CF-100 prototypes' wing-flex snag extended back to January 1948. Construction of the first prototype was sufficiently advanced at that point for wind-tunnel testing to begin. John Frost, the project's chief engineer since the previous June 14, had been shocked when he saw the plywood mockup of the fighter then being called the XC-100 at Malton on his return from England. One of a number of changes Frost made to the design that had been given three-dimensional shape was to lower the fuselage-mounted engines from their positions above the wings to a level where the undersides of their nacelles coincided with the ventral fuselage and wing under-surfaces in a more or less smooth cross-sectional sweep. "This greatly reduced the frontal area of the aircraft," Frost recalled many years later, "since the bottom of the engine was now level with the bottom of the wing, and not sitting on top of it as previously."

By January of 1948 Frost was back in England, dropping in on the manufacturers of the XC-100's engines (the first three prototypes would be powered by Rolls-Royce Avons), ejection seats (Martin-Baker), and landing gear (Dowty). In Frost's absence, aerodynamicist Jim Chamberlin interpreted the wind tunnel data to indicate that the fighter's centre of lift was too far forward. With Avro chief engineer Edgar Atkin's approval, Chamberlin moved the engines about one foot aft.

While that modification had the aerodynamic effect of creating a larger area of undersurface aft of the wings and thus moving the aircraft's centre of lift backward, it also had a structural effect. The engines tapered toward their tailpipes, and a larger-diameter cross-section now met the main wing spar, which passed underneath. The spar carries much of a wing's bending loads. To cater to the larger diameter of the engines at that point, a dip was introduced into the upper surface of the main spar. Thus, as engineer Waclaw Czerwinski put it, "Suddenly the aircraft got a main spar that carried all the load but [was] very much weakened."

The flex now designed into the CF-100's wing tore up the wing-engine fairing, a light, concave-shaped piece of aluminum rivetted over the wing-engine-nacelle joint that smoothed airflow over the wing's upper-surface root.

Turbulent air downstream from the fairing, at the tail, was Waterton's warning that something somewhere was very wrong. He took responsibility. "Quite simply," he writes, "I 'bent' the aeroplane."

Waterton says he was restricted to gentle manoeuvres during the four flights he was able to make that February. John Frost came along for the ride on his eighth CF-100 flight, "another delightful contrast to England, where I was never able to find a designer with spare time enough to fly in his own creation." Frost also accompanied Waterton to a demonstration in Ottawa for the governor general and Belgium's Prince Bernhardt—"a tremendous success," Waterton thought, "despite my 'bending' the plane for a second time—even though it had been reinforced."

Waterton approved of the approach of the stress office at Avro in moving slowly on the modifications to the wing spar. He felt that the British firms were all too likely to put test pilots' bodies on the line to prove ill-considered modifications to troublesome designs. Avro added doubler plates to thicken the spar caps where they dipped under the engines.

During May Waterton demonstrated the CF-100 to the U.S. Air Force over Washington. On the way, he averaged 575 mph at 25,000 to 30,000 feet and set a new Toronto-Montreal speed record of better than 638 mph.

The second CF-100, 18102, or FB K, flew July 10, 1950. Waterton did the first flight, then quickly checked out Bruce Warren on 18102. "Duke" Warren, a 1949 ETPS graduate, would take over as CF-100 project test pilot from Waterton in February 1951. He was killed in 18102, along with his observer Robert Ostrander, when they flew straight into the ground east of London, Ontario, on April 5, 1951. An oxygen system malfunction was blamed.

The demonstration trips to Washington and an appearance at an airshow at Boston's Logan Airport (where Waterton met then-Capt.

Chuck Yeager, the first man to fly at the speed of sound) raised the CF-100's profile, especially after Waterton survived his most hair-raising moment in 18101. Bruce Warren was there to provide a running commentary on loudspeakers as Waterton performed his death-defying routine. "It was my custom to fly at about twenty feet from the ground with flaps partially extended, just staggering along above the stall, and then—in front of the spectators—open the engines to full power and roar upwards in a steep climb. It was both noisy and impressive.

"It was in the middle of the operation—when opening up the engines from about 105 mph—that I was nearly caught out. I had already pulled up the nose, and had the throttles fully opened, when the starboard engine stalled. It's always at such times that things go haywire . . . At low altitude, the flaps giving high drag, and with virtually no speed . . . a prang was inevitable. Yet I didn't crash. I managed to get the nose down, and gently nursed the aeroplane along until I had sufficient speed to climb away, then, when I had gained sufficient height, I raised the flaps and carried out a normal single-engined circuit and landing."

Meanwhile, Warren's eyes were on his script: "As Warren described the CF-100's incredible climb rate," Larry Milberry tells us, "Waterton was staggering along above the runway, just managing to keep airborne."

Fresh from its triumphs elsewhere, the first CF-100 returned to Toronto during September 1950 to perform at the Canadian National Exhibition on the Toronto waterfront. "One incident [at the CNE airshow] was particularly frightening," Waterton relates. "While pulling up into the vertical climb of a loop, I heard a violent crack: a sharp thunderclap of sound clearly audible above the engine and wind noise. Something had gone—but what? I smartly rolled out at the top of the loop, ready to head for open spaces and bale out. Nothing drastic seemed to have occurred, however, for the plane flew on without further trouble.

"But I had the wind up and wasn't taking chances. I cut short the display and came in. The crack, we discovered, had been caused by the rupture of metal: the skin of the wing and centre section had again split—and this time worse than ever."

BACK IN BRITAIN after handing the CF-100 test program over to Don Rogers, Bruce Warren, and Mike Cooper-Slipper, Waterton became a hero in Britain after twice crash-landing Gloster Javelin prototypes that had lost their elevators in flight. For the second of these accomplishments, in which he barely escaped from the exploding aircraft, Waterton was awarded the George Medal, Britain's highest peacetime award for bravery.

Yet today, living not far from the Great Lakes port of Owen Sound, Ontario, Waterton is forgotten, a prophet without honour in Britain and a kind of exile in his own land. In immediate postwar Great Britain, he could never be more than an energetic, temporarily useful colonial. To Canadian eyes and ears he had also seemed foreign— more British than the British. In a Britain exhausted and still rationed years after the great struggle for its life, the bad news he reported (as a test pilot, an author, and a newspaperman) about the nation's postwar fighter designs—the Javelin in particular—was accurate and only more unwelcome for that. Waterton's firsthand examples of deadly negligence, lack of accountability, and industrial revolution work practices at Gloster embarrassed the company and the rest of the Britsh aircraft industry, which blackballed him.

When he left Canada on February 7, 1951, to return to England, Waterton was "proud to have played some part in the birth of Canada's jet aircraft industry . . . What had been planned as a six months' trip to Canada had lasted for fifteen. When I left Toronto, the structural weaknesses of the CF-100 had not yet been overcome, but the 'plane had established an outstanding pattern of behaviour and performance.

"The CF-100 has been," Waterton wrote in 1956, at the height of the Cold War, "for many years the West's top night and all-weather fighter . . . No other night fighter has its range and it can undertake night interception and intruder roles beyond the capability of other fighters which have a drastically limited range in order to gain in rate of climb. Canada can take great credit for the CF-100. It had its set-backs, but no more than many others and less than most. The troubles were mainly of an engineering nature and not aerodynamic, for the CF-100's appearance differs little today"—he was writing in the mid-1950s—"from the aeroplane I left in 1951."

The CF-100 was Canada's most impressive military aircraft program. Nearly 700 were built, and into the 1960s they were Canada's first-line protection against the main perceived threat to the continent: Soviet bombers. Bill Waterton still believes Canada can take credit for the CF-100, but Canada has never returned the compliment.

5

> **PETER COPE:**
>
> ## FLIGHT TEST
>
> ## PROFESSIONAL

CHRONOLOGY: Peter Roland Cope, b. Croydon, December 7,
1921. Degree in science, majors in physics, chemistry, pure
and applied maths. Volunteered for RAF, tested, put on nine
months' deferred service, worked as research chemist.

August 1941 called up to RAF but no flying training being done in U.K.; to
Maxwell Field, Alabama, November to May 1942, graduated as USAAC lieutenant. July–September 1942, OTU. To January 1944, 170 Sqn., Mustang Is in
low-level photo-recon role. February–April 1944, flying instructor school,
Montrose. May 1944–end 1945, No. 12 AFU Spitalgate (near Grantham) as
instructor. January–May 1946, Empire Test Pilots' School, first half No. 4
Course, Cranfield (made top 10; top 10 rushed mid-course to RAF test centres). May–August 1946, Aeroplane & Armament Experimental Establishment, Boscombe Down. September–December 1946, ETPS No. 5 Course;
joined second half of course. Beginning 1947–November 1949, Royal Aircraft
Establishment, Farnborough (Exceptional Rating).

Joined Armstrong-Whitworth as civilian test pilot November 1949,
testing two-seat Meteors. Hired by Avro Canada April 1951, replacing Bruce
Warren in CF-100 development program. Recommended Jan Zurakowski to

Avro Canada, 1952. November 25, 1952, first air firing of CF-100 machine guns. By May 1956 had completed 1,000 hours of CF-100 flight testing.

October 3, 1958, flew CF-105 for first time. Remained with Avro after CF-105 cancellation February 20, 1959. Continued to July 6, 1960, last CF-100 flight. Retired as test pilot with 102 models of 62 types of aircraft flown, including the Avrocar flying saucer.

Mid-1961 to end 1986, Boeing Commercial Airplane Co. customer support. Supervised introduction of new models with airlines: 727, 737, 747, 767. Finally, manager of wide-body 747/767 customer support.

                              ∨ ∨ ∨

T WAS AS IF PETER COPE'S flight test observer
knew what was in store before the two of
them got off the ground that summer's day
in 1954. Test pilots are inclined to ignore omens; after all, Cope had
fired the T160 cannon from CF-100s on the ground and in flight before. The difference was that this time he would be flying and shooting faster.

As it happened, the CF-100 cannon tests were the closest Cope
ever came to killing himself. He understates the risk today: a misfire
during the cannon tests, he says, was "the one thing that might have
happened."

When it came into service in 1953, the CF-100 all-weather interceptor was as fast and almost as heavily armed as any aircraft of
its kind in the world. Of course it was never put to the ultimate test.
It is reasonable to believe that it would have been effective against a
Soviet threat consisting of propeller-driven derivatives of Second
World War bombers. With jet bombers appearing in Western air
forces and the likelihood of the Soviets developing their own, however, the Royal Canadian Air Force wondered whether the CF-100
might need more teeth.

The CF-100 Mk.3, the first production model, was armed with four .50-calibre machine guns arranged in a semi-circular belly pack below and just behind the engine intakes. On later models, the guns were augmented with wingtip pods containing unguided folding-fin aircraft rockets (FFARS).

Another idea was to replace the Mk.3's .50-calibre machine guns with four 20-mm cannons. Whereas a machine gun fires rifle-type bullets, a cannon fires bigger explosive shells. A few of those shells, in the right place, could disable a bomber.

Flight testing the T160 cannon installation, like most armament tests on the CF-100, fell to the CF-100's project test pilot, Peter Cope. Aircraft armament testing is inherently dangerous. It involves working with explosive devices, often in unproven applications. There were many armament upgrades proposed for the CF-100, and testing them cost lives. Cope did more than anyone on Avro Canada's flight test staff to transform the new fighter from a 640-mph two-seat sportster into an effective weapon of war.

The cannon test in question took place June 18, 1954, in CF-100 18103. That aircraft was the third prototype CF-100 and the first of its kind powered with the Canadian-built Orenda engines the fighter was designed to fly with. The four cannons were installed in the ventral gun bay of 18103, replacing the machine guns. In a period when real-time data transmissions from aircraft being tested to the engineers on the ground were limited to voice messages over the radio, the CF-100's two-seat cockpit afforded the bonus of a second pair of eyes on the instruments while the pilot flew the aircraft.

"Prior to this flight," Cope recalled with a wry smile 45 years later, "the flight test observer was so nervous he had to pee beforehand. So he had the traditional pee at the back of the aeroplane first. And then in getting back into the aeroplane, he broke all the pencils he had in his left sleeve pocket. So we had to give him another lot of the pencils . . .

"In the meantime, he made the usual intercom check, and his headset wasn't working. And while all this was going on, he fiddled around with his parachute harness. And, believe it or not, he managed to jam the quick-release buckle. I'd never heard of anyone doing that before. If anyone could do it, he could do it, and he did it. So we had to get him out of the aeroplane, get him out of the harness, and get another parachute. So, finally, after these setbacks we set forth."

It was not as if the cannon-firing trip had looked like a snooze beforehand. Both the CF-100 and its experimental gun installation would be tested at their maximum outputs. Anything that could go wrong with aircraft or gun was more likely to go wrong with both pushing the limits.

"I think this particular run called for max continuous firing at 5,000 feet and max speed [640 mph or 556 knots]," Cope says today. "And those cannons would belt out 16–17 seconds' continuous firing at about 550 knots. The recoil would knock about 5 to 10 knots off the aeroplane's speed.

"I got 17 seconds' continuous firing on the cannon. It all seemed to be working very nicely. I'd just finished, and as [the shooting] stopped, there was the most god-almighty bang. There'd been an explosion under the port engine. It blew both port cowls off. The upper came across the cockpit and knocked most of the clear Perspex out of the canopy frame, leaving shards at both front and rear ends. And then the lower cowl going along the leading edge of the port wing didn't do that any good.

"Directly this happened, my first reaction was *Gain as much height as possible.* So I throttled back and got climbing for altitude. I chucked the aeroplane around. The power and controls were all right. Tended to be a little bit one-wing-heavy. But anyway I knew I hadn't got a major problem. Nothing else was broken.

"And this guy in the back, he was so nervous, I had a helluva job to restrain him in the aeroplane. I called up Avro and told them what had happened and that we were coming back there. The observer wanted to jump. In that aeroplane, if you jumped, you were going to tear your head apart on the canopy shards. Then he said, 'Well, just go in to Downsview.'" Downsview, de Havilland of Canada's airfield, was closer.

"But I was thinking, *We can get into Malton without any trouble, the aeroplane is perfectly flyable, might have to land a little hot.*

"So I checked the stalling speed: *We might have to land a little hotter.* But that was no problem on the longer runway we had there [at
Malton], other than the damage we'd got. I had to go in at 140 knots
[161 mph] just to play it safe, and take it from there. No problem."

On the ground, the observer had to have his hands pried from
the ejection seat firing handle. Had he pulled that handle, the rear
Martin-Baker Mk.2 ejection seat would have launched him to an
uncertain fate. It was still not known on that day whether the rear
seat in a CF-100 was usable. It was certainly suspect. A little more
than two months later, another flight test observer would become the
thirteenth CF-100 fatality, killed when he was unable to activate his
seat after the airplane he was in became uncontrollable. As it was,
Cope's terrified observer was lifted out of 10813, unable to move for
himself.

THE FACT COPE CONSIDERS that flight his most dangerous says a
lot about his flying career up to mid-1954. It is not as if his life in aviation had been uneventful. Plenty had gone wrong. His mounts had
tried to shoot themselves down four times while he was testing guns
or rockets on fighter aircraft. He had experienced engine failure on
takeoff; in one case, twice in a row, in another, three consecutive
times. In each instance he brought the stricken airplane home. By
1956, he had accumulated 1,000 hours of experimental test flying on
CF-100s, much of it fraught with danger but, thanks to Cope's skills
and judgement, not lethal.

It would be easy to conclude that Cope lived a charmed life as a
military and test pilot. He is quick to say today he has been lucky
throughout his career, and while it may sometimes be better to be
lucky than to be good, Cope was both. The type of wartime operational flying he did, low-level photo reconnaissance, emphasized precision and discipline, the same qualities needed for experimental test
flying. The RAF schooled him in weapons testing. His talent was recognized with an appointment to the Empire Test Pilots' School. Cope
was the first ETPS graduate to join a Canadian aircraft manufacturer's
flight test staff. He is one of the few test pilots of his time who never
got himself into a situation where he had to abandon an airplane.

"I always maintain," he said recently, "that the only reason I would leave an aeroplane was (a) if it was on fire, or (b) if I could not maintain control of it really well. Fortunately, I never had to leave one."

If personality has anything to do with success in this line of work, Cope's sunny outlook must have helped. Cope is an open, friendly fellow, the kind others like to hire and work with. People like Cope get breaks in life: when his station commander refused to endorse Cope's ETPS application after he and a colleague sang all the verses of a bawdy ditty in the officers mess, an RAF air vice-marshall stepped forward to sign it.

Becoming a pilot was Peter Cope's life's dream. He spent his first 10 years living in a London suburb near Croydon, London's prewar airport. He often wondered whether the Lufthansa pilots he met after they arrived at Croydon in Junkers trimotor airliners returned during the war flying Heinkel bombers. By the time the RAF called him up, Britain was not a safe place over which to solo in a slow, bright yellow airplane. Cope feels that his first big break was being sent that November to Montgomery, Alabama, for basic training.

"Luckily, when I first started flying at primary school in the United States, I had an instructor that, when you lined up looking at the instructors, I thought, 'I'd like that little guy. He looks a happy fellow.' I got him.

"He was the base aerobatic nut. And after we'd soloed—I finished first in the class—he got working on the aerobatic stuff. We covered all the required, routine flying: chandelles, lazy eights, forced landings, all that sort of thing. And then we got into aerobatics. He did everything with me the Stearman PT-17 could possibly do. Now the Stearman hadn't got enough guts to do an outside loop, but we did everything else. Then he taught me inverted spins." (An inverted spin is like a normal one, except that the airplane is upside down, on its back.) "And he said, 'Don't you ever do these on your own until I give you the okay.' Well, after I'd demonstrated several times that I could recover from an inverted spin, he said, 'Okay, when you want to, try it on your own. Just take it calmly, just like you do normally.' So with great trepidation one day I launched myself into my first [solo] inverted spin, and everything worked out beautifully. No trouble . . .

"One time in the Royal Air Force, when I was testing the Seafire"—
a carrier-borne development of the Spitfire—"we were working on
the Pilot's Notes, and we wanted to find out what would happen if
you mishandled the controls at the stall. So I brought this machine
into a stall—kicked in hard right rudder and stick hard back. It
flipped right over into an inverted spin. Naturally I thought, 'What
have we got here? Oh, yeah, we're going the wrong way.' I applied the
normal corrective technique, and we came out quite happily.

"I figure old Norman Reed, who was my instructor, he helped
save that aeroplane, because otherwise you'd be in a position where
you'd like to leave that aeroplane, [because an inverted spin] is so
damn hairy."

DURING SEPTEMBER 1942, after a couple of months at an Operational Training Unit, the British military pilot's finishing school, Cope
was posted to the only outfit he would ever fight with, 170 Squadron,
a low-level photo-recon (PR) unit equipped with the Allison-engine
Mustang I. One-seventy was a kind of Commonwealth foreign legion
consisting of Australians, New Zealanders, Canadians—and even a
Trinidadian—which may be why 170 Squadron's tours kept being extended. No nation's air staff kept track of them. As time passed, the
members of 170 found themselves with more and more to do. They
started by doing before-and-after photo shoots of less than a dozen
v-2 rocket sites on the Cherbourg Peninsula before D-Day and ended
the war having photographed 150 of them. It was fast, precise flying
rather than the usual freelance fighter buccaneering.

Ironically, pilots of 170 Squadron were more likely to suffer at the
hands of their supposed friends than from German attacks. Meeting
the Luftwaffe 176-victory ace Johannes Steinhoff in Canada after the
war, Cope learned that the pilots of FW 190s, the premier German
fighters, avoided descending to the level of the Mustang Is, which
could out-turn them near the ground. On the other hand, Royal Navy
gunners in the English Channel routinely opened up on anything
flying west over the ditch. And, for some reason, Spitfires flown by
Americans (of all people to mistake American-built Mustangs for
Bf 109s) were constantly bouncing Cope and his squadron mates.

It was while Cope was between tours with 170 Squadron that he took courses in gunnery and rocketry—skills he had already shown talent for by learning to fly exacting straight and level photo passes.

"During the war I was a PGI, pilot gunnery instructor. I'd done a lot of work on cannon, machine guns, and rockets. That was squadron stuff; I'd picked up my PGI by going to Sutton Bridge on a course old Screwball Beurling"—Canada's leading fighter ace and a dead-accurate shot—"was on too. I got the gunnery work there."

Cope was still with 170 Squadron when the war ended. He applied for the Test Pilots School No. 3 Course, the first postwar ETPS session, but was too late with his application. As Cope recalls, the minimum qualification was to have flown 10 types, accumulated 1,000 hours' flying, and have a degree.

Cope had a number of entries on his service record that would have impressed anyone reading his application. There was the time he flew his Mustang to an RAF maintenance unit for a routine 50-hour engine change. The first two zero-time units installed at the MU failed on takeoff. This made his third takeoff with a new engine a special kick.

He is one of a very select few pilots to have studied with two ETPS courses. (Others would be Neville Duke, of Hawker Hunter fame, and F/L A. W. "Bill" Bedford, famous as the test pilot of the P.1127, later the Harrier.) Cope was accepted into ETPS Course No. 4, starting January 1946 at Cranfield. But so short of test pilots was the postwar RAF that, by design, Cope and the other top nine of his classmates were diverted to the RAF's test establishments halfway through their curriculum, in May. They had by then mastered the basics of performance testing. Cope was posted to the Aeroplane & Armament Experimental Establishment (A&AEE) at Boscombe Down from May to August 1946. He and the other refugees from the interrupted No. 4 Course were invited back to join No. 5 Course for the second half of its program, which covered aircraft test handling techniques, from September to the end of December, 1946. There, Cope and classmate Neville Duke joined, among others, Peter Lawrence, who would be killed in a prototype Gloster Javelin. (In fact, six of the 33 on the No. 5 Course would be killed in flying accidents, a higher-than-average survival rate for ETPS classes at the time.) Then, for most of 1947, Cope was posted to the Royal Aircraft Establishment (RAE) at Farnborough. Being posted to both the A&AEE and RAE during his training in test flying was the equivalent to doing postgraduate work at Oxford *and* Cambridge.

Cope's specialty throughout his test flying career was the sporty trade of aircraft armament testing. "I did a lot of rocket work at Farnborough because I was a very good shot, accurate and so on. What we were doing at Farnborough for a while was developing flight paths for rockets launched into water. And we had Lake Alwyn, up in Wales, where they had eight lanes marked out on the lake with submersed screens to pick up depth and positioning of the rockets. What I did was make, with eight rockets, eight passes, put one rocket down each lane, one after the other, to measure the underwater ballistics." This called for pretty accurate firing from Cope's Mosquito fighter-bomber.

"One day, I got one nicely away, something went wrong, it nipped out of the water, clobbered my port wing, and bashed a hole right through to the main spar. I think something went wrong with the [rocket's] fins ... whether they got bent or something, it just came out, *whissh!* And clobbered the port wing."

ALTHOUGH COPE WAS an outstanding pilot by then—rated "exceptional" even among the RAE Farnborough elite—he was soon inspired to raise his game to a new level. He flew the Martin-Baker MB.5 fighter prototype at Farnborough, which was impressive enough. But then he saw Jan Zurakowski's legendary demonstration of the MB.5 at the June 1946 Society of British Aircraft Constructors (SBAC) airshow at Farnborough. And although he cannot imagine how Zurakowski could have done it, Cope recalls the Polish flyer doing a Falling Leaf— a manoeuvre characteristic of twins, in which power can be alternated between the two engines to produce yaw to one side, then the other—in the MB.5, a single-engine fighter.

"Just brilliant flying" is what Cope remembers of that performance. "Perfect positioning over the crowd so they saw as much of the aeroplane as possible. Basically, it was one of the most crisp displays you could get. Funnily enough, I always admired Jan's demonstration flying because of the crispness. I figured I could do a pretty good demonstration job, but I was definitely, you might say, a softer pilot. I think I had more feel for the aeroplane in some respects than Jan. But I liked his demonstration better than mine."

Zurakowski's mastery of flying technique set a new standard for Cope. Cope was obligated to the RAF until late 1949, when he joined Armstrong-Whitworth as a civilian test pilot to fly new Meteor Mk.8s off the line and develop the two-seat Meteor Mk.11 night-fighter jet project A-W had taken on while the Meteor's originator, the Gloster Aircraft Company, was fully occupied producing single-seat Mk.8s and Mk.9s. Zurakowski was with Gloster, so his and Cope's professional destinies were now linked.

Cope stayed at Armstrong-Whitworth for about 16 months, from late 1949 to April 1951. A-W, like Avro Canada, was part of the Hawker-Siddeley Group. Early in 1950, A-W was looking for someone to ferry Hawker-Siddeley managing director Sir Roy Dobson and Avro Canada vice-president and general manager Fred Smye to a company sports day on the south coast of England in a de Havilland Rapide twin-engine cabin biplane. Cope volunteered, and he made an immediate impression as a safety-conscious pilot by forbidding Dobson to smoke his cigar in the airplane. Cope also discussed with Smye the idea that Avro Canada would soon be needing test pilots for the CF-100 program. When the RCAF's test pilot Bruce Warren was killed in the crash of the second CF-100 prototype on April 5, 1951, Cope wired Smye offering his services.

"And I got a wire back from Fred: 'Fly over immediately. All expenses paid. Terms discussed on arrival.'" A-W's managing director offered to keep Cope's job open in case things didn't work out in Canada.

But they did. Cope first flew the CF-100 May 7. His assessment was different from Bill Waterton's. Waterton had rated the CF-100 superior to the Meteor in a number of respects.

"Now, I was bitterly disappointed when I finally got to fly that CF-100. I mean, it was so overrated. It was vastly inferior to the Meteor. And it was a messy aeroplane. Because some aeroplanes, you fit in, and you're part of the aeroplane, you're with it. With the CF-100 it was an awkward seating position, you sat so relatively stiffly up. You got the impression you were the man put in just to fly it rather than be part of it. It didn't have that wraparound feeling at all. You take something like a Vampire, Spitfire, or Martin-Baker 5, they were just fantastic aeroplanes. Whereas with the CF-100, you felt you were [just along for the ride]. When I got my hands on it, I was very disappointed with its overall performance, and just the aeroplane itself as a fighting machine. I had a 19-point input in my flight report outlining where this lacked [the qualities of] a good operational aeroplane.

"In those days, when you wrote a flight report on the aeroplane, apart from being copied to Avro top management, it was also copied directly to the RCAF. And the air force saw the write-up before it got into Fred Smye's hands. So they called Fred up and he got very upset at this, and naturally he called me and said, 'What do you mean by all this?' So I went over with him what the shortcomings were, a 19-point negative approach to it. He was very appreciative of this and said, 'I don't like how it got to me, you were just following procedure, but if this is how you feel, then we've got to do something about it.' Fred always said to me, 'Any time you have problems, call on me.'

"They decided to have a good session on this, so they called in Avro Manchester's chief designer, Stuart 'Cock' Davidson," whose nickname is believed to have been short for Cockney. "We had a session with him and the Avro design people. With Davidson's drive, he backed me up on 18 of the 19 where they said they'd do something to fix them. Which I thought was a pretty good batting average . . .

"One of my points was the damn canopy. There was just one pivot point at the back for that damn big canopy. Obviously, you needed two pivot points, one on each side, so that it would swing back evenly. As it happened, going with the one, under G, you didn't know which way it was going to go."

In fairness to Waterton, he knew about the canopy, which had blown off 18101 at nearly 400 mph April 29, 1950, with Don Rogers in the back seat. Waterton had criticized its dive brakes and had brakes with serrated edges, similar to those on the Meteor, installed. But, on the whole, Waterton found himself testing a prototype with a wing spar flex problem that was tearing the root fairings up. The flex persisted for most of his time with the CF-100. That problem was his main preoccupation.

The CF-100's gestation was long, although not especially so by British standards of the time. The 30 months from the prototype's first flight January 19, 1949, to the June 20, 1951, first flight of 18103—the Mk.3 with Orenda engines and therefore the first real CF-100—were time enough for the Opposition in Canada's House of Commons to call the CF-100 program "if . . . not a fiasco . . . at least a very, very costly experiment." There was the sham handover of a not-ready-for-primetime CF-100 to the RCAF on October 17, 1951, and, finally, the delivery of three CF-100s to North Bay for crew training in July 1952. Nearly four years from first flight to first handovers—and most of another year to squadron service in April 1953—for a conservative design that aviation historian Larry Milberry has called "basically a jet-powered World War Two fighter" is a long time.

With Waterton back in England and Bruce Warren dead, Cope found himself starting almost from scratch on his first CF-100 flight May 7.

He spent the rest of 1951 and much of 1952 determining the big fighter's performance and handling characteristics. Thus Cope's logbook comes close to being the history of the CF-100's development, a point-by-point gimlet-eyed examination of what was, at the time, one of Canada's great engineering achievements. No sooner does any aircraft take to the air than ways to improve it are being thought up.

One idea for improving a fighter designed to shoot down bombers as far away from Canadian cities as possible was to enable it to operate from short runways in the Far North. Jet Assisted Take Off (JATO) bottles, attached to the belly between the main landing gear, did give the CF-100 a takeoff boost in tests that Cope started August 12, 1952—but there were not enough tests for the bottles to be used operationally.

The CF-100 was a fighter, the intended armament of which were the eight machine guns first fired in the air by Peter Cope November 25, 1952. If FFARs would augment the CF-100's lethality, one question was where to store and fire them from. Cope spent almost 18 months, from January 12, 1953, to June 1, 1954, testing an internally mounted belly pack that would drop down in .33 seconds, release a fusillade of as many as 48 FFARs, and retract. But at anything over 345 mph, deployment of the rocket pack caused buffeting that only got worse at higher speeds. On August 23, 1954, that buffeting led to the death of the flight test observer hit by the errant canopy. That September the ventral rocket pack was abandoned.

From May 1954 to April 1955, Peter Cope made 36 flights to evaluate the T160 cannon's suitability for use in CF-100s. At least the conclusion was clear: it wasn't suitable. The T160 program was duly dropped 10 months after Cope's—and his flight test observer's—most exciting aerial adventure.

Air-to-air missiles (AAM) make sense as armament for an interceptor, and Avro proposed a CF-100 armed with Canadian-built Velvet Glove missiles in April 1954. Within two years Canada's AAM project had been overtaken by American developments such as the Sidewinder heat-seeking AAM and the Sparrow radar-guided AAM. Cope did 10 flights in the summer and fall of 1957 with Sparrows, firing one or more missiles at altitudes from 10,000 to 45,000 feet on eight of those trips.

The Sparrow CF-100 was cancelled that October in favour of the supersonic CF-105, which had first flown the previous March. The CF-100 was still fast enough to intercept American B-52s, and presumably also the jet bombers the Soviet Union had by then, but by the 1960s the Soviets were thought to be working on supersonic bombers.

Even at that, the CF-100 was faster than its designers in Avro's engineering department thought it was. Soon after Jan Zurakowski joined Avro, he dived the CF-100 past the speed of sound on several occasions. Cope repeated the experiment January 22, 1953, registering Mach 1.05, and recording what it was like to fly (to the best of Cope's knowledge) the first straight-wing aircraft to exceed the speed of sound without rocket power and live to tell the tale:

"It's not a move you wanted to do repeatedly, because that airplane wasn't designed for it. The technique was at 45,000 feet you roll over on your back and just go straight down in a vertical dive. First of all, the aircraft starts rocking its wings, and you're having to fight that. Then the aircraft starts kicking its tail—directional problems. And you have to deal with that, possibly combined with an aileron twitch. And, finally, the needle will go just over the One Mach. From about nine-six or nine-seven to about One. And then, it's very short-lived because your dynamic pressure is rising as you are dropping and you can't maintain the speed. It depends so much on the cleanliness of the aeroplane. Some will, and some won't. And nothing you can do about forcing it. You can't do anything more than go straight down under full power."

COPE DID THE LAST of his Sparrow AAM firings from CF-100s October 25, 1957. Three weeks short of a year later, after much careful training and preparation, he became the fourth (and last) pilot to fly the CF-105 Arrow. His first CF-105 flight October 3, 1958, in the second prototype Arrow, 25202, lasted an hour and five minutes, from 4:15 P.M. to 5:20 P.M. What a way to round off a long working day: at Mach 1.5.

"We had a cockpit layout on the Arrow that was the best I have ever had in an aeroplane, because the cockpit engineer was Wilf Farrance. (Farrance exchanged personal visits with Sir James Martin, maker of the Arrow's Martin-Baker ejection seat. Martin came to Toronto twice, and Farrance visited the M-B facility in England, where he was invited to tour the country for a week while drawings of an upgraded seat from the one Avro had specified were prepared.) There's always a great controversy between the pilots and the engineers about what they want in the cockpit, and where it should be. Farrance was the section chief responsible for getting a good cockpit. Perfect gentleman, too. Very easy to work with. So we got a cockpit where we had a slightly reclining seat, so it was very comfortable. He worked with our engineers and ourselves, gave us the best cockpit, we thought, in the world.

"The displays and controls were arranged as we wanted them, the main engine controls and gear controls were nicely sorted out. And then on the electronics, we had double banks each side. The most in-board bank was the stuff you used more frequently than the others, the outboard bank was the stuff [we used] on a secondary basis . . . But they were all there, a good layout. It was easy to be seen.

"Starting this darn aeroplane"—Cope laughs out loud—"was just brilliant: push one button. That was it. Looked after itself. You had to have the throttle in the right place, of course. Throttle at idle. Then press the button. The button was up on the forward left side, near the throttle.

"And then, okay, from the taxiing-out point of view, you had to be a bit careful at first, because you sat so far ahead of the gear that you had to make sure you didn't shortcut turns. Stick your nose well into the turn before you brought the rest of the aeroplane around. But that was no problem. It was a question of getting used to it after a shorter-gear aeroplane.

"And then, at Toronto, we didn't use afterburners at takeoff because it gave us too much darn kick." An afterburner injects raw jet fuel into a turbine engine's hot exhaust, increasing power dramatically, but at an equally dramatic fuel consumption rate. "If you used afterburner on takeoff you had a job to keep the speed down to the gear retraction speed. So normally you took off on just non-burner power, which was plenty, and then lit the burners as you wanted during the flight.

"On my first flight I did a conventional [non-afterburner] takeoff. It felt beautiful, and climbing through 17,000 feet I lit the burners, and maintaining that climb, I went supersonic climbing through 40,000 feet! You can say, Wow! That's most impressive. I was going up to 50, but through 40 I'd already gone supersonic. But the big beauty of the Arrow was, you had no change of trim going from subsonic to supersonic, above about 17,000 feet. You could do it hands-off, basically, it was so good. And below 17,000 feet you just needed two or three pounds' back pressure on the stick, elevator control, just to hold level flight during the transition phase, and then the airplane was back in trim again. No problems . . .

"And the big difference between subsonic and supersonic, was, as you went supersonic, all your pressure instruments of course reacted to the transition, made the jump from just about nine-seven to [Mach] 1.02, if I remember correctly. And then, of course, you lost your engine noise, because the engines being behind, you didn't pick up any more engine noise, but you got quite a bit more slipstream noise across the canopy. It wasn't enough to worry you at all, but it was just the change in the pattern: losing the back-end noise and picking up front-end noise.

"And basically that was it, you were flying supersonic in a slightly different-sounding aeroplane but a beautifully controlled aeroplane. And it gave you a great deal of confidence in this machine. I was most impressed with it.

"The beauty of this aeroplane, the Arrow, was that people often think of delta-wing aeroplanes as hard to fly. A delta is an easy aeroplane to fly. They're not quite like conventional aeroplanes. You have no flaps, for one thing. On the approach, you set up the angle-of-attack [nose-up trim] at whatever you need, and that aeroplane is completely speed-stable. Bring it in, at whatever speed you want, and it's dead stable, it'll sink nicely, then if you're very gentle and not coming in too steeply, the ground effect will land you."

ON FEBRUARY 2, 1959, Cope was involved with a small departure from routine during the CF-105 test program when he was diverted in 25204 to land at Trenton, Ontario, 87 miles east of Toronto. A Trans-Canada Air Lines Viscount airliner had been involved in a minor mishap at the intersection of the two longest runways at Malton. Cope returned to Toronto by land, and Spud Potocki returned 204 to Malton.

His total time at the controls of the most sophisticated fighter-interceptor of its time was five hours, 25 minutes. Eighteen days after Cope's excursion to Trenton, on "Black Friday," the Arrow program was cancelled.

Peter Cope was among the 35 Avro employees at work the following Monday. There was still much to be done. Although Avro Canada did not long survive the loss of the Arrow program, there were still CF-100s to be finished, flight tested, and delivered. His last flight in a CF-100 was July 6, 1960. Cope logged more than 1,600 hours in 1,900 flights in CF-100s, including the first and last ones built.

facing page: Don Rogers built one of the foremost high-performance flight test sections in the world as Avro Canada CTP. He was more than just the boss. In 1953 he did dangerous icing tests on the CF-100, intended to fly and fight over the arctic. The temporary windscreen wiper was part of those tests. AVRO CANADA

above: Mike Cooper-Slipper, *left,* being briefed on the Avro Jetliner by Avro Canada flight engineer Bill Baker and Avro U.K. CTP Jimmy Orrell, *right,* before the Jetliner's first flight, August 10, 1949. Orrell made 16 test flights in the Jetliner, his last on October 27, 1949. Cooper-Slipper became the third pilot of the world's second-ever jet transport. AVRO CANADA

facing page: Battle of Britain ace Mike Cooper-Slipper in front of the port engine of the wartime B-25 Mitchell in which he and Tommy Thompson flew chase during the first flight of the Avro Jetliner, August 10, 1949. After just under two years in Canada, he looks thoroughly North Americanized. AVRO CANADA

above: Edmonton-born RAF Squadron Leader Bill Waterton, drawn by Cuthbert Orde, summer 1946, when he was with the Royal Air Force's High Speed Flight, which set a new absolute world speed record of 616 mph. He was back in Canada in December 1949 to prepare for the first flight of the Avro Canada CF-100 fighter the following January 19.

above: Peter Cope examines the knee-mounted scrolling notepad he devised for recording flight test data before recording devices replaced handwritten notes. Cope did most of the CF-100 armament flight testing. He had an experimental cannon installation explode in flight, but his record of never bailing out of an airplane stayed intact. AVRO CANADA

facing page: Although remembered best for making the first flight of the Avro CF-105 Arrow March 25, 1958, Jan Zurakowski spent 7 years before that milestone developing the CF-100, one of which he is pictured beside. Zurakowski dived a CF-100 supersonic, achieving a speed the Avro engineers believed might endanger the aircraft. AVRO CANADA

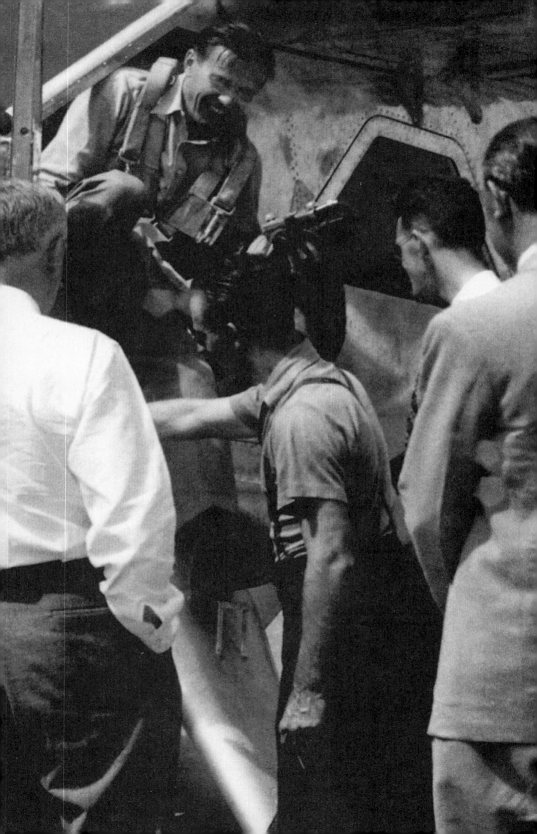

George Neal started out at de Havilland Canada building engines. As a former mechanic, he understood what information flight test engineers wanted and tried to get it for them. *Below,* Neal flies the Beaver prototype CF-FHB-X over Toronto after Bannock turned over its flight testing to him in early October 1947. Neal eventually certified the Beaver airworthy on floats. He went on to do the first flights of the DHC Otter and Caribou. DHC

facing page: WW2 night-fighter ace Russ Bannock climbs from DHC-2 Beaver prototype August 16, 1947, with good news for DHC chief engineer Doug Hunter, in white shirt at left, and chief design engineer Jaki Jakimiuk, in suit at right. Richard D. Hiscocks, in front of Jakimiuk, reshaped the Beaver after Christmas 1946. Bannock did two first flights that day. A malfunction ended the first. DHC

Of 5 de Havilland Canada types whose first flights Bob Fowler did, the one he took least seriously beforehand was the Twin Otter. It was small, slow, and had fixed-wheel landing gear. It also sold more than any of them, 844. *Above,* he holds the first Twin Otter in an eye-catching roostertail pose for photographer Reg Corlett, circa 1965, with Toronto Island coming up fast. But Fowler could stop it on a dime. DHC

6

➤ **JAN ZURAKOWSKI:**

THE DOUBLE-

SUPERSONIC MOMENT

CHRONOLOGY: Sqn. Leader Janusz Zurakowski, Polish Cross of Valour with two bars, Polish Virtuti Militari, four times Mentioned in Dispatches (RAF ret'd). b. September 12, 1914, at Ryzawka (then in Russia), moved to Poland at age 7. First flew gliders 1932. Attended Officer's School, Deblin, Poland, 1934–37, first powered solo flight 1935. Joined 161 (Lvov) fighter sqn., Polish Air Force, 1937. Became instructor at Central Flying School, Deblin, March 1939. Flew obsolete PZL P.7 fighter in defence of Deblin early September. Escaped Poland mid-September, via Rumania. To France, then England in January 1940.

Posted as Pilot Officer to RAF 152 Sqn. August, then 234 Sqn. September, both on Spitfires. Shot down on August 24, crash-landed September 5 (both in U.K.); posted 609 Sqn. in November, at which time credited with two Bf 109s, two shared Bf 110s and one more probably shared. To No. 57 OTU Hawarden as instructor March 1941; to 61 and 58 OTUs to December, then back on operations with 315 (Polish-Deblinski) Sqn. To 306 (Torunski) Sqn. April 1942 as Flight Lieutenant; promoted Sqn. Leader and CO 316 (Warszawski) Sqn. that June. (Both squadrons part of Polish Wing at Northolt.) To HQ Stn. Northolt end of 1942. In 1943 Sqn. Leader, Flying, at Northolt (also Sector Gunnery Instructor, first half 1943, led 46 fighter sweeps over France).

Then to HQ Fighter Command (developing fighter tactics) November 1943. Awarded Virtuti Militari, Poland's highest military honour.

Attended Empire Test Pilots' School No. 2 Course during 1944–45. Then to Aeroplane & Armament Experimental Establishment (A&AEE), Boscombe Down, testing Fleet Air Arm and U.S. Navy aircraft and the first British jet fighters, the Gloster Meteor and de Havilland Vampire. At Society of British Aircraft Constructors (SBAC) Farnborough airshow June 1946 demonstrated Martin-Baker MB.5 fighter prototype. Following year joined Gloster Aircraft Co. as chief experimental test pilot on Meteor development. Did first flight Meteor F.Mk.8, most numerous Meteor version, October 12, 1948. Performed new manoeuvre, "Zurabatic Cartwheel," in ground-attack prototype Meteor 8 at 1951 SBAC show. Also flight tested Gloster Javelin.

Joined Avro Canada as CF-100 chief development test pilot 1952. Late that year dived CF-100 Mk.4 prototype past speed of sound. Bailed out of same CF-100 during rocket belly-pack testing, flight test observer John Hiebert killed. Demonstrated CF-100 at 1955 SBAC show entirely within airshow perimeter; said to be first-ever demonstration of non-British aircraft at show. Totalled 1,278 hours in CF-100s.

Performed first flight, CF-105 Arrow, March 25, 1958. Total CF-105 time: 23 hrs., 45 mins. on 24 flights in three Arrow prototypes. Highest speed, 1.89 Mach. Retired from the Avro Flight Test Section October 1958. Awarded Trans-Canada (McKee) Trophy for that year. Built and operated Kartuzy Lodge, Barrys Bay, Ontario, from 1960 to present with wife, Anna. Inducted into Canada's Aviation Hall of Fame, 1974. Honorary Fellow, International Society of Experimental Test Pilots, 2000.

The **MARTIN-BAKER** MB.5 fighter prototype remains one of aviation's fascinating might-have-beens. In 1946 the MB.5 was being tested at the British Aeroplane & Armament Experimental Establishment (A&AEE) test centre, Boscombe Down. It was the latest in a series of highly regarded prototypes starting with a 1937 design intended to compete with the Spitfire and the Hurricane. The MB.5 has been called "possibly the finest all-round single-seat piston-engine fighter ever designed."

The MB.5 was a real pilot's aircraft, combining advances in cockpit layout with quick throttle response—especially as compared with the jets then in service, in which sudden throttle movements often caused flame-outs, or engine stalls. The MB.5 had contra-rotating propellers, which eliminated the yaw (sideslip) effect of piston engine torque, especially on takeoff, and had a wide-track undercarriage for assurance on landing. Squadron Leader Jan Zurakowski, one of the MB.5's test pilots at Boscombe Down, knew and admired the man behind the MB.5, Sir James Martin (whom Zurakowski still calls Jimmy). Martin's small but ingenious staff of about 30 engineers endowed the

MB.5 with such practical features as a hinged instrument panel for easier maintenance access, a single knob to blow the canopy off for safe emergency egress, and engine cowling panels that could be opened with a halfpenny.

Notwithstanding the MB.5's many detail advances, the British Ministry of Aircraft Production (MAP) had its doubts about, among other issues, the durability of the MB.5's contra-rotating propeller hub and the small Martin-Baker company's production capability. The MB.5's fate, however, was mostly a matter of timing. It first flew in May 1944, when the MAP had one eye on the imminent availability of jets.

When Jan Zurakowski took the one and only MB.5 into the air at Farnborough in 1946, there was only faint hope of the aircraft ever reaching production. The display Zurakowski flew that June at the Society of British Aircraft Constructors airshow has been called "breathtaking" and "brilliant and sparkling." The July 4, 1946, issue of *Flight* reported, "The M-B was swung from bank to vertical bank at a speed which, allowing 40 mph or so of mid-upper wind, cannot have been much above its stall; previously it had been flying in a series of stalled falling-leaf manoeuvres." The Falling Leaf became Zurakowski's aerobatic signature—at least until he invented an even more spectacular stunt five years later.

If ever an aircraft might have won a production contract on the basis of a memorable demonstration by a great pilot, the MB.5 was that aircraft. The MB.5 represented the peak of piston power technology, which was still superior at that time to the next wave—jets—but it was doomed to be surpassed by them. No contract was forthcoming. James Martin went on to develop the modern aircraft ejection seat—driven, perhaps, by the death of his partner Capt. V. H. Baker in the wreckage of the MB.3 in 1942.

And Zurakowski, who had escaped an overrun Poland to become one of the Royal Air Force's few in the Battle of Britain and one of the most highly regarded postwar test pilots in the world, became famous as an innovator who could make airplanes do things their designers never imagined. He would begin and end his spectacular career as a test pilot flying prototypes that have become legendary: they were too good to be mass-produced.

THERE IS SOMETHING very Canadian about Jan Zurakowski, the country's best-known test pilot. His English was heavily accented when he arrived at Avro Canada's Malton, Ontario, base in the spring of 1952. As gifted as he was as a pilot, as quickly as he had risen in the wartime RAF, and as famous as he was by then for devising new aerobatic manoeuvres and flight test techniques in Britain, he struck Canadian aviation beat reporters as, well, not quite the test pilot type. Small, quiet, with a scientific turn of mind, Jan Zurakowski communicated best in the universal language of flight.

For Janusz Zurakowski (pronounced Yah-NOOSH Zhura-KOFF-ski) was utterly fluent anywhere around airplanes. He could make airplanes do things that sounded impossible when he explained them beforehand, as he often did. But what sounded like a daredevil stunt when Zurakowski outlined it always turned out to have a perfectly logical purpose. He could explain the physics of anything he was proposing to do, but it was at the controls of an aircraft that his intentions became crystal clear. Pilots, more than others, understood the precision of his display flights. Zurakowski would find some engineering feature of an aircraft and give it three-dimensional expression on his personal canvas, the sky.

In Canada, at least, Zurakowski is immortal for having made the first flight of the Avro CF-105 Arrow. The Arrow was among the first aircraft equipped with an early electronic fly-by-wire autostabilizing system that corrected deviations from the intended flight path at supersonic speeds, before the pilot could react. At such speeds, sudden changes in attitude or direction can be catastrophic. Many pilots were killed in early supersonic fighters when their airframes broke up from the excessive strain imposed by sudden loss of control due to design flaws or the failure of the crude computers that governed these early systems. Zurakowski's first flight in the CF-105 March 25, 1958, was carefully controlled to the point where the aircraft's landing gear remained down for much of the flight, just for simplicity's sake. Still, more than most first flights of combat aircraft, it was a flight into an uncertain future.

In Zurakowski's hands, the Arrow spoke for itself in a way that makes that big white bird a heartbreaker for Canadians more than 40 years after it was cancelled. Merely by speaking out against the government's cancellation of the Arrow project, as he has in forewords to some of the dozen-odd books published on the Arrow project and on several websites about him and the aircraft, Zurakowski has become something of a cult figure. He still decrys Canada's willingness to, as author Grieg Stewart put it, "shut down the national dream."

Janusz Zurakowski was born on September 12, 1914, in Ryzawka, then part of Czarist Russia. At the time, Poland did not exist as a nation, being divided among Prussia, the Austro-Hungarian Empire, and Russia. When Poland became independent and the Communists took power in Russia in 1921, the Zurakowski family fled west. Jan was seven. The move involved three weeks' travel by night for eight people—Dr. and Mrs. Zurakowski, five children, and a cousin—in a small horse-drawn cart. The family bribed a series of guides to tell the authorities the Zurakowskis would be visiting the next town to the west. They crossed the Soviet frontier in darkness. Once the family was established in Garwolin, Poland, Jan's father became the city's medical officer. Jan was expected to become a doctor himself.

But as a teenager, Jan was more interested in aviation. His first flight, in an LKL.5 biplane, came when he was 15. It was the prize in a national model airplane contest that he won. Like many outstanding fighter pilots, Zurakowski flew gliders, starting in 1932. He once remained aloft for 15 hours, 15 minutes. He flew gliders at night, too, dismissing one prang as the result of there being no moon. He soloed in an RWD-8 high-wing monoplane in May 1935. One of 40 successful applicants among 2,000, Jan was educated at the Officer's School at Deblin from 1934 to 1937. He joined the Polish Air Force (PAF), or Lotnictwo Wojskowe, shortly after graduation. At about the same time, he met his future wife, Anna Danielska. He served with the 161st Fighter Squadron (Lvov), stationed near the Soviet border, from October 1937 to March 1939. Just prior to the German invasion, he instructed at Poland's Central Flying School in Deblin. In defence of the airfield, Zurakowski carried out five flights in obsolete PZL P.7 fighter-trainers, damaging a Dornier 17 bomber.

With Poland's defeat, Zurakowski, like many experienced Polish pilots, made his way back to the Allied cause. In his case, that meant crossing into Rumania on September 18, 1939, from the small south-east portion of Poland not occupied by German or Soviet armies, catching a ship to Beirut, and making his way from there to France in November 1939. He arrived in England just in time—with a few months' training on British aircraft types such as the Tiger Moth and the Hawker Hector army co-operation biplane—for the Battle of Britain.

In Polish aircraft, the pilot pushed the throttle lever forward to kill the engine. Zurakowski did the same in a Tiger Moth, taking off instead of stopping. On being posted to the RAF 152 Squadron in Scotland and being given a Spitfire, the former fighter pilot instructor naturally did some aerobatics. On landing, he was paraded by his squadron CO before the station commander, who chewed him out until Zurakowski was able to produce his logbook. The logbook, of course, contained proof that following his second Spitfire outing at No. 5 OTU Zurakowski was authorized to do aerobatics. This came as a surprise to 152 Squadron, where pilots needed 50 flying hours on Spitfires and written permission from the base commander to even begin practising aerobatics.

Like most Polish fighter pilots, Zurakowski was very aggressive in combat. He has been described as having "a cool, clinical approach" to air fighting, and his combat reports often read like flight test evaluations. Still, Zurakowski took hits on five separate occasions while flying Spitfires in combat—typical of the highly motivated Polish pilots.

On August 24, 1940, Zurakowski attacked a formation of Do 17 bombers over Portsmouth. "But," as he later told the story, "they got me instead."

Subsequent research suggests Zurakowski's nemesis that day might have been a Do 17 gunner, as he thought, but more likely it was then-Oberstleutnant Hans-Karl Mayer, a Spanish Civil War veteran and eventual 38-victory ace. Zurakowski's Spitfire, N3239, had its tail shot up. He could get no response from the rudder or elevator, so he bailed out at 18,000 feet.

Even outside his aircraft, Zurakowski brought his natural test pilot's presence of mind to the task at hand. The unoccupied Spitfire began flying tight rings around its pilot, so Zurakowski waited to deploy his parachute to avoid getting it tangled up with his airplane. He found himself spinning in free fall, more than once directly in the Spitfire's corkscrewing line of flight. The Spitfire's descent resolved itself into a flat spin, and Zurakowski found himself underneath it— not much of an improvement—but falling a little faster.

"Finally, when I was so low I knew I would die *unless* I opened the parachute, I pulled the cord. The plane hit the ground with a great racket, and I hit a second later. It was that close. The plane did not catch fire," Zurakowski recalled years later.

Waiting on the ground was a threat with which Zurakowski was less well equipped to cope. Somewhere on the Isle of Wight, he found himself standing beside an elderly Home Guardsman pointing a shotgun at him with trembling hands.

"I'm sure the crash scared him, and now he didn't know whether I was a German who would kill him or not. He looked at me and asked if I spoke English. Imagine! The way I spoke English at the time would not help. He would likely think I was a German who was *trying* to speak English."

Zurakowski's survival tactic was to gather up his parachute slowly and with great attention to detail, taking as much time as possible. He was extricated from this jittery standoff by the arrival of a lieutenant assigned to pick him up and start him on his way back to 234 Squadron's base at Middle Wallop.

ALREADY ZURAKOWSKI was expressing himself in test pilot terms, matter-of-factly concluding his first one-on-one victory claim a few weeks later, on September 5, by noting, "The Me 109 out-dived me, but I overtook him easily flying straight and level." By October, with three and a half victories, he was posted to 609 Squadron. The following February, he was decorated with the Polish Virtuti Militari (or Cross of Valour) and bar. After a series of instructional postings, he returned to operations during December 1941 with 315 Polish (Deblinski) Squadron.

In the three months from April to June 1942, Zurakowski rose from flight lieutenant with 306 (Torunski) Squadron to squadron leader, commanding 316 (Warszawski) Squadron, both based with the high-scoring Polish RAF wing at Station Northolt. After a six-month stint at the station HQ from December 1942 to July 1943 (during which he was sector gunnery instructor and was awarded a second bar to his Cross of Valour, the equivalent of winning it three times), he was designated Squadron Leader, Flying, at Northolt. At the end of October, he was freed from flying a desk and made deputy wing leader of the Polish squadrons at Northolt. By then, he had accumulated a total of 209 RAF fighter sorties, a dozen as a squadron leader and 44 as a wing leader.

His next posting was to Fighter Command HQ, where he specialized in developing fighter tactics. While there, Zurakowski learned there was an opening for a Polish pilot at the second-ever session of the Empire Test Pilots' School (ETPS) starting in March 1944. It was customary to lose a wartime rank at ETPS, and Zurakowski was reclassified as a flight lieutenant. After three months, he was back to squadron leader. He stands out, even in the 36-man group photo of his ETPS class. At 30 and balding (but hardly the oldest in this historic class, which included the middle-aged Jimmy Orrell and the Canadian Shan Baudoux, one of the RCAF's first three jet pilots), Zurakowski is the only one who, head cocked, eyes focussed, appears to be interrogating the camera instead of simply having his presence recorded by it.

In January 1945, Zurakowski joined the A&AEE, Boscombe Down, the centre of British flight testing, once again retaining his rank. This was highly unusual: senior officers often lost a grade or two in the smaller postwar RAF.

Zurakowski was posted to C Squadron (Navy aircraft) at A&AEE, then to A Squadron, which evaluated new fighter prototypes. One of his assignments was to test the de Havilland DH.103 Hornet, a twin piston-engine derivative of the famous wartime Mosquito. The Hornet was a smaller aircraft than the Mosquito, with more power, making it the fastest piston-engine fighter to see service with the RAF. With its pair of 2,030hp engines, it was all the more sporty when one engine failed on takeoff.

This engine failure was the pilot's nightmare Zurakowski was ordered to explore. More than that, he was asked to delay taking any corrective action for three seconds after chopping power to the "failed" engine, just after leaving the ground. This was to simulate the panic of an average pilot, who would be dismayed to find himself rolling upside down, entering a spin, and about to fly the short distance into the ground.

Ever game, Zurakowski tried it. It was, he recalls, "just too dangerous."

He decided to try it at 10,000 feet. The same roll-spin sequence occurred. Zurakowski was given permission to wait just one second before correcting. That worked better, although Zurakowski, as a stand-in for the average pilot, was not satisfied with that solution. Tossing the DH Hornet about at an altitude at which he was visible from the ground made Zurakowski's flight testing something of a spectator sport at Boscombe Down. His eye-catching loop of the Hornet, in his words "as a glider," engines-off, was a big hit. Lewis G. Cooper, author of a book on the Hornet, recalls that "Zura never let an opportunity pass by without giving the staff a display which usually included single-engine aerobatics."

Zurakowski did explore the idea of a controlled 360-degree "flat turn" on just the one operating engine. Not even he could pull that off. As he recalled during the mid-1980s, "Even at stalling speed [the minimum speed necessary to maintain controlled flight], the asymmetric power [from one engine] was not enough to overcome the drag of the fin and rudder [which, in a spin, meet the air broadside]. The only way to do a cartwheel was to reduce speed to about half stalling speed. This was not possible in horizontal flight but possible in vertical flight ... In vertical flight I could reduce the speed to a lower value. To zero."

This was the inspiration that would result a few years later in the most sensational new aerobatic stunt of the postwar period. "And," Zurakowski says today, "I forgot about it."

AS THE FIRST ALLIED operational jet fighter of WW2, the Gloster Meteor's place in aviation history is secure. By the late 1940s, though, it was becoming, in a climate of rapid combat aircraft development, long in the tooth. In 1947 Jan Zurakowski joined the Gloster Aircraft

Company (GAC) as a test pilot and began, consciously or not, working on the aerial manoeuvre that became known worldwide as "the Zurabatic Cartwheel."

Exactly how the engine-out controlled spin, which could not be accomplished in the DH Hornet in horizontal flight, came to be a much more spectacular vertical pinwheel manoeuvre in the jet-powered Meteor has long ago passed into legend.

The two aircraft were as similar in layout as a propeller-driven and a jet-powered fighter could be: both were twins, with their engines set well out along their wingspans. On the Hornet, the engines were set far enough from the fuselage for the big propeller arcs to clear the nose. On the Meteor, as with its contemporary, the German Messerschmitt Me 262 jet, two engines were required to produce the necessary power. The Meteor's engines were set well out on the wing so the jet exhaust would clear the tailplane. So, like the Hornet, the Meteor had tricky engine-out flight characteristics.

Early jet engines were prone to flaming out. A flame-out is a condition in which the fire in a turbine engine is unintentionally extinguished. In an engine flame-out, often caused by coarse use of the throttle, it took quick action by the pilot to maintain directional control. The power-on engine, well out along its wing, gave it the aerodynamic leverage, if unchecked, to send the aircraft into a flat spin.

The pilot faced a sudden, tricky dilemma: did he have the altitude and airspeed to try a restart? Was there enough altitude to keep the nose down in order to keep airspeed above 184 mph, the minimum speed at which, with landing gear down, a pilot could hold the rudder so the aircraft flew toward the working engine? If not, a fully developed spin in the Meteor was likely and, especially near the ground, irrecoverable.

RAF pilots new to the Meteor were carefully drilled in engine flame-out procedures, "as the Meteor had a very bad reputation," remembered Mike Retallack, then a flight lieutenant, in a short memoir he published in 1993. During the late 1950s Retallack converted from piston-engine fighters to the Meteor. It had "killed so many pilots over the years, mainly due to the inherited principle that a [malfunctioning jet] engine had to be shut down [as a piston engine had to be], not throttled back, as was done later," he recalled. One training technique was to reduce speed at low altitude and gradually increase the power on one engine to show how slowly the Meteor would fly. The limiting factor was the pilot's ability to hold the rudder deflected toward the functioning engine with his foot pedals.

"As the speed fell away," Retallack writes, "the foot loading to prevent yaw became intolerable, so much so that, even with a locked knee, one's whole leg was trembling. When the load became impossible to hold this was called an individual's critical speed, and usually occurred between 120 and 125 kt [143.8 mph]." Below that critical speed, whatever it was for any particular pilot, the Meteor was in trouble. The pilot faced a dicey choice: either losing control, if the operating engine's power was maintained at its maximum, or losing climb performance, if power was reduced in order to maintain control.

No one can convince Jan Zurakowski that there was much wrong with the Gloster Meteor. For him, there wasn't. But one interpretation of the origin of the Zurabatic Cartwheel is that he was working on turning what for many pilots was the Meteor's liability into a sensational aerial stunt, and he discussed it with various people. It may have been late in 1949 that he had the conversation reported in Don Middleton's *Test Pilots* by Fred Sanders, who was head of Gloster's flight test department. "Jim Hayworth, chief test pilot at Rolls-Royce, was in Zura's office . . . when the subject of aerobatics and display flying arose. Zura said that he had discovered a new aerobatic manoeuvre and demonstrated the theory of it on paper— he had worked the whole procedure out mathematically and proceeded to blind Jim with complex formulae which lost him completely. Zura was convinced that this spectacular 'cartwheel,' as he called it, would be a show-stopper at air displays, but he would require more power before it [would be] feasible [with the Meteor]. Rolls-Royce gave [the Meteor's R-R Derwent engines] more thrust and the result delighted audiences for several years afterward."

But, as Zurakowski remembers it, the availability of the right equipment was a secondary factor in his decision to do the Cartwheel. As with so many innovations, his main motivation was more human than that.

At some point, perhaps late in 1950, Gloster's flight test centre at Moreton Valance and Zurakowski, its distinguished Empire Test Pilots' School graduate, were visited by the current ETPS class. Naturally, with Zurakowski present, the subject of aerobatics came up. Zurakowski recalls, "I mentioned it [the Cartwheel]. I told the test pilots that I could do this. They accused me of what they call 'shooting a line.' Which means presenting a story [that is] completely fantastic. So that upset me a bit, and I decided to show it at some opportunity . . . From then on, the Cartwheel was inevitable.

"Meantime, Gloster, they realized the Meteor was getting older . . . To keep it in production, they had to find some other use for it. An idea was to use it as ground attack or army co-operation, whatever you call it. So we had to convince the Ministry of Aircraft Production, which was controlling aviation at the time, that it was a good idea. Gloster's put up some money, got the aircraft, got the wingtip tanks, which were not typical for standard Meteors, got eight rockets under the belly—the same not typical—a few more rockets under the wings, and I had been asked to demonstrate this aircraft to convince the experts on the high levels that the aircraft is acceptable for ground attack, that it had a range and carrying capacity good enough, and is manoeuvrable still. That is what I was supposed to show.

"So then I decided that I would try to show this aircraft to the officials to bring a bit of attention to the old Meteor design. Remember, that is 1951, and the Meteor has been flying for eight years. It is an old aircraft, from a fighter point of view."

If it was a spectacle the Gloster company was looking for, Zurakowski delivered. It may have been, as Zurakowski family friend W. L. Bialkowski reports, that the immediate impetus was a request from the GAC staff to demonstrate the power of the heavily armed ground attack prototype they knew as the Reaper "by lifting it off the runway and pointing it vertically upwards at some 120 kts [138 mph]. There was a slight risk of what would happen should there be a failure of one engine at this time."

There certainly was. Bialkowski mentions the 16 underwing rockets the Reaper carried, giving the aircraft, in engineering terms, "extra rotational inertia." For most pilots, the loads far out on the wing would only make the yaw effects of a flame-out worse. For Zurakowski, they were an encouragement. He tried the Cartwheel for the first time after a routine development test flight in the Reaper, setting it on its tail to begin his first practice Cartwheel at 10,000 feet for safety reasons.

Zurakowski would initiate a zoom-climb at 350 mph and fly straight up until the Meteor had slowed to about 80.5 mph, then chop the power on the engine on the side he wanted to turn toward. The Meteor would rotate like a pinwheel on the thrust of the outboard engine. When the aircraft's nose was pointed straight down for the first time halfway through the first revolution, Zurakowski cut the other engine. Momentum then carried the Meteor through another full 360 degrees. As the Meteor's nose slowly edged straight up, airspeed fell to zero. The Meteor pinwheeled through 540 degrees, or one and a half complete revolutions, all in the vertical plane. Once the aircraft's nose was again pointed straight down, "a slight pendulum oscillation set in," as Peter Cope described it in *Flying* magazine. The Meteor began to fall, "and the airplane flicked into a spin."

This was where mistakes exacted their price from less exceptional pilots than Jan Zurakowski. "The entry angle was critical," Cope writes. "It had to be a 90-degree climb. If the entry fell *short* of the vertical, the nose dropped forward at the start of the rotation, and a normal spin resulted." Normal spins of more than two revolutions in the Meteor were severely restricted for service pilots, for whom they were often irrecoverable. "If *past* the vertical, the airplane would flip on its back, followed by an inverted spin." An inverted spin *was* irrecoverable.

Zurakowski next tried the Cartwheel at his home aerodrome, Moreton Valance, where he started from a low-level fly-past at something below 575 mph, then pulled up and did the rotation at 6,000 feet, leaving "a comfortable margin for spin recovery," as Cope succinctly put it, "provided your name was Zurakowski."

"Basically, it was a very simple manoeuvre," Zurakowski explains today. "The only problem was that you had to climb vertically. And the vertical climb was without reference points. Just the blue sky and clouds on top. It was very difficult to assess that you were really climbing vertical.

"So, climbing up, it was really keeping vertical, nothing more simple, just close one engine sharply. And wait. After a half turn, you close the other engine, and the aircraft will stop itself."

The beauty of the Zurabatic Cartwheel, in Zurakowski's mind, was that it was a straight up-and-down stunt. Everything but the entry fly-past could be done at airshow centre stage. And it finished with a dive, providing plenty of energy for the next act. Often, Zurakowski would spin the Meteor deliberately after completing the Cartwheel, just to get down on the deck faster.

The fact that Zurakowski first did the Cartwheel in the Reaper prototype G-AMCJ inspired a widespread belief that an outboard wing-load with rockets and full tanks was essential to doing the stunt. Not true. He points out that, to begin with, he never did Cartwheels in the Reaper with fuel in the tip tanks. Ever the scientist, he also performed it in a clean F.Mk.8 Meteor "without anything added . . . And I didn't find any difference."

Part of the legend of the Zurabatic Cartwheel is that, within weeks of Farnborough 1951, five Meteors were lost when squadron pilots tried to emulate Zurakowski. One of the imitators who lived to tell the tale, Max Bacon, a flying officer with the Battle of Britain Day demonstration team at the Meteor Advanced Training School, Worksop, Nottinghamshire, was apparently surprised to be able to perform the Cartwheel in a Meteor without wingtip rockets, and he wrote to Zurakowski to ask him if he thought such a thing could be done. F/L Retallack watched Bacon do it, and he tried it himself. In Retallack's case, a pilot who had, with good reason, dreaded trying to fly the Meteor straight and level with an engine out was only months later trying to cartwheel a Meteor.

Although the Reaper was never produced as a ground-attack aircraft, the Meteor would go on in its many versions to have a much longer career with the RAF than might have been anticipated for a fighter rushed into service late in the war. It seems fair to say that Zurakowski made a vital contribution to the Meteor's record of being the sole fighter to see combat in WW2 still in production 10 years later.

"Up to the end of 1955," he notes, "about 3,500 Meteor aircraft were produced in more than 10 variants, and about 600 aircraft were exported to seven countries." Zurakowski made the first flights of three of those variants, including the most heavily produced, the Meteor 8. Some Meteor F.Mk.14 two-seat night-fighters were still active as trainers as late as 1965.

THE PARADOX OF Jan Zurakowski is that the inventor of one of the most outlandish aerial manoeuvres ever is a careful, thoughtful, and quiet individual whose charisma comes entirely from his accomplishments. In his flying days, he had a wiry, restless presence that was more compelling than sheer bulk. He looked then, and still does, like the actor Robert Duvall. He plays a typical Duvall role: the get-on-with-it skeptic, the guy who knows more than he lets on. Zurakowski uses terms like "the experts," "my boss," and "high-level officials" as double-edged swords—mild insults in one intonation; people you have to deal with in another.

Zurakowski has often been called a quasi-engineer, an aerodynamicist with everything but the degree. Military academies such as the one at Deblin do offer a solid grounding in engineering. The curriculum at the ETPS leans heavily toward understanding and expressing aircraft behaviour in engineering terms.

In fact, Jan's older brother Bronislaw, with whom he says he has been confused, *is* an aerodynamicist. So Jan has had access to good advice. "I am a very good aerodynamicist," Jan jokes, "[but] my knowledge [of aerodynamics] was only that *they*"—some of the engineers he worked with at Gloster Aircraft and Avro Canada—"were bad."

At Gloster, "five years of experimental testing taught me not to accept much at face value, to doubt nearly everything until proven, and to respect evidence and the importance of collecting flight test information by special instrumentation," he told the Canadian Aviation Historical Society 20 years after the first flight of the Arrow.

By the time the Arrow flew, Zurakowski had developed a simple philosophy of flight testing. His job, as he saw it, was "to discover as soon as possible anything that [would] have to be corrected." Why the time element? Because, as he had discovered, the bad-news messenger is seldom believed. Design engineers, he learned again and again, would control flight test programs so that their outcomes agreed with expectations. The resulting losses were measured in time and money, if not lives.

"Sooner or later," as he recently recalled thinking at the time, "any Arrow that gets into service will [have its deficiencies] discovered. [More likely] later. So," he concluded, even then an older and wiser man, "it is economical to keep test pilots."

Flying the Avro Canada CF-100 Canuck supersonic looked a lot like another of Zurakowski's stunts. The CF-100's nearly straight leading-edge wing and tail and its huge, drag-producing engine nacelles produced, with the fuselage, the aerodynamic cross-section of three of the proverbial manhole covers, arranged side by side. Even if you could somehow make a CF-100 fly at the speed of sound, the idea seemed foolhardy at best.

Nobody knew how this two-seater crammed with fragile vacuum-tube electronic gear might react to reaching the speed of sound. But to Zurakowski, that was the point. It was not long after he joined Avro Canada in April 1952 that he began to wonder. The CF-100's radar was primitive and unreliable. What if the pilot, flying on instruments in the dark or in heavy weather, was betrayed by a loose tube or other equipment failure and so was unknowingly flirting with Mach 1 in a dive?

"I asked the experts," Zurakowski related 25 years later. "The answer was that wind-tunnel tests indicated the aircraft would become uncontrollable, and that besides, the Pilot's Notes clearly showed Mach .85 to be the limiting speed . . . For me, this answer was not satisfactory."

Acting largely on his own, a mere seven months after joining Avro, Zurakowski made three flights to test the CF-100 supersonically. On December 4, 1952, he dived 18112, the prototype Mk.IV—the first major production CF-100 variant—and read Mach 1 on his Mach meter. In an attempt to get independent verification of this speed, Zurakowski flew 18112 to Ottawa on December 16 to dive it in formation with a specially instrumented F-86 Sabre. But the Sabre was unable to hold formation.

"Back at Malton two days later," Larry Milberry writes in *The Avro CF-100,* "all doubts were dispelled about the CF-100's supersonic capability. Zurakowski took 18112 to 45,000 feet and put it into a steep dive. [When 18112 reached] 33,000 feet a sonic boom shook the Malton area as the aircraft broke the sound barrier. On that flight 18112 registered Mach 1.06. It was now clear that the CF-100 could handle such performance with no repercussions."

By 1954, the RCAF had become concerned that the CF-100 might be falling behind newer jet-powered types. One interim answer was heavier armament. The RCAF suggested adding a belly-pack of 50 unguided rockets in addition to the wingtip rocket pods then being tested. The rocket pack would extend from the lower fuselage aft of the ventral gun-pack, fire, and retract in less than a second. Testing had revealed vibrations caused by deployment of the rocket pack and a critical trim change. Even with an automatic pitch correction system installed, unacceptable levels of vibration accompanied each lowering.

Most of the CF-100 armament testing had fallen to Peter Cope. But on August 23, 1954, Zurakowski and flight test observer John Hiebert were testing the belly-pack (in the same 18112 Zurakowski had dived supersonically) when an explosion occurred somewhere behind the cockpit. The controls were frozen with the aircraft in a left-turn bank. Zurakowski jettisoned the rocket pack and called for Hiebert to eject. He then heard another loud noise behind him, which he assumed was Hiebert leaving. Zurakowski followed. When his parachute opened, Zurakowski realized he had broken his leg. The CF-100 crashed near Ajax, east of Toronto. Only in hospital did Zurakowski learn that John Hiebert had died in the crash. He was the thirteenth CF-100 fatality so far.

The sequence of events was adjudged to have been started by a spark igniting kerosene from a fuel line cracked by vibration caused by lowering the ventral rocket pack. The final noise before Zurakowski's ejection may have been the canopy release mechanism, which malfunctioned, incapacitating Hiebert.

Zurakowski had worked on developing the canopies on the newer two-seat variants of the Gloster Meteor in England. One of his (and Peter Cope's) first concerns upon being introduced to the CF-100 was its canopy's rear anchor pin, which was half the gauge of the Meteor's. Numerous times the CF-100 canopy had spontaneously blown off, or, when blown off intentionally, separated on only one side. The canopy blew off accidentally on 18101 once when Bill Waterton was checking out Don Rogers on the prototype. There was suspicion that, if the canopy departed, a CF-100 back-seater would be unable to lift his hands behind his head in a 400-mph slipstream to operate the ejection seat handle. As early as mid-1952, Avro had expressed doubts about observers being able to escape from the rear seats of CF-100s. An accident leading to a partial canopy release in 1953 caused an observer to be struck by debris and by the canopy itself, and to have his helmet ripped off by the slipstream in a turn at 345 mph and 2.5G. One Avro observer refused to fly in CF-100s until a windshield was installed over the rear-seat instrument panel.

But the RCAF was taking its time ordering the windshield. To make the point, observer Geoff Grossmith volunteered to fly without a canopy to see whether he could operate the seat trigger mechanism. At 288 mph his arms were sucked out of the aircraft as he shouted to pilot Peter Cope to slow down.

One month after Hiebert's death, the belly rocket pack requirement was dropped. By early 1955, production CF-100s were being equipped with a back-seat windshield to allow observers some protection from wind blast after loss of the canopy, intentional or otherwise.

NOT ALL OF Jan Zurakowski's duties as chief experimental test pilot involved death-defying acts. The great ones do the routine stuff in a special way. Chris Pike, an Avro Canada production test pilot, remembers watching Zurakowski do two of his pre-flight walk-arounds.

The first instance involved Zurakowski helping out during a time when the production test staff was overwhelmed with work. Zurakowski spent more than the usual time underneath a brand-new CF-100 instead of giving it the usual topside once-over and climbing in. Somewhere within the shadowy recesses of the landing gear bays, he looked up and found an empty threaded hole. Not a rivet hole, but a machined receptacle for a set-screw that was structurally important. "I'll bet you," Pike said recently, "the rest of us wouldn't have found it."

Another time, Pike, who with Stan Haswell flew almost every CF-100 built, was flight testing a newly assembled aircraft that exhibited far from the usual gentle CF-100 behaviour at the stall. Usually, Pike explained, you could hold the CF-100's stick back, forcing stall after stall; the nose would fall of its own accord and the aircraft would recover, time after time. But this one was different: "All of a sudden, it stalled and dropped the left wing between 75 and 85 degrees. This shook me. I tried it a total of three times."

On the ground, Pike called the experimental office. Chief test pilot Don Rogers flew the aircraft and reported the same results. Then Zurakowski joined them. He walked over to the CF-100 and began examining it closely. Pike doesn't remember whether Zurakowski usually carried a straight-edge with him or found one for this examination, but he did observe the chief experimental test pilot placing the straight-edge on various dorsal and upper-wing skins. In all but one location, the surfaces were convex.

"He found a dip underneath the straight-edge where there should not have been one," Pike marvelled in 1999—an indentation on the upper surface of the offending wing. Filler was applied and smoothed out. The CF-100 then stalled normally.

"That's only one example of his intense understanding of problems," Pike adds. "I'd think to myself, 'Why didn't *I* think of that? Why didn't one of the other pilots think of that?' Here's a guy that *did* think of it."

THE CF-100'S DEBUT at Farnborough, originally planned for Waterton in 1951, materialized for Zurakowski four years later. Three Canucks had crossed the Atlantic in March, two of them to be evaluated by the RAF. They were stored in the U.K. until August, at which time a major effort by Avro Canada's five-man team of technicians was required to have two of the Mk.IVBs, 18321 and 18322, ready for the SBAC airshow. They were flown to Farnborough September 3 and displayed by Glen Lynes and Jan Zurakowski. Lynes was an impressive display pilot, but Zurakowski stole the show.

"Although far from new, the Avro Aircraft CF-100 Mk.4B was a welcomed newcomer to Farnborough," *The Aeroplane* reported in its September 9, 1955, issue, "and was magnificently displayed by Jan Zurakowski. His imaginative approach to demonstration flying was shown by his sequence of a half-bunt from the inverted position; several rolls; a four-turn oscillary spin; a vertical upward roll; and a most impressive prolonged falling leaf, with the Orenda 11s idling."

Zurakowski and Lynes were a good team. Lynes always made an impression on the crowd. His colleagues felt Lynes, a talented pilot who was later killed doing a CF-100 display at Malton, was continually pushing to be a more impressive performer; he was very competitive. "When he flew up to you," Chris Pike recalled, "he could scare you with how close he could come to you."

On the other hand, said Pike, "when Zurakowski did a display, other pilots would look at the display and say, 'That's a great pilot.' I could swear that [when he was doing low-level passes] I could reach up and touch the airplane as it went by. His flying was absolutely amazing from the point of view of other pilots. You felt this. He was a man who, as a pilot, was head and shoulders over everybody else. He didn't have anyone come close to him. He was natural born. He was born good."

Almost by accident, Zurakowski's frequent back-seater Hugh Young was aboard CF-100 18120 when Zurakowski did an impromptu airshow, giving us a rare account of what it was like inside an airplane being demonstrated by Zurakowski. "The flight of June 2, 1953, was the most strenuous I had during my five years on the CF-100," Young would recall many years later.

The Brampton Flying Club had organized an airshow to celebrate the queen's coronation. Avro had agreed to supply a CF-100. Zurakowski and Young were doing handling tests, which were to be finished in time for Zura to return to Malton, switch to another aircraft, and do the show at Brampton, northwest of Malton. But Curly Ridley radioed from Flight Test that the other aircraft had a snag. Could they do the airshow in 18120?

"Zura insisted that he had too much fuel onboard 120, making the aircraft too heavy for aerobatics," Young remembered. "There was Curly on the ground sweating bullets, Zura squeaking away in his mike apparently being awkward (anyone who ever heard Zura transmitting will agree he literally squeaked into the mike), and I in the back seat chuckling to myself because I knew what Curly didn't: Zura was burning off fuel just as fast as he could—full power at 100 feet altitude.

"I was in for the ride of my life. I remember the first low pass towards a grass field, and then Zura rolled inverted and I found myself hanging from my straps like a pendulum. Heaven knows how you fly an airplane like that. After that, my world toppled. At one point, the Brampton Flying Club was revolving slowly in plan view but dead ahead, i.e., we were going vertically straight down. Zura did some tail slides (by closing both throttles in a vertical climb until the aircraft stopped and slid backwards). This later became a commonplace airshow demonstration among the [Avro] pilots, and would kill Glen Lynes.

"Zura then did the only falling leaf I ever was to experience in any aircraft, a sort of extreme alternating side-to-side sideslip. The airflow must have been mostly sideways across the canopy because there was a very loud swooshing noise I had never heard before, nor have heard since. In fact, we did everything but spins."

IT IS OFTEN FORGOTTEN that Jan Zurakowski retired from test flying in October 1958, nearly four months before the cancellation of the Avro CF-105 Arrow program that made him a household name in Canada. The act said much about Zurakowski's character. He retired at the peak of the Arrow's test flight program and the height of his own status and fame. Zurakowski, who attained his Canadian reputation in barely more than six years of active test flying at Avro, was one of those rare individuals who walk away from the work of a lifetime on their own terms.

By retiring when he did, Zurakowski fulfilled a promise he had made to his wife, Anna. He had promised her that he would quit the dangerous work he had been doing since 1944 by the time he was 40. Zurakowski kept his promise four years late. The Arrow, which looked to become the outstanding combat aircraft of its type, was just too mouthwatering an opportunity for him to pass up. Where Zurakowski had plunged deep into the unknown in diving the CF-100 through the sound barrier, the CF-105 was designed from the outset to fly at twice the speed of sound.

"In 1958, when the first CF-105 flew," Bill Gunston wrote during the mid-1970s in *Early Supersonic Fighters of the West*, "it was by a wide margin the most advanced fighter in the world. In its airframe, avionics, weapons and—by no means least—flight performance, it set standards which nothing else actually built in the West could rival until today's F-14 and F-15 ... The thunderous white Arrows were in 1958 the only aeroplanes, military or civil, under development anywhere in the British Commonwealth that appeared to be indisputably better than the opposition."

The design development of the Avro Arrow has been extensively documented in the largest number of books ever devoted to a single Canadian aircraft type—including one book consisting of nothing but declassified company, flight test, and RCAF memos, and another on how the RCAF planned to operate its new weapon. All this in honour of an aircraft that, rightly or wrongly, never attained production. Zurakowski's career at Avro coincided with the development of the CF-105, making him something of a proud parent.

Zurakowski joined Avro Canada in April 1952, one month after the company received an ambitious operational requirement from the RCAF for an all-weather interceptor to succeed the CF-100. That June, Avro presented the RCAF with proposals. A year later, after extensive exchanges with the air force and the National Aeronautical Establishment in Ottawa, Avro handed the RCAF its CF-105 proposal and was authorized to proceed with design.

Models were flown in wind tunnels in Ottawa and at Buffalo, Cleveland, and Langley Field, Virginia, and rocket-powered models were flown into Lake Ontario. The key engine decision was made in late 1954. The prototypes would fly on Pratt & Whitney J75 power while Avro's engine department, Orenda, developed and tested its Iroquois for the production Arrows.

Zurakowski has reminded us what a leap into the unknown the Arrow airframe and engine were. "As design investigation progressed it became apparent that there were new problems connected with the increase in speed from [the] Mach 0.87 of the CF-100 to the more than Mach 2 of the new interceptor," he noted in a 1987 article for *Wingspan*. "This increase of more than 750 mph called for a lot of electronic systems needed for successful interception, automatic flight, weapon fire controls and navigational systems. I would like to point out that during the [six] years of ww2, a time of most intensive development, the speed of RAF fighters increased by only about 100 mph."

One of the critical breakdowns within Avro's engineering department late in the gestation of the Arrow was the alienation of the Flight Test Section from the design office. Zurakowski has complained many times that reports on the predicted aerodynamic behaviour of the CF-105 were denied the flight test staff, because, as he recalls, the engineers said "there could be a wrong interpretation of the reports by the pilots."

The most compelling specific issue for Zurakowski as chief experimental test pilot was whether the Arrow would be subject to the same instability at supersonic speeds that plagued such American breakthrough designs as the F-100 Super Sabre. The F-100 had its vertical tail and wingtips extended after being grounded in late 1954, when some squadrons had already been equipped with early models. Mike Cooper-Slipper experienced the same know-it-all attitude from Orenda engineers when he flight tested the Iroquois turbojet engine. The inability of Avro to include its test pilots in its everyday design development work was a serious flaw in its corporate culture. When a report suggested that the landing speed of the Arrow would be "much higher" than predicted, chief engineer Jim Floyd turned to Zurakowski at a meeting and asked him what he thought. "My answer was that I did not know, because my request for reports had been refused. It was a bit of a shock to him [Floyd], because he had previously instructed that reports be made available to the Flight Test Section."

With the landing speed of the Arrow revised upward, Zurakowski's experience with the big fighter's brake specification is instructive. At an early design stage, he could express in precise engineering terms what had gone wrong with vital components on which his life would depend.

"An engineer was instructed to write the specification for wheel brakes of the Arrow," he recalls in his *Wingspan* article. The engineer mistook the figures used to calculate an estimated landing speed by assuming the delta-wing Arrow would land at a much higher nose-up angle than the landing gear would permit. In reality, the CF-105 would touch down with its nose almost 30 degrees lower, and therefore at much higher speeds than this estimate foresaw.

To make matters worse, the usual increase in aircraft weight attended the Arrow flight test program, when hard figures replaced estimates. "A fast program to develop new brakes was required to prevent delay in the flight testing," is how Zurakowski sums up that episode.

In retrospect, the one aspect of the five CF-105 prototypes that fulfilled all expectations was their performance. "The first flight of the Arrow on 25 March 1958 was very simple. Just check the response of controls, engines, undercarriage and air brakes, handling at speeds up to 400 kts [460 mph], and low speed in a landing configuration," Zurakowski writes in *Wingspan*. "The aircraft flying characteristics were similar to those of other delta wing aircraft like the Gloster Javelin or Convair F-102." Zurakowski had flown both, "but the Arrow had a more positive response to control movement." So positive, in fact, that in his report on the Arrow's flying characteristics quoted in *Avro Arrow*, Zurakowski concludes that "some longitudinal pitching at medium speed [was subsequently] eliminated after first flight by alterations to the elevator control circuit and, in the last flight, longitudinal behaviour of aircraft was much better . . . Lateral and longitudinal was sensitive, and the pilot's tendency to over-control was present."

In other words, normal control inputs resulted in larger-than-intended changes to the CF-105's attitude and direction in flight. Adjustments were made to the aircraft's electronic stability augmentation system, which compensated for the pilot's tendency to over-correct.

"The unpleasant part of my first flight," Zurakowski writes, "was the feeling of responsibility, combined with the realization that the success of this aircraft depended on thousands of components, especially electronic and hydraulic, with only a small percentage under my direct control." The flight lasted 35 minutes.

According to a CF-105 flight log published in *Avro Arrow*, Zurakowski did Mach 1.1 on the third flight of 201, the first prototype, on April 3, 1958. "On flight Number 7, climbing at 50,000 feet, I exceeded 1,000 mph [or Mach 1.52], and that was the only performance [figure] released at that time by air force headquarters."

The accountability Zurakowski felt arose on 201's Flight 11, Wednesday, June 11, after an uneventful sortie of one hour and 20 minutes.

Zurakowski touched down at the extreme threshold of Malton's Runway 32, deployed his braking chute immediately, and had it blossom behind the aircraft within the first 1,000 feet of its landing run. At about 4,000 feet, however, the aircraft veered to port. The left main landing gear dug into the runway's soft shoulder, pivoted the Arrow around it, and snapped off all three undercarriage units.

The first Arrow prototype ended up on its belly, mostly in the grass, at right angles to the runway with the nose facing away, at the end of a long skid mark. Zurakowski was unhurt. From his point of view inside the cockpit, as recalled in 1987, "During a landing run in 201 I suddenly realized that the aircraft was pulling to the left and I could not maintain direction. Suspecting that the braking parachute had not opened evenly, I jettisoned it: there was no improvement, and at about 30 mph the aircraft left the runway and the undercarriage collapsed in the soft ground.

"On investigation it was established that the left undercarriage leg had not completed the lowering cycle, and during the landing run the wheels were at about a 45-degree angle to the direction of travel, producing a higher drag than the brakes on the right side could compensate for. With decrease of speed, rudder effectiveness decreased and the aircraft could not be prevented from changing direction.

"This accident probably could have been avoided if the warning light had indicated that the undercarriage had not locked properly, or if the chase plane pilot had watched me during landing and reported the trouble by radio. Unfortunately, he was short of fuel and landed first. If I had known of the fault, I could have landed slightly across the runway, making correction for the expected turning moment."

This and a subsequent landing accident in 202, with Wladislaw (Spud) Potocki at the controls, generated speculation at the time (and since then) that the Arrow's landing gear systems were faulty. Actually, Potocki's incident had little to do with the landing gear system itself. It was caused by the flight control system deploying 202's massive flaps shortly after touchdown, in such a manner as to increase lift just as Potocki was applying the brakes, causing all six wheels on the three landing gear units to lock up.

Zurakowski regarded his accident as a normal part of the flight test process. There were aspects that demanded answers: No landing gear warning light? Insufficient fuel in the chase aircraft (of which apparently there were two) for a one-hour-and-20-minute flight? For *those* reasons Zurakowski was not warned that one of his main undercarriage units was askew?

The longer view showed that the landing gear themselves were quite exemplary: two known malfunctions in 66 test flights. (The other: a nose gear door that failed to close on June 4.) Bill Gunston has singled out the Arrow's landing gear for special praise. "If I had to select anything [on the Arrow] for a special bouquet it would be the landing gear," he writes. "The main gears were by Dowty in Ajax near Toronto, while the nose unit came from Jarry Hydraulics in the French part of Montreal, and in an age when advanced designs of undercarriage were ten-a-penny I can think of nothing—not even the B-58 gear—that could equal these for beautiful engineering."

It was typical of Jan Zurakowski that his overriding concern, and the point with which he would later introduce his account of the accident, was the time lost to the flight test program. Two-oh-one returned to the air October 5 but didn't make its second post-accident flight until December 11, by which time 202, 203, and 204 were involved in the flight test program.

Zurakowski made 21 flights in Arrows 201, 202, and 203, exceeding the speed of sound on 203's first flight September 22. By then he had checked out both Jack Woodman of the RCAF and Spud Potocki, who succeeded him as Avro's chief experimental test pilot, on the CF-105. Zurakowski made his last flight as a pilot in an aircraft of any kind September 26, 1958, when he spent an hour aloft, reaching Mach 1.55, in 202.

Canada's most famous test pilot became a staff engineer at Avro Canada, working there until the Arrow program was terminated by the federal government February 20, 1959.

DE HAVILLAND

PART TWO

CANADA

> ## DE HAVILLAND CANADA:
COMPANY OF TEST PILOTS

"**W**E DIDN'T EVEN THINK OF the de Havilland guys as test pilots," kids Stan Haswell of Avro Canada, who with Chris Pike flew most of the nearly 700 CF-100 jet fighters built. "I mean, they were flying single-engine piston types."

True. But then one reason de Havilland of Canada (DHC) still exists—as part of Bombardier Aerospace's Regional Aircraft Division—is that, from 1946 to the end of 1998, the company sold 4,271 airplanes of eight different types of its own design. The DHC-2 Beaver is the best-selling Canadian aircraft of any kind, at nearly 1,700 units—most of them still airworthy. The demand for 50-year-old DHC products, such as the Beaver, makes clear that the company could have sold hundreds more. In fact, a modified version of the Twin Otter, a DHC design that has been out of production since 1988, is still being produced in China.

DHC's test pilots had a lot to do with those sales. They advertised the company's aircraft with breathtaking demonstrations that had little to do with speed or altitude and everything to do with bringing the necessities of modern life to some of the most remote corners of the world. From its origins in 1914 as the Aircraft Manufacturing Co. Ltd. (Airco), and then, from 1920, as the British de Havilland Aircraft Co. of Stag Lane and Hatfield, England, de Havilland had a test pilot culture that was unique among airplane manufacturers. That culture was continued at the company's Canadian affiliate: test pilots have always been valued at DHC. *Valued?* Capt. Geoffrey de Havilland himself, co-founder of de Havilland in England, was often his own test pilot. Two test pilots, Phil Garratt and Russ Bannock, have run the Canadian company. Garratt's early-WW2 assistant, John McDonough, was also a test pilot.

By the late 1940s, the de Havilland company had built innovative organizations on both sides of the Atlantic, generating more prototypes and more racing and special-purpose aircraft than any other manufacturer anywhere. They simply had more test flying to be done. By then, too, de Havilland's son Geoffrey Jr. was CTP at Hatfield. From the top down, de Havilland was a test pilot's company, an organization where test pilots often had long and productive careers. As aircraft became more sophisticated, test pilots at DH and DHC were relied upon for vital engineering contributions to new designs.

In January 1915, Geoffrey de Havilland made the first flight of his first combat aircraft design, the Airco DH.1, without any of the usual preliminary hops—just to show his confidence in his own handiwork. He performed the first flight of another of his company's products in 1937, 22 years after he had begun designing aircraft. Two of his three sons became test pilots.

Capt. de Havilland has written about his routine in testing the first of his important Moth series of light airplanes. The DH.60 Moth, so named to reflect de Havilland's interest in natural history, had its initial flight February 22, 1925. If the Moths did not bring the joys of flight to "the masses," as de Havilland hoped, they at least extended those pleasures to new classes of airmen, "the amateur, the weekend flyer, and for instruction."

"As the actual construction advanced day by day," de Havilland explains in his autobiography, *Sky Fever*, "I watched it with growing interest, looking forward to the time when I would step into the cockpit and do the first test flight. A keen eye was kept on safety, from the strength of the structure to the smallest items of the controls. I had the elevator and rudder control cables duplicated so that if a turn-buckle was not locked after adjustment there would be no disaster ...

"The day arrived when the Cirrus Moth, as we called our first Moth, was standing on the aerodrome with its dark blue fuselage and light cream wings. The registration letters were G-EBKT. The first test flight of a new aeroplane was always for me a mixture of concen-trated interest, some excitement and a little apprehension; but the intense interest always overcame the thought of any danger.

"Testing all aeroplanes in the early days ... was straightforward, in comparison with the much more complex aeroplanes of today. A series of taxiing trials were usually done first to test control on the ground, functioning of the landing gear on rough ground and, perhaps most important of all, the tail skid behaviour. It is a strange fact that for many years on our new aeroplanes, tail skids collapsed in a monotonously regular way until we made them about four times as strong as seemed reasonable. There is no easy way of 'stressing' a tail skid.

"My thoughts before opening the throttle for a first flight were about the tail 'setting.' There were few wind tunnel tests to go by and the [horizontal] tail setting was usually a matter of a close guess. But if set at too great a [leading edge up] angle it might result in the pilot not being able to hold the nose up, and if at too negative an angle, in not being able to hold it down.

"Once in the air I always felt much happier and could test elevator, aileron [and] rudder controls and engine revs at leisure. The first flight was always short, because it usually showed the need for small adjustments.

"Then I carried out a more extended flight intended to test stall performance, which was critically important in testing for 'wing drop,' then climbing to a good height to test spinning and recovery. Periodi-cally I would fly straight and level for a few seconds to make notes on a knee pad. Finally I ended up with a long, full throttle high speed run.

"In testing the first Cirrus Moth, this same pattern was followed, and yet there was a difference. This difference was, I believe, to be found in the complete confidence I felt that this was going to be not just a good aeroplane, but that the Cirrus Moth was going to lead to a new period of simpler and easier flying for the masses. After five minutes in the air I knew my hopes were justified. We had produced something outstanding in light aeroplanes . . .

"We soon started on a small production batch of Moths and these quickly created a demand for more. Flying clubs were started at home and overseas, and production had to be speeded up to satisfy increasing demand. Soon they were being flown by men and women to India, Africa and Australia and most other countries. They were fitted with floats and used on water, and with skis for use on snow."

Nowhere were Moths fitted more frequently with floats and skis than in Canada, where, at Mount Dennis (now within Weston, a suburb of Toronto), de Havilland Aircraft of Canada was created March 5, 1928, in a canning shed on a railway spur near an adjoining open field. Its purpose was to funnel Moths into, as de Havilland's sales genius Francis St. Barbe saw it in 1927, "a set of geographical, climatic, economic and social conditions providing aviation with an ideal breeding ground. Splendid openings for the speed of aerial transportation are everywhere and one of the most encouraging factors in the situation is the Canadian character. Coupled with a measure of good old British caution, you find a people with a big outlook, with imagination and courage."

ERSKINE LEIGH CAPREOL was DHC's first test pilot. On April 18, 1928, Capreol flew the first two Moths shipped to Mount Dennis and assembled there. One of them was G-CAJU, "The Sir Richard Wakefield," one of many Moths donated to flying schools by the head of the Castrol motor oil empire. Capreol flew AJU for 15 minutes. AJU went on to accumulate more than 3,000 hours in flight, most of them training pilots at the Toronto Flying Club, before being retired in 1940. In the fall of 1928 Capreol flew a display at the Canadian National Exhibition on Toronto's Lake Ontario waterfront, for which DHC was paid the handsome fee of $2,000. Besides providing a useful addition to the nascent company's cash flow, Capreol's aerobatics set a standard for future DHC test pilots, for whom demonstration flying was as important as experimental test work.

Capreol was a classic case of an infantryman risen from the trenches in the First World War. He was seconded into the Royal Flying Corps from the army, having served in France with three battalions of the Canadian Expeditionary Force. He was commissioned in the RFC in 1917—still only 19 years old—and was posted to the School of Special Flying to become an instructor. Seriously injured in a flying accident, Capreol was hospitalized for 18 months and unable to return to Canada until 1920. For the rest of his life he walked with a cane. In 1927 he was cleared, despite his handicap, to resume flying with the Royal Canadian Air Force at Camp Borden, Ontario, where he served for 14 months as an instructor before joining DHC.

Capreol's credentials as a flying instructor were at least as important to DHC as his flight test skills. An important de Havilland customer before DHC existed was Ontario's Department of Lands and Forests, which started its Ontario Provincial Air Service (OPAS) in 1924 to patrol the province's vast northern timber tracts with war-surplus Canadian Vickers-built wooden Curtiss HS2L flying boats. The OPAS took delivery of four DH.60X Cirrus Moths on floats in July 1927, and the service was so pleased with them that another six were ordered for 1928. OPAS soon operated a fleet of 14 Moths, some of them operational until 1948. Capreol flew the assembled Moths and gave instructor courses to OPAS pilots, who then checked out others on the new floatplanes.

During the late 1920s, Capreol may have been the only A Category instructor in Canada. He has been credited with training 11 of the first 14 Canadian flying club instructors, most of them on Moths. He also trained Chuck and Jack Austin, heirs to a timber fortune. They were impressed enough to offer Capreol a partnership in the air service they would form six years later.

DHC's incorporation in March 1928 took place within 19 months of the Great Depression. Moth demonstrations and sales enabled the company to survive, then thrive. The OPAS Moth sales not only helped underwrite de Havilland's Mount Dennis startup, they began a business relationship that led directly to DHC's postwar bush plane designs, starting in 1947 when OPAS was launch customer for the DHC-2 Beaver. During 1928, Capreol happened to take a teenaged

Torontonian named Richard D. Hiscocks on the Gipsy Moth flight that was Hiscocks' prize for winning a model airplane contest. Hiscocks would return to DHC three times, leaving an indelible imprint on the company as aerodynamicist on the Beaver and the Otter and, eventually, as its vice-president, engineering.

Aside from flight testing most of the aircraft shipped in crates from England and assembled at Mount Dennis and Downsview (to which DHC moved in September 1929) until 1934, Capreol helped develop and test modifications such as canopies (or "coupe tops," as they were often referred to in the days of open cockpits) and ski-equipped landing gear that made de Havilland aircraft more useable in Canada's North. He demonstrated various subsequent Moth biplane models, such as the DH.60M "metal Moth," which replaced the usual fabric-on-wood frame construction with a welded steel-tube fuselage in response to Canadian requests for a tougher airframe. The RCAF bought 50 in 1929. Soon thereafter 90 more were shipped to DHC for the OPAS and flying clubs all over North America.

Buyers included such celebrity airmen as the Australian Bert Hinkler, who flew an Avro Avian (powered by the DH.60's Cirrus engine) from London to Darwin in 15 days in January 1928—the longest solo flight on record at the time. Hinkler bought and modified a Puss Moth at Downsview in 1931, crossed the South Atlantic in it the same year, and was lost with it in the Italian Alps two years later.

Capreol and the DHC hangar crew also helped prepare the twin-engine DH.84 Dragon, Seafarer II, which replaced the similar aircraft that Jim and Amy Mollison crashed at Bridgeport, Connecticut, ending the first-ever husband-and-wife east-west trans-Atlantic crossing. Capreol accompanied Jim Mollison on his half-hour first flight in Seafarer II on September 20, 1933, the replacement aircraft a gift from another of the Castrol Wakefields, Sir Charles. Along on the flight as moveable freight was George Blanchard, who crawled back and forth within the fuselage to establish fore-and-aft centre-of-gravity limits.

The flight was a routine production test hop that nevertheless attracted wide news coverage in Toronto because of the objective of "the flying sweethearts," as the Mollisons were dubbed, to fly to Baghdad and set a new nonstop distance record. They attempted to take off from, of all places, Wasaga Beach, north of Toronto. The beach did provide a runway of almost unlimited length for the over-loaded Dragon, but its prevailing crosswind doomed the attempt, which ended with a collapsed landing gear wheel.

As successful as the new Canadian de Havilland operation was in selling airplanes shipped from England, by 1934 the Depression forced a reorganization in which Capreol left to join his former students, the Austin brothers, and become general manager and founding chief pilot of Capreol & Austin Air Services, a charter outfit that flew from Toronto Harbour to northern Ontario and Quebec mining camps. Austin Airways became, in time, the oldest airline in Canada.

FORTUNATELY, IN THOSE hard times there were experienced test pilots at DHC who considered the opportunity to fly payment enough. Phil Garratt first joined the company in 1928 as a volunteer production test pilot. Garratt, a former barnstormer with Canadian WW1 aces Billy Bishop and William Barker, did test flying for fun over the eight years he spent building his fortune in chemicals. He came to DHC full-time as its first Canadian managing director in 1936.

On December 21, 1937, Garratt handled the first flight of a Canadian-built DH.82 Tiger Moth, the first of more than 1,500 of the biplane trainers DHC turned out for the war effort. As with de Havilland in England, the company's guiding light was also test-flying its products. Garratt was one of his company's test pilots for nine years (and managing director for 30).

DHC's test-pilot ethos became more of an advantage as its products became more sophisticated. Even the biggest aircraft manufacturers, such as Boeing and Curtiss, usually hired test pilots on a contract basis, which is why the great Eddie Allen did the first flights of both Boeing's giant Model 314 trans-oceanic flying boat (which became the largest production airplane in scheduled service in the world) and Lockheed's Model 049 Constellation airliner. To have the company's chief executive as an active or former test pilot was an advantage that few, if any, companies other than the British and Canadian de Havilland organizations ever enjoyed. It eliminated much of the suspicion that divided engineers and test pilots at other companies.

G. Ralph Spradbrow, DHC's CTP for a bit longer than two years during WW2, took DHC's first Avro Anson Mk.II (of 375) aloft for the first time September 21, 1941. Then, a little over a year later, he moved into a whole new high-performance dimension. He took the first of 1,133 Canadian-built twin-engine Mosquitoes, RAF serial KB300, up for its first flight September 23, 1942. In his short time with the company, Spradbrow had gone from production-testing slow, fairly docile trainers to flying the first of nine different versions of the world's first genuine 400-mph combat aircraft.

Spradbrow seldom gets credit for his wartime contribution at DHC. A number of authoritative sources credit the first flight of a Canadian-built Mosquito to Geoffrey de Havilland Jr., who was scheduled to fly its debut but was unable to leave England because of bad weather. In de Havilland's absence, Spradbrow not only had to make his first flight in a Mosquito in an airplane that had itself never flown; he was required, in addition, to fly "some kind of a demonstration," as one observer put it, for the DHC plant personnel and their VIP guests. He did it all with DH England liaison engineer F. "Peppy" Burrell pointing out knobs and switches in the cockpit as he flew.

Spradbrow loved flying Mosquitoes, DHC photographer/writer Joe Holliday tells us in his 1970 memoir of those wartime days, *Mosquito*. "Up to this moment Sprad had been laughed at by the pilots of the faster ships in the area as he tested the slower Ansons. Now it was his chance to turn the tables. He would have dearly liked to have the chance, he had been heard to say, to blast past one of those Trans-Canada Air Lines Lockheeds [in a Mosquito] with one prop feathered!"

Ralph Spradbrow was a compact man, about five-seven, and a snappy dresser (as befits one who had been the Eaton department stores' executive pilot), given to tweed sports jackets and plaid ties. He had "a very pleasant attitude whenever I was in his company," remembers Blanche Warren, the wife of DHC's original Canadian employee and wartime flight test supervisor, Frank Warren. "Not pushy, but easy to know. Just a quiet, conversational type."

Although Spradbrow and his staff—Jim Follett, Frank Fisher, and Mike de Blicquy—were production-testing a type of aircraft already certified airworthy in Britain, they were soon climbing into Mosquito models that were different from the British ones. KB300 and those that followed were powered with Packard-Merlin engines built to American standards and fitted out with vital equipment, such as cockpit instrumentation, that was American as well. DHC built both fighter and bomber versions of the Mosquito. There were considerable differences between them, from how the crew climbed into the aircraft to the more forward centre-of-gravity the fighter's nose guns created. There was plenty to go wrong. Among DHC's innovations was a formed-plywood slipper-type drop tank devised by Waclaw Czerwinski, one of DHC's brilliant coterie of Polish-émigré engineers. With all of these changes, Spradbrow and his staff were doing something in between production and experimental test flying.

Spradbrow left Downsview in late 1942, soon after rising to the occasion for KB300's first flight. He would upgrade his skills at the English parent company's flight test centre. He was replaced at Downsview by three memorable personalities from Britain. In January 1943 the DHC flight test staff was augmented by C. W. A. Scott, co-pilot of the de Havilland Comet racer that won the 1934 London-Melbourne MacRobertson race. The following month Pat Fillingham began the first of several extended visits to Downsview. Fillingham, an easy-going, popular production Mosquito test pilot from Hatfield, brought with him RAF F/L Gerry Wooll.

That April 26, not long after arriving, Wooll and his observer Tim Stone would bail out of a Mosquito at 17,000 feet when, after seeing smoke from its right nacelle, Wooll feathered the propeller. The power-plant burst into flame. Both crewmen barely managed to avoid parachuting into Lake Ontario. The burning plywood Mosquito shed debris for miles before crashing near a barn. An oil line in the starboard engine nacelle that activated the hydraulic prop-feathering mechanism had ruptured, and the oil was ignited by a faulty exhaust manifold. Better to have the problem surface near Toronto than over Berlin.

At about the same time, Jim Follett began setting a series of spectacular city-to-city speed records as part of a series of U.S. tours designed to overcome American reluctance to buy the Mosquito. "Tall, lithe, thin-faced and wearing a neat mustache" is Joe Holliday's description of Follett. An insurance man who started taking flying lessons at the Toronto Flying Club in the early 1930s, Follett became an instructor within a year. He came to DHC from Trans-Canada Air Lines. Follett made the transition from the slow Anson, nicknamed "Faithful Annie," to the Mosquito so well that he got to fly Canadian-built Mosquitoes from Toronto to New York in 55 minutes; from Toronto to Kansas City in two hours 45 minutes; and from Toronto to Burbank, California, in seven hours, 20 minutes.

Pat Fillingham took what Holliday called his "carefree, happy attitude" on to de Havilland Australia to introduce Hatfield's Mosquito flight test procedures there in October 1943. Ralph Spradbrow, back from England, became service liaison test pilot, working directly with air arms using the Mosquito and reporting directly to chief engineer Doug Hunter. As Fillingham's farewell, Jim Follett and the English test pilot performed a mock duel over Downsview. Follett flew a Mosquito bomber, Fillingham a Mosquito fighter. The dust-up demonstrated the Wooden Wonder's versatility and left the audience "looking on with their mouths agape." Follett was named CTP that same month.

In time, DHC management acknowledged that its test pilots were doing something more challenging than production test flying—as exciting as that was for Gerry Wooll. The admission came with the addition of a designated experimental test pilot to Follett's staff: Ian G. Ross. (Where production test pilots fly new examples of proven designs, experimental test pilots do first flights of new designs and unproven modifications to existing aircraft.) Ross was a former bush pilot with 14 years' experience as an airman on 55 types of aircraft. Older and quieter than most of his colleagues (Holliday called him "taciturn"), Ross had a long list of personal credits, including overseeing the construction of the vital trans-Atlantic departure base at Gander, Newfoundland. He pioneered what became the RAF's Ferry Command, making the first Atlantic crossing in a PBY Catalina flying boat.

THE END OF THE WAR saw DHC's impressive flight test department reduced to the single person of George Turner, who split his time between flying and the engine shop. With the company subsisting on overhaul and modification work on Catalina flying boats and Lancaster bombers, Phil Garratt authorized plant manager Bill Calder to resume building the DH.83 Fox Moth, a prewar design combining plentiful Tiger Moth biplane wings, tails, and engines with a fuselage deepened to accommodate a four-seat cabin. DHC built them with up-rated 142hp Gipsy Major engines and coupe tops and sold them to such important future customers as the bush-flying entrepreneurs Arthur Fecteau and Max Ward. Turner took the first of 53 postwar DH.83CS, CF-BFI, up on December 5, 1945. Ward's Fox Moth, CF-DJC, cost him $10,000—much more than comparable war-surplus aircraft. But it was a wise choice. DJC was the founding equipment of an airline, Wardair, that would eventually span the Atlantic with Boeing 747s.

The decision to build Fox Moths adapted to Canadian conditions with more powerful engines, three kinds of landing gear, and neat weatherproof teardrop canopies was a small but critical first step in DHC's progress from assembling airplanes from kits built in England to licence-building the leading-edge multi-role Mosquito combat aircraft, to designing its own types of airplanes. The first of these was the Chipmunk trainer, which changed the affiliation between the parent English company and DHC. Most of the Chipmunks ended up being manufactured by de Havilland England. One outcome of this role reversal within the DH family was the need for a new type of test pilot at Downsview. The first of these would be Russ Bannock.

8

➤ **RUSS BANNOCK:**

FROM CTP TO CEO

CHRONOLOGY: Wing Cdr. Russell Bannock, DSO, DFC and bar (RCAF ret'd), b. Edmonton, Alberta, November 1, 1919. Interest in aviation sparked by working in mining exploration in the Yellowknife, NWT, area. Became private pilot in 1937, qualified for a commercial pilot's licence the following year. Joined RCAF autumn 1939, receiving wings at Camp Borden, Ontario, early 1940. Posted to 112 (Army Co-operation) Sqn. for service in France but transferred with that country's collapse to instructional duties at Trenton, April 1940–June 1942. After several months with RAF Ferry Command, became chief instructor at No. 3 Flying Instruction School, Arnprior, Ontario, to October 1943. Then posted to No. 36 Operational Training Unit (OTU), Greenwood, Nova Scotia (Mosquitoes).

Arrived in England February 1944, attended No. 60 OTU. Joined RCAF 418 (Edmonton) Sqn. that May, flying Mosquito VI fighters in the night intruder role. Teamed with navigator F/O R. R. (Bob) Bruce, shot down first enemy airplane, a Bf 110, within a week of joining. 418 Sqn. directed to intercept flying bombs; by mid-August Bannock and Bruce had destroyed 19 V-1s— four in one hour the night of July 6–7—plus another airplane. Between late August and end of September, Bannock and Bruce scored three more air-to-air victories and made epic 600-mile return by day on one engine from an intruder mission to the Baltic coast. Both awarded DFCs. Bannock became 418 CO with rank of Wing Commander.

November 1944 Bannock took command 406 night-fighter Sqn. (Bruce became navigation training officer), converting to intruder role. He and his new navigator, a F/L Kirkpatrick, claimed four additional victories, and he and Bruce awarded bars to their DFCs for their work with 418 Sqn. Wartime score, *Aces High:* 9 destroyed, 4 damaged, 2 destroyed on ground, 18 (and 1 shared) V-1 flying bombs.

Bannock left 406 May 1945 to become director of operations, RCAF HQ, London, until August, when awarded DSO for his work in leading 406 Sqn. After leave in Canada, returned to England to attend RAF Staff College 1945–46.

Bannock became CTP and operations manager at DHC May 1946. Began development testing of DHC-1 Chipmunk trainer later that year. Performed first flight of DHC-2 Beaver bush plane August 16, 1947. Hired most of DHC's outstanding staff of test pilots, including George Neal, Bob Fowler, Dave Fairbanks, Mick Saunders, and Don Rogers.

In 1950 became manager, military sales, as well as flight test director. Made several important sales (Beaver, Otter, Caribou) to U.S. Army. Rose to vice-president, sales; sat on DHC's board of directors from 1956 to 1968, when he resigned over Hawker-Siddeley Canada ending production of Beaver and Otter bush planes. Started Bannock Aerospace with son Michael to trade and lease DHC aircraft. Returned as DHC president and CEO July 1975, after Canadian government bought company, and remained until DHC's biggest-ever project, four-engine Dash-7, was into quantity production three years later. Retired again from DHC mid-1978.

Member, DHC Hall of Fame. Voted into Canada's Aviation Hall of Fame 1983.

▼ ▼ ▼

R USS BANNOCK'S Second World War and
that of his navigator, Bob Bruce, almost
ended seconds after they shot down their
first German aircraft. Bannock and Bruce were far from home, alone
over the Luftwaffe base at Bourges Avord, about 62 miles south of
Paris, around midnight. They stalked a Messerschmitt Bf 110 from
one end of the landing pattern to the other, so that, even in the dark,
the Germans knew they were there. When their victim exploded, all
hell broke loose over Avord. For four years, almost to the day, Bannock had been awaiting this moment.

The wait was all the more frustrating because he had come close
to being with one of the first Canadian squadrons to see action. He
had packed his bags at Rockcliffe, near Ottawa, in late May 1940, with
every expectation of sailing to France with 112 (Army Co-operation)
Squadron, Royal Canadian Air Force. There he would have flown the
Westland Lysander, doing reconnaissance and artillery spotting for
the First Canadian Division in skies dominated by the Luftwaffe. But
Dunkirk intervened. Winston Churchill's preference for "a thousand
pilots from you later, [rather] than ten today" sealed Bannock's fate.

Not that Bannock resented having to produce his share of the 50,000 pilots the British Commonwealth Air Training Plan (BCATP) turned out. Disappointed as he was not to be going into combat, he couldn't help noticing that "out of a class of 50 wings graduates, the top 10 usually went to instructor school." Bannock was an examining instructor at Trenton, Ontario, when the movie *Captains of the Clouds* was being filmed at the base in 1941.

An early Technicolor production, the movie is as well produced as any aviation movie of its time. It is about a skilled Canadian bush pilot who, ordered to instruct fledgling fliers instead of fighting the Germans, fights his superior officers instead. James Cagney's role was somewhat reminiscent of Bannock's situation. Bannock was from Edmonton, Canada's bush-flying Gateway to the North. He had flown at the right hand of Grant McConachie when the future Canadian Pacific airline-builder was operating Yukon Southern Airways, a northern bush outfit. Bannock flew the Edmonton–Fort St. John–Whitehorse route as McConachie's co-pilot during the summer of 1939. Bannock was recommended to the RCAF by the great Wilfrid "Wop" May, a 13-victory Royal Flying Corps ace who became the first commercial bush pilot to operate out of Edmonton.

The difference between Bannock and the Cagney character was that Bannock obeyed orders. In September 1942, he became chief instructor at Arnprior, near Ottawa, Ontario. During 1943 Bannock's oft-expressed wish for combat duty was finally granted when he was sent to Greenwood, Nova Scotia, to fly the twin-engine de Havilland Mosquito VI fighter.

The four years that passed between Dunkirk and D-Day, when Bannock and Bruce joined Bannock's hometown RCAF 418 (Edmonton) Squadron, made their first aerial combat that much more memorable. They were flying a night-intruder sortie June 14–15, 1944. The intruder mission, code-named "Flower," involved flying alone to Luftwaffe bases and attacking night-fighters as they returned from defending against bombing raids. Bourges Avord was on Bomber Command's track to and from the railway yards at Lyon that night, and that is where Bannock and Bruce stalked and shot down a returning Bf 110 night-fighter on final approach. A searchlight came between the Mosquito and the Messerschmitt as Bannock attacked.

"They knew we were there," Bannock told Ted Barris, author of *Behind the Glory,* a history of the BCATP. "They opened up on us. As soon as we opened fire, one end of the airfield to the other lit up. [The Bf 110] exploded just as it touched down. Then the whole airfield was like the Canadian National Exhibition—coloured lights coming up at us from all directions." The Mosquito was coned and approaching the basewide belt of anti-aircraft fire: tracers of yellow, green, blue, "a multitude of colours." Bannock turned hard left at an indicated 300–350 mph, trying to avoid the heaviest AA fire.

"We did a tight 180-degree turn at 100 feet," he recalled. Bannock could tell his altitude because his wing was nearly vertical and the treetops 100 feet below were lit up like day. "I was really reefing hard ... I had turned so tight, though, that the Mosquito actually flicked on me." Turning hard left, the fighter suddenly went into a high-speed stall and flicked over into an equally tight, equally vertical right-hand turn. The upper wing had stalled and dropped just as the lower wing added lift. The natural impulse to correct with the control wheel would have been fatal so close to the ground. It was at that moment that those interminable months of flying instruction paid off.

"I instinctively let go [of the control wheel]. The thing you mustn't do in a high-speed stall when it flicks over is to attempt to correct it with aileron. If you do that, it will just whip right around. Instead, I just let it go and let it unstall itself, and carried on the other way. I chalk it up to instructing experience." The flick sent Bannock and Bruce west. They kept right on going.

Bannock and Bruce were almost incredibly prolific. Four days after their Bf 110 success, the squadron's priority shifted to the V-1 buzz bombs that were killing Londoners. The two shot one down over the English Channel, again on their first try. The night of July 3–4 they pounced on three V-1s not far from their launch point at Abbeville, France. Three days later they shot down four V-1s within an hour, and the next night two more.

The night of September 23, on their final long-range intruder mission with 418 Squadron, Bannock and Bruce had an engine disabled by a thumb-sized fragment of perspex from one of the two Bf 108 trainers they shot down at Parow, on the Baltic Sea almost due north of Berlin. It penetrated the radiator in the left wing leading edge, draining that engine's coolant. Bannock flew on the right engine at treetop level over more than 600 miles of German-held territory—seven hours and 15 minutes of intense flying and precision navigation—over the Baltic, then over Denmark, to base at Middle Wallop. Each man was awarded a bar to his Distinguished Flying Cross.

WHEN THE POSTWAR De Havilland of Canada began designing and assembling its own airplanes, a new kind of test pilot was required to test them. The prototype de Havilland Beaver, DHC's second original postwar design, was registered CF-FHB-X, in honour of Fred H. Buller, its designer. The "x" meant experimental. Experimental aircraft are flown by experimental test pilots. If an ideal for that new kind of test pilot could have been dreamed up, he would have been a lot like the 27-year-old Wing Commander Russ Bannock, DSO, DFC and bar, who joined DHC in April 1946.

As impressive as Bannock's war record and experience as a pilot were, he was hired for DHC by Hatfield's sales director Francis St. Barbe for his organizational abilities. In less than a year on operations, Bannock and his navigators had destroyed nine German aircraft in the air, damaged four, destroyed two on the ground, and accounted for 18 V-1s destroyed and another shared. Bannock became renowned as "The Saviour of London." Nonetheless, St. Barbe liked him better as the CO of 418 and 406 Squadrons. Under Bannock, 406 Squadron, the RCAF's first night-fighter unit, became the most efficient intruder squadron in the RAF's Fighter Command, claiming 23 air and 10 ground victories during the final four months of the war. Bannock acquired executive know-how as director of operations at RCAF HQ just after the war—experience that was polished at the RAF Staff College over the winter of 1945–46.

Bannock did not seek work at de Havilland. He was being groomed for higher things by the RCAF, who offered him a posting to Moscow after his stint at the staff college. Bannock jokes that he preferred Toronto. But, while in Toronto, Bannock called upon interim wartime DHC manager J. Grant Glassco to express his sympathy at the loss of Glassco's brother on Mosquito operations. Glassco contacted St. Barbe to let him know Bannock was available. St. Barbe's judgement of Bannock's abilities beyond his skills as a pilot was, as usual, acute.

During May 1946, DH Hatfield hosted Bannock for a month of check flights on such DH products as the twin-engine DH.104 Dove feeder airliner and the DH.100 Vampire fighter, the RAF's second jet-powered combat aircraft (and the RCAF's first to be used operationally). He was also briefed on such upcoming projects as the DH.115 Vampire trainer, the DH.112 Venom, and the DH.106 Comet, which became the first jet airliner to fly in 1949. While at Hatfield, Bannock met an easy-going DH test pilot named Pat Fillingham, who had spent much of 1943 at Downsview test-flying Canadian-built Mosquitoes and was involved in all of the above projects.

Together, those designs made up the most complete and advanced lineup of any combined airframe–aero engine builder in the world. DH's engineering advancements, however, were not necessarily reflected in its everyday procedures. The Vampire first flew at Hatfield in 1943, but it didn't go into service until the month Bannock was in England, May 1946. The Vampire trainer did not fly until the end of 1950, so British pilots had to make the transition from piston to jet-powered flight by climbing in and lighting it up.

Bannock's checkout on the Vampire was typically terse: "Geoffrey de Havilland Jr. put me in the cockpit of a Vampire and said, 'There's the throttle. You push this tit to start the engine. There's the brakes, there's the dive brake. Good-bye.'

"And I remember the first flight I did, when I put the gear down, the lights didn't come on. There was no radio at the time in it. I flew slowly by the control tower a couple of times. A guy stood up and went like that"—Bannock pointed down—"So I presumed the landing gear were okay, and I came in.

"I remember Geoffrey asked, 'What did you fly it down low for?' I told him the lights didn't come on.

"He said, 'That's okay.' And that was my indoctrination on the Vampire."

Francis St. Barbe stayed in touch with the Canadian operation. Shortly after the war, during one of a number of visits, he saw a model of a trainer project on the desk of DHC's wartime chief design engineer, Wsiewolod "Jaki" Jakimiuk, and remarked, "If you make a good trainer I'll sell it."

By October 1945 the trainer's lines were being drawn full-size onto brown paper. At the end of the month, the company was committed to two prototypes. Parts began to be made in late December. From lofting to first flight took seven months, 22 days. The DHC-1 Chipmunk was the company's initiation into modern all-metal aircraft design, and, although it was a very simple airplane, it was sound aerodynamically and would be used by the RAF's volunteer reserve for nearly 50 years. Because DHC chief engineer Doug Hunter wanted the Chipmunk tested by a DH England pilot, Pat Fillingham returned to Downsview to fly the prototype, CF-DIO-X, for the first time May 22, 1946. Bannock, who had just returned from Hatfield, believes Fillingham flew the Chipmunk, at most, half a dozen times before Bannock took over its development.

On the whole, DHC historian Fred Hotson tells us, Chipmunk testing was routine, with the sole early modification a minor one to the rudder control mechanism. There was also a problem with wing-drop upon deploying the Chipmunk's landing flaps that required some ingenuity to diagnose. Bannock regarded the Chipmunk as a strong airplane, stressed to a "pretty high G factor of plus-6 and two and a half Gs inverted," although you couldn't fly its stock Gipsy Major engine upside-down for long.

The Chipmunk program was the occasion for one of Bannock's early hires for the Flight Test department: thirty-four-year-old RCAF S/L Charlie Stockford, "who I knew was a very good flying instructor." Bannock was already heavily involved in sales. Stockford had been working for a week early in 1947 gathering data from a series of spin trials with the second prototype's centre-of-gravity being moved aft, bit by bit. On January 19 Stockford was flying with CF-DJF-X's centre-of-gravity in its aftmost position—rear-loaded, in other words. This is the most difficult loading with which to recover from a spin. He was doing the last of the final series of aft-loaded spins when it began to appear to onlookers on the ground that Stockford would not recover.

He and DJF did recover, but too late. Aircraft and pilot bounced and ploughed 100 yards across a farmer's field. Stockford struck his head on the windshield, suffering a fractured skull. One landing gear leg was driven up through the DJF's wing; its fuselage was twisted and its engine dislocated. As Bannock remembers it, DJF wasn't written off, although Stockford's career as a test pilot was.

DJF's replacement as an experimental airframe was the sixth Chipmunk off the line, CF-DJS-X, which was used for, among other experiments, trials with ski landing gear and a more powerful 190hp Lycoming engine. Replacing the Chipmunk's 142hp DH Gipsy Major 1C engine with the Lycoming on the production line would have involved buying the American engines with hard currency the company did not have, so the idea was shelved. Many ex-service Chipmunks now in private hands are powered by Lycomings.

Bannock took over development testing through to the Department of Transport (DOT) civil certificate of airworthiness trials: "There was lots of measurement flying—measuring speeds, rates of climb, stalling speeds at different weights, range. We developed it as a basic trainer and a fully aerobatic aircraft. So there was quite a bit of aerodynamic testing to be done. We put stall strakes on the inboard section of the wing leading edge to give a straight stall [without having a wing drop], and I think we added some rudder to hasten the spin recovery. The Chipmunk was a very good spinning airplane—to teach people spinning—because it went into a stall and spun properly. It took about three turns to recover once you'd let it wind up. I remember doing a lot of spins."

The only crisis—if you could call it that—the Chipmunk faced lasted as long as it took DJS to spin from about 6,000 feet down to 2,000. The DOT test pilot in charge of the Chipmunk's civil airworthiness trials, who was in the front seat and had control, was unable to recover DJS during the time it took to lose 4,000-odd feet of altitude. He properly applied opposite rudder to counteract the rotation but was moving the stick back and forth sideways, reacting to the spinning, instead of pushing it forward, to lower the nose and gain airspeed, which would give the rudder some bite. Bannock remembers:

"He shouted at me, 'It won't come out! It won't come out!'

"I said, 'Push the stick forward!' By this time we were down to about 2,000 feet. So I shoved the stick forward. It came out . . .

"He said, 'This is not a good spinning airplane.'"

Bannock thought otherwise. So they went back up, spun again, and Bannock recovered. The DOT man never mentioned the subject again.

BY NOVEMBER 1946 the DHC sales department was circulating a questionnaire to northern flying services asking them what features they wanted in a new bush plane. At that time DHC was proposing a neatly streamlined, all-metal single-engine utility aircraft powered by a 295hp DH England Gipsy Queen inline engine. The Gipsy Queen was still being tested at Hatfield. The DHC-X concept was given its elegant form by Jaki Jakimiuk and had its systems designed by Fred Buller, author of the Chipmunk's tail and landing gear.

One reply to the questionnaire came from the veteran bush-flying great C. H. "Punch" Dickins, who thought the new design needed more power than the Gipsy Queen would deliver. Dickins passed his verdict to Phil Garratt in person, and he ended up joining the company to sell the improved bush plane he wanted to see. It so happened that DHC's new chief technical engineer, Dick Hiscocks, agreed with Dickins.

Hiscocks, like Garratt, was a DHC postwar returnee. Following the Moth flight with Leigh Capreol he won in 1928, he returned to Downsview as an engineering physics student during the summer of 1937 to assemble the twin-engine DH.89 Dragon Rapide "flying newsroom" for the *Globe and Mail* newspaper. After a wartime career at the National Research Council, Hiscocks accepted Garratt's offer around Christmas 1945 to became DHC's aerodynamicist. The first hand Hiscocks shook at the Downsview plant was that of Buller, who for some time had harboured private misgivings about using the unproven Gipsy Queen in the bush plane.

Hiscocks began by designing a lighter strut-braced wing with the extra lift of drooped ailerons that, together with the Beaver's flaps, would give the bush plane STOL performance, even with an engine in the 300hp class. Then, in March 1947, the solution to the new design's power problem appeared: a flood of war-surplus Pratt & Whitney R-985 Wasp Jr. radial engines developing 450hp apiece, two from every war surplus Avro Anson V, appeared at p&w's Longeuil (Montreal) plant for overhaul. All the elements were in place for a quick redesign of the bush plane around the r-985. The resulting DHC-2 Beaver made the company.

It was understood that, as had been the case with the Noorduyn Norseman, the Beaver would operate primarily on floats. There were not many airfields in northern Canada at the time, but there were thousands of lakes. Bannock had flown on floats, but that had been eight years before. He spent some time flying Phil Garratt's DH.87 Hornet Moth on floats, notably a trip to Montreal where Garratt and his temporary personal pilot learned of the availability of the r-985 engines. But Bannock needed to hone his float skills on a bigger airplane than the two-seater Hornet Moth.

"The Beaver was coming along, and I knew I was [going to have to test it on floats]. The Ontario deputy minister of Natural Resources, Frank McDougall, said, 'Why don't you go up and spend a few days with George Phillips in Algonquin Park?' Phillips was the superintendent [of the Ontario Provincial Air Service, or OPAS] and they had Stinson Reliants [on floats]. So I spent two weeks with him. George is the one who taught me float flying. That was a very interesting two weeks. We got up at six in the morning, we did calisthenics, we swam across the lake and back, then we went out and flew for an hour, and then we came home and had breakfast. Then we'd go flying again and visit camps in the park. I spent the better part of two weeks up there, so I got a pretty good hang of float flying. It was the last couple of weeks of June of '47."

Bannock's busman's holiday paid off in spades. First, there was no better float-flying finishing school than OPAS anywhere in the world. Second, they were flying the aircraft Phillips wanted replaced. The contenders were the Beaver and the Fairchild Husky, which had already flown June 14, 1946. The OPAS was dangling a 25-plane contract for one or the other. That order would determine which aircraft reached production. Third, there's nothing like getting to know your customer personally.

The Beaver prototype, CF-FHB-X, first flew August 16, 1947, on wheels, from Downsview. Actually, it had two first flights. The first takeoff was at 10:00 A.M. Ten minutes later, at 3,000 feet, Bannock noticed the oil pressure, ideally 60 psi, drop quickly to 35, then to 10. He pulled the throttle lever back to idle and dead-sticked FHB to a spot just in front of the DHC hangar.

An oil return valve, installed upside-down, had drawn lubricant out of the Beaver's oil tank instead of replenishing it. With no other damage done, Bannock took off again after lunch for a one-hour flight. His all-important first words to the two dozen engineers present were, "It's a delightful aircraft to fly and I do not think we need to make many changes."

But he did make one of those changes clear when he took Dick Hiscocks by the elbow "and dragged me to the tail," as Hiscocks remembered it, "where the hinge wire in a control tab had backed out and partially jammed the elevator."

Bannock's memories of the Beaver flight test period are not all warm nostalgia. One recurring motif was the elevator hinge that kept jamming. But there is no question that everyone was on the same team, facing in the same direction.

"In the early days of the Beaver, as soon as I'd come down from a flight, I was in [chief engineer] Doug Hunter's office with Dick and Fred and Jakimiuk. They were firing questions at me. After each of those test flights I'd sit down with Fred and Dick, explaining to me what they were looking for, more particularly Dick on aerodynamic stuff . . .

"We ended up having to put more chord on the elevator of the Beaver. I remember discussing that with Dick at some length, and Fred. And I remember giving Fred hell—I almost had to bail out of a production Beaver because the elevator jammed on me. On the elevator tab the hinge was held with a piece of piano wire. They stuck a piece of piano wire in, but they didn't pinion it at each end. I was doing stalls, and all of a sudden I got up elevator and I couldn't put it back down again. It was jammed. I shook and shook and shook. Fortunately, I was up at around 4,000 or 5,000 feet. Eventually I found that by getting both feet on the control column I could push it enough that, with a little bit of power, I felt I could control it.

"Fortunately I was still at about 3,000 feet when suddenly it let go.

I'd had a box full of sandbags at the back and a lot of these sandbags came up and hit me, because suddenly it pitched forward. Well, then it jammed the other way. With it jammed the other way, I, with a little bit of power, could steer it in onto the long runway, and land it.

"What had happened was this piece of piano wire, which was pretty stiff wire, had slipped out, and it jammed against the fairing at the back end of the fuselage. When I got 'up,' it jammed underneath the fairing. And it kept bending, sprung, and jammed on the other side.

"You know, Fred didn't think too much of that. Fred said, 'We can fix that. We'll just put a pinion at each end.'

"I said, 'Well, why didn't you think of that beforehand?'"

UNKNOWN TO BANNOCK, George Neal had rejoined DHC on July 14, 1945. Having left the DHC engine shop with his pilot's licence to join the BCATP to test-fly repaired and overhauled training aircraft, Neal, like so many others, returned, overqualified, to his old job. Neal was returning not just to DHC but to his family, six of whom worked for the company at one time or another. His father, John F. Neal, put in 20 years at DHC. Neal's sister Kay spent the war making Mosquito self-sealing rubber fuel tank liners in a dangerously fume-ridden room and helped organize the DHC plant for the United Auto Workers. His older brother, John, headed a number of shops in the plant over the years; at the time it was Propellers. That was where Neal was working in 1947 when Bannock circulated a memo saying he was looking for test pilots.

"Eventually," Bannock recalls, "I hired George Neal. I advertised for a test pilot. This fellow appeared in my office in a leather jacket and a leather baseball cap, and he sat down and he never took his cap off. Here he was, in front of an air force hidebound guy. I wondered, 'Who the hell is this guy?'

"I didn't know anything about him. His brother was head of the propeller shop. George handed me a resumé, and I was quite impressed that he had done a lot of test flying during the war as a civilian pilot for an air observer's school in Moncton, New Brunswick. I was surprised to find a guy who had 4,000 hours of flying, half of it test flying of Ansons that were overhauled or repaired. On the strength of that I felt it was worth giving him a try. And it didn't take long to realize that he was quite a capable, efficient guy for test flying."

Bannock checked out Neal on FHB September 27, 1947. "So after I did the first two, three months of the Beaver, he took over. I did the initial float work—probably a month of float flying. I remember going down there in a Fox Moth almost every morning to [Toronto] Island to do float flying and speed measurements and so on.

"The reason I got George to do it, I was getting married on the fourth of October. September the sixteenth, we started float flying. So I flew it [on floats] for another three weeks. I was still float flying the day before I went to Ottawa to get married. And then George took over."

It was not long before Neal became CTP at Downsview. Bannock was already vice-president, sales, and most of his flying involved demonstrating the Beaver in imaginative and dramatic ways to possible customers. Bannock's emphasis on hiring test pilots who could sell airplanes by showing what they could do was a key factor in DHC's rise to become the pre-eminent builder of bush and commuter aircraft in the world.

The most spectacularly successful sales demonstration of any Canadian aircraft, measured by the sales it led to, was Bannock's mid-July 1949 fishing trip to an unnamed grayling stream just south of Northway, Alaska. Bannock treated the brass of the U.S. Air Force's 10th Search and Rescue Group to the outing. They included Arctic flying pioneer Col. Berndt Balchen and his superior officer, Brig. Gen. Dale Gaffney, second-in-command of Alaska Air Command; aircraft dealer Charlie Babb; and three other officers. That made a total of six men and their fishing equipment, plus the pilot, in the float-equipped CF-FHS, an early-production Beaver. Normally, Balchen, Gaffney, and their fishing buddies took a Jeep the 30 rugged miles to this stream. Bannock carefully scouted the stream for sandbars before he set FHS down on it and unloaded.

Landing was the easy part. As impressive as the Beaver's STOL performance is, it won't necessarily take off within the same distance. So Bannock spent two hours while the others fished wading the stream bed, staking out a 20-foot-wide channel within the less-than-half-mile stretch between bends from which he figured he could take off with a load that would include the added weight of the fish. The eight-knot current gave him a rolling start, and he had to execute a turn on the climbout to clear the trees at the downstream end of his watery runway.

"It looked okay," Bannock recounted nearly 50 years later. Balchen and Gaffney were impressed. They ordered a dozen. With time and further demonstrations, including a late-1950 flyoff against 13 American types decisively won by the Beaver at the USAF's Wright-Patterson test centre, Dayton, Ohio, the U.S. military eventually bought 976 Beavers, easily the biggest sale of Canadian aircraft ever.

THE RCAF ACQUIRED 86 Vampires as its first jets to see squadron service and operated them from 1949 to 1956. DHC not only assembled and test-flew the Vampires but overhauled the Vampires' DH Goblin engines over their operational lives. Bannock checked out George Neal, with whom he shared Vampire production test flying, in more or less the same way he had been introduced to it.

"I just put him in the airplane," Bannock smiles. "He'd never flown a jet before. I gave him a little pep talk on it, and I said, 'You know it's going to take a little longer for the engine to accelerate when you're coming in to land.' And away he went.

"George gradually did more and more. Then he did the first flight on the Otter [December 12, 1951]. I did a little flying on the Otter at times, just to satisfy myself that [everything was fine]. And I took the second prototype, CF-CGV-X, to show it off. That is where we really sold it to the RCAF. As soon as we put it on floats I took it to Goose Bay. I took a few people fishing. Prior to that I'd been going to Ottawa, and there was an air marshall, I forget his name, who kept saying, 'We still have 40 Norsemen, and they're gonna be good for the next 10 years, so don't waste my time.' I remember him telling me that. But, as a result of this fishing trip, Wilf Curtis turned to Doug Smith and Johnny Plant and said, 'Let's buy six of these.' And that's how we started.

"That particular airplane, I took it to St. John's and sold the idea of using Otters to Eastern Interprovincial Air Service—the Crosbys. I don't think they bought that airplane. I think they bought the next one off the line.

"But George did the development flying. Including, I remember, one day, on one of the early airplanes, they'd done some changes to the back end. As George started his takeoff run it started to swing, and the more he put in opposite rudder the more it continued to swing. And he taxied back in. They'd crossed the rudder cables. It normally does swing a little bit with all that engine torque effect. When it did that you just put on a little opposite rudder. When he did that all it did was turn the rudder the wrong way. You're not supposed to design airplanes so that that can happen, but it does happen. Anyway, they fixed it."

After the Otter was launched and DHC became a major manufacturing concern with three aircraft types in mass production, Bannock, still nominally responsible for DHC's Flight Test department, fine-tuned his sales instincts to the point where he was practically guaranteeing quantity production of the company's designs by offering the U.S. Army exactly what it was looking for—whether they knew it or not. And what the U.S. Army ordered usually became something other armed forces had to have.

The concept was impressive enough: a twin-engine transport that could deliver a three-ton payload to a half-mile dirt strip. George Neal flew the prototype DHC-4 Caribou CF-KTK-X for the first time July 30, 1958, and was at the controls of third prototype CF-LKI-X with DOT test pilot Walter Gadzos in the right-hand seat the morning of February 4, 1959, when LKI crashed after losing an elevator to high-speed flutter. Neal and Gadzos escaped by parachute.

The U.S. Army stood by its orders for the Caribou. But the crash dampened enthusiasm for the transport among other air arms. Three world tours led to the Caribou's respectable sales of 307, and a total of 121 for the Caribou's successor, the turbine-powered DHC-5 Buffalo. It took a three-year intensive effort from the engineering and flight test departments at DHC to deliver on Bannock's sales pitch at the Pentagon, but deliver they did.

So, by the late 1950s, Bannock was conceiving new DHC aircraft types, guaranteeing production by selling them to the U.S. armed forces, and directing their flight test programs: taking them from a raw idea to certification. The final expression of his knack for divining the future of air transportation was the Twin Otter. Important customers, such as Max Ward, had been arguing for an Otter-type airplane with twin-engine reliability for years—ever since shortly after the original Otter flew in late 1951. It was a case of the excellence of one aircraft seemingly showing the way to its successor.

But it took new-technology engines to make this new type of aircraft possible. The Pratt & Whitney Canada PT6 turboprop engine, first flown by DHC test pilot Bob Fowler in 1961, promised 50 percent more power for 30 percent less installed weight than the single Otter's R-1340 radial. The improved power-to-weight ratio paid a safety bonus: with twin PT6s, a loaded Otter-class airplane could climb on one engine.

During the spring of 1963, Russ Bannock found himself touring U.S. Army Otter bases in Vietnam. The Americans loved the Otter, but as always they were looking for improvements. They wanted twin-engine reliability and nosewheel gear for safer crosswind landings. On his trans-Pacific flight back to Downsview, Bannock drew up specifications for a twin-engine version of the Otter with turboprop engines. He then presented his brainchild to the DHC board. Management thought the revisions necessary to transform single-engine to twin Otter would be fairly simple. They weren't. But then the post-Caribou DHC of 1963 was not the DHC of the 1950s.

The wrinkles that beset the Twin Otter were ironed out in static tests and its flight-test program. In the end, however, the biggest handicap the Twin Otter faced was the fact that its primary customer, the U.S. Army, was unable to buy it. So the Twin Otter created its own market—the feeder airline industry. Bob Fowler and Mick Saunders took Twin Otter prototype CF-DHC-X aloft May 20, 1965. It was the first of 844. Today, Twin Otters on floats are the ultimate bush planes, able to turn 360 degrees on water within their own wingspans with reversible propellers.

EVEN AFTER HE RETIRED in 1968, Russ Bannock retained a proprietary interest in the aircraft he had personally flight tested (Chipmunk, Beaver, and Otter), launched as director of military sales (Caribou and Buffalo), and, in effect, conceived (Twin Otter). One reason he left the company was his belief that DHC's new Hawker-

Siddeley management was making a mistake by terminating production of the Beaver and the Otter, a few unsold examples of which lit-
tered the Downsview tarmac in the late-1960s recession. He founded
Bannock Aerospace to sell and lease DHC aircraft, putting his money
where his sales pitches had come from.

But DHC was not quite finished with Russ Bannock. He returned
in 1975 as president and chief executive officer, taking the controls
during the company's difficult period of Canadian federal government ownership, a period when the chief executive of DHC had to answer to the usual stakeholders—customers, his board, the work
force—plus the federal Department of Industry, Trade and Com-
merce, its shifting cast of ministers, and any number of individual
politicians. Bannock's foremost task was to raise the capital required
to finance the production launch of what he has called DHC's "biggest
engineering project" up to that time, the four-engine Dash-7 STOL regional airliner. It first flew March 27, 1975, with Bob Fowler, Mick
Saunders, and engineers Jock Aitken and Bob Dingle.

Bannock later recalled his three years of running the company as
"an interesting challenge." Much of his time as CEO was spent secur-
ing, then reconfirming, the government's 60-percent share of the
Dash-7's developmental costs while reinvigorating the ongoing Twin
Otter and Buffalo programs. Out of those came the company's share
of Dash-7 costs and, Bannock noted, "a small profit each fiscal year."

The four-engine Dash-7, which sold 113 units, led directly to the
Dash-8 twin, of which 511 had been sold as of 1999. It was still in production in developed forms, such as the ultra-quiet 70-passenger
Q400 Dash-8, at the turn of the twenty-first century. Bannock's three-
year second career at DHC positioned the company for a future far
beyond his tenure.

Bannock was inducted as a member of Canada's Aviation Hall of
Fame in 1983, for perhaps the most wide-ranging set of accomplishments—flying instructor, fighter ace, test pilot, top salesman and
company CEO—in the modern airplane business anywhere. He is one
of those rare individuals who do better at successively bigger tasks.
Like Sir Geoffrey de Havilland and Phil Garratt, Bannock was a test
pilot who ended up running the company.

➤ **GEORGE NEAL:**

TESTING FROM

THE INSIDE OUT

CHRONOLOGY: George Arthur Neal, b. November 21, 1918, at Downsview, a suburb of Toronto. Attended Northern Vocational School, Toronto, 1932–36. Auto mechanic apprentice, 1934–37. Began flying at the Toronto Flying Club's airfield (first instructor Ken Main) 1935. Soloed in Gipsy Moth CF-CAA; awarded flying licence following year. January 1937 hired by DHC, worked in engine shop for $67.20/mo. for first six months and $76.80/mo. thereafter. Joined No. 1 Air Observer's School in Toronto August 1941 to fly Avro Anson twin-engine bomber crew trainers, some of which he had helped assemble at DHC. Joined RCAF at Moncton, New Brunswick, then posted to No. 10 AOS Chatham, New Brunswick, where became flight commander, test pilot, instructor pilot, and assistant maintenance superintendent, accumulating more than 2,000 hours on Ansons alone.

Rejoined DHC postwar, began test flying July 14, 1946, on overhauled Anson Mk.V. Tested Cansos, demonstrated DH.104 Dove and DH.114 Heron feeder airliners, and production-tested newly assembled DH.83 Fox Moths for bush plane market. Also tested Mosquito fighters converted to trainers for China. Among later overhauls and conversions Neal tested were Search-and-Rescue Lancasters, Canadair North Stars, B-25 Mitchells, Douglas Dakotas, and Noorduyn Norsemans for Dutch Air Force.

March 13, 1947, DHC CTP Russ Bannock turned over development of DHC-1 Chipmunk (first flight May 22, 1946) basic trainer to Neal; September 27, 1947, Neal checked out on DHC-2 Beaver prototype CF-FHB-X (first flight August 16, 1947), on which he did remaining developmental and certification test flying, including float certification. January 20, 1948, became DHC's CTP and one of first civilian pilots to fly DH.100 Vampire jet fighter.

December 12, 1951, performed first flight of DHC-3 Otter prototype CF-DYK-X. During 1956 investigation of two Otter crashes, he and Bob Fowler flew a specially equipped Otter through the manoeuvres that had resulted in the crashes, making an important contribution to the Otter's ongoing record for reliability. May 31, 1956, Neal and Tony Verrico did first flight of DHC's licence-built Grumman CS2F-1 Tracker anti-submarine aircraft. Neal, Dave Fairbanks, and flight test engineer Hans Brinkman performed first flight of the DHC-4 Caribou prototype CF-KTK-X, July 30, 1958. March 24, 1959, near conclusion of Caribou certification tests, modified third prototype CF-LKI-X crashed after shedding an elevator during a maximum-speed dive test, with Neal and Department of Transport TP Walter Gadzos parachuting to safety.

Became DHC manager of flight operations, 1975; later director of flight operations. Retired from DHC, November 1983. Honoured with the Trans-Canada (McKee) Trophy, 1989. Retired 1991 as chief pilot for Canada's National Aviation Museum, Ottawa, with the end of the NAM's program of flying (he flew the museum's historic aircraft, including its Avro 504K, Sopwith Pup, and Nieuport 17 WW1-era biplane fighters). Inducted into the Canadian Aviation Hall of Fame June 1995; October 18, 1997, admitted to the DHC Hall of Fame.

V V V

I HE DE HAVILLAND CANADA DHC-4 Caribou is a medium-sized, twin-engine, short take-off and landing transport that can deliver a couple of Jeeps or 30 fully equipped paratroopers—nearly three tons of payload—to a dirt airstrip only three football fields long. In military terms, that means the Caribou can operate much closer to the front lines than other tactical haulers—in fact, it can operate from the same improvised strips as DHC's single-engine, one-ton-payload DHC-3 Otter.

That kind of performance made the Caribou so irresistible to U.S. Army aviation procurement officers that DHC's proposal was ordered off the drawing board after a few days' study at the Pentagon during September 1956. "Off the drawing board" means the customer is so impressed with a proposal that the order comes before the proto-types fly, with the objective of saving time. Any problems have to be discovered during the flight test program and rectified on the proto-types; changes are made on production models already moving down the line. This is an enormously expensive process.

The initial prototype, CF-KTK-X, was the product of an intense design effort. It flew for the first time July 30, 1958. The Caribou redefined the battlefield tactical transport role. No fixed-wing aircraft came close to the Caribou's front-line capabilities until a redesigned, slightly larger turboprop successor, the DHC-5 Buffalo, appeared six years later.

A total of 307 Caribous were built, of which 293 were sold to military air arms in 19 countries and 14 more to civil operators. At least four were used by the Central Intelligence Agency for clandestine operations. The U.S. Army, which ordered 169 and designated them AC-1S, used Caribous during the Vietnam War to supply such besieged mountaintop redoubts as Khe Sanh, where they usually attracted enemy fire. Twenty were lost on operations. The Royal Australian Air Force, the second-largest Caribou user after the U.S. Army with 31, decided during the summer of 2000 to keep its surviving Caribous, many of them Vietnam veterans, in service for a further five to eight years. In 2005 the RAAF's oldest Caribous will be 41 years old.

For all of its seeming ease of gestation, bringing the Caribou into production nearly bankrupted DHC. Its difficult test-flight program, only hours from being finished, culminated in an unexpected episode of high adventure for George Neal and his Department of Transport co-pilot, Walter Gadzos, in the late morning of Tuesday, February 24, 1959. It was a beautiful, clear, crisp Ontario winter's day. Neal and Gadzos took off in the third prototype Caribou, CF-LKI-X, just after 11:00 A.M.

Neal and Gadzos were flying LKI that day because it was the first of the seven prototypes to be modified with a 42-inch extension to the fuselage just behind the cockpit. Loading tests had shown that the Caribou, as designed, had a narrow centre-of-gravity loading range. That is, the prototype's load had to be concentrated within a relatively short space fore and aft of the airframe's balance point. The longer fuselage would give more generous centre-of-gravity limits, and thus more flexibility in loading under operational conditions. Lengthening the fuselage was a major modification, and such a change required that certain tests, including maximum speed dives, be repeated. In fact, the Caribou was required to meet the U.S. Federal Aviation Administration's Civil Air Regulations (CAR) 4b certification standard—a more stringent airworthiness criterion than military requirements. The earlier, shorter prototypes had, with some difficulty, already done so.

As always in new aircraft test programs, time was a factor. The number one prototype Caribou flew for the first time at about the 18-month mark of DHC's 24-month schedule to deliver early army Caribous. The U.S. Army's initial order was for five Caribous. These would be service test models. They were to be delivered two years from contract signature, at $500,000 apiece—a price more than five times that of DHC's most recent type, the Otter. Such was DHC's financial commitment to the program, and the army's eagerness to get their hands on the Caribou, that when the five test models, designated YAC-1s, became available for testing in late 1958, there were 22 more Caribous at various stages of assembly along the line.

So LKI (U.S. Army serial 57-3079) was a critical aircraft in the biggest and most challenging program DHC had ever committed itself to. LKI was the first of those five YAC-1 service test aircraft. A lot was riding with LKI when Neal and Gadzos took her up to 10,000 feet, on a northeasterly heading, with the intention of, as DHC historian and test pilot Fred Hotson put it, "clearing up outstanding items."

"We were supposed to demonstrate that maximum dive speed was free of flutter, on any of the controls," Neal explained almost exactly 40 years later, every detail of that flight still clear in his mind. Flutter is defined by Dale Crane's *Dictionary of Aeronautical Terms* as "Rapid and uncontrolled oscillation of a flight control surface on an aircraft caused by a dynamically unbalanced condition. Flutter normally causes the loss of the control surface and a crash." A flag flutters in the wind, but aircraft control surfaces are balanced and stiffened to withstand that tendency.

"We *had* dived it," Neal insists. "We did the first [dive tests] with Number One, KTK. We had had a flutter problem"—with a spring tab on an elevator—"at 160 mph in level flight, just by increasing the speed. But the engineering department stiffened the tab up. And they got it okay, so that we eventually got up to a max speed of 285. And now, in our testing, we discovered that the centre-of-gravity range was too narrow. And so, to make it a viable airplane to use, we had to move the C of G—centre of gravity—range further forward."

"The only way they could do that was to extend the fuselage just behind the cockpit. So they put an extension in. Well, it just lengthened everything"—including, of course, the control cables to the tail. "The engineers felt that everything was stressed [that is, strengthened to withstand foreseeable stress levels]; everything was okay.

"But they didn't do a flutter analysis on it. Because it was felt that, you know, it was all stiffened up, so the extension wouldn't make any difference. Engineering was quite confident that it was okay. But since it was a new—well, it was a major revision to the airframe—DOT said, 'You'll have to prove that it's flutter-free with this new length of fuselage.'

"We were almost through the testing for DOT. And this was one of the last things we had to do. It was a beautiful morning, and cold. Weather was CAVU and smooth, light winds, less than eight miles an hour. So the program of the flight was to demonstrate the dive to CAR 4b requirements for flutter purposes.

"Anyway, we climbed out of Downsview heading up to 12,000 feet. This was just before lunchtime. I said, 'Well, this won't take long. Let's just do this dive and come back and have lunch.'

"We climbed out in LKI," Neal continued, "got up to 12,000 feet just northeast of Downsview, still heading northeast, levelled off and set up 2,250 rpm on the props. And then I started the dive. I increased speed to 200 mph and trimmed it at that speed, hands-off, with the elevator trim—and then from there on I just pushed ahead [with the control wheel] and trimmed as I went, nose down, to keep that speed increasing. At 265 mph, I wrote in my report, 'a high-frequency buzz was felt from the elevator.'

"I felt it right in the palm of my hand. Just a *buzz*. Like a bee stinging. And I knew right away the elevator tab was fluttering because I'd had it before"—with first prototype KTK.

"So I chopped the power and pulled the propeller pitch all the way back. That meant they were in minimum governing [coarse pitch] and the throttles were at idle. And, of course, I was trying to bring the nose up, to reduce the speed.

"The buzz increased, and in a few seconds the elevators started to flutter in sympathy. It was a little bit slower, but it was three or four inches' movement back and forth. Whereas when the tab was fluttering, the elevator didn't move, just the tab fluttered." A spring tab is a moveable, spring-loaded, small aerodynamic device hinged to the trailing edge of a control surface to reduce the force necessary to move it or to trim it for hands-off flight. "The tab then got to the frequency where it excited the elevator and the elevator started to flutter.

"The elevator forces were fairly heavy, and the speed slow to decrease. At a speed somewhere around 250–200 mph both engines were feathered." Strictly speaking, it is the propellers that are feathered, but pilots usually refer to feathering the engines because one object of that precaution is to prevent damage to the engines from over-revving. "I felt they were dragging. You know, when you have a flat pitch on the prop and the engine's just idling, the airflow is trying to push the propeller and turn the engine faster than it's going. So there's a lot of drag—it's barn-door drag—and that was holding the nose down. And I was trying to fight to get that nose up. I recognized this [situation] and I reached up, pulled the mixture controls, and then I feathered both props. This certainly helped the nose to come up.

"But the elevator kept on fluttering. I thought it might stop with the decrease in airspeed, but it didn't. Then Walter got on the control column on his side to help me in pulling it up. Seconds after he did this, my control wheel pulled out of the control column, and I immediately wrapped my arms around the remainder and let the wheel dangle free on its wires.

"As the airspeed was coming back through 180 mph, there was a loud bang and a few heavy jerks on the control column. At this point the rapid motion on the control column ceased, but the elevator was still fluttering, making considerable noise and vibration. You could hear it going *toof toof toof,* and you could feel the vibration. Aside from that, it was quiet.

"I said to Walter, 'I think we've lost something,' after that bang. So he got up out of his seat and he looked back at the tail.

"He said, 'Oh yes, your right elevator's gone.'"

What Gadzos saw from the right-hand seat of LKI was the left elevator fluttering. The right elevator was, at that moment, holding steady, making it appear not to be there.

"This was all happening within a few seconds. We were now at 10,000 feet. Walter held on to his control column and I picked up my control wheel in order to transmit to base the following message: 'We have lost our right elevator, and it looks like we'll have to leave.' But the message never got through. I'm not sure whether one of the wires had broken or it was the pipsqueak of a transceiver that we had for emergencies. We left it on that emergency frequency. I still had my headset on with its mike and so on.

"After I did that I put my arm around the control column and I told Walter, 'It looks like we're going to have to leave this thing; go back and have a look and start getting the emergency doors ready.' They just pushed out and away they went. He was going to do that.

"The airspeed was in the order of 160 mph, and while Walter was trying to open the front hatch, I found that I could reduce speed by using the elevator trim wheel with rather large movements. The trim wheel operates an adjustable tab on the right elevator only.

"Walter pulled the release cable for the front hatch, near the cockpit floor, but it wouldn't go. So I asked him to go back to the side cabin windows, which he did. It's an oval window, one on each side, bigger than the others, almost in line with the undercarriage. These had the English-style handles on them, in that, from the inside, the handle protruded so a rescuer outside could open it. But from the inside, you had to push a button to get the handle to engage. He was struggling with the handle. He'd forgotten to push the button. So I yelled at him: 'Push the button!' And he pushed the button, and then he was able to turn the handle and push the hatch out. Then he put the left one out.

"I reduced the speed on the trim [raising the nose] slowly, and at 140 mph the aircraft began to do violent pitching and shuddering. It pitched up and down like a snake. I reduced speed further to 120 mph and the pitching ceased. On further reducing the speed to 110, the violent pitching again occurred, so I returned to the 120 where it was steady.

"Walter came forward and said the side hatches were gone. And I said that I didn't know whether I could land the aircraft or not.

Naturally, I wasn't sure! No wheel. Engines idling at that time. Here we're still coming down and the flutter's still going on ... How long can the airframe last with that flutter going on?

"These questions were going through my mind, and at that point I still regarded removing the hatches as a precaution. Then I said, 'Get the floor hatch out now, in case we have to go.'

"He leaned down and pushed the button. When he pushed the button, the door was gone. The hole is about two feet deep, from the sub-floor up the cockpit wall. He was leaning down to reach this button. He'd already pulled the emergency pins [when he pulled the cable earlier], so it was only the latch that was holding. The latch released when he pushed the button and the door was gone. But, in pushing the button, he lost his balance.

"And out he went. Just like that. But as he went, his left foot caught the cabin floor under his knee for just a few seconds, and when I looked down and saw him there, he was moving back and forth in the hole there, and he had his hand looking for the parachute ring. As soon as he had the ring, he straightened his leg and out he went. That's the last I saw of Walter until later.

"This was at approximately 6,000 feet so he had time to get going.

"I then unfastened my harness, hung my headset on the storage hook, and climbed down to the cabin floor. I went back to the cabin and looked out the side opening but decided the floor hatch was better, so I returned to the front.

"Just then the left wing dropped, so I climbed back up to straighten it out with the co-pilot's control wheel. It would not move, so I put my finger in the gear sprocket in the pilot's side [which was exposed by the missing control wheel], and then moved the co-pilot's wheel to level the aircraft. It moved just enough, and then it wouldn't move any more.

"At this point, I reconsidered trying to land the aircraft. It was steady at 120 mph, but it started oscillation above and below that. So I thought, 'Well, who knows?' I headed for a large bush area and noted the altimeter was at 3,000 [not enough altitude to get back to Downsview]. This changed my mind.

"I did one more check. I shut off all electrical switches and fuel valves, and tucked my pencils and clipboard under the co-pilot's seat cushion. I went down to the floor hatch, took off my cap and threw it back into the cabin, removed my screwdriver from the sleeve of my flying overalls, leaned down to the hatch opening, and the wind caught my head and I let go.

"Once free of the aircraft, I counted to three, pulled the ring, and was jerked upright by the canopy opening. I looked up to the Caribou and could see it slowly turning left. The left elevator was fluffing quite rapidly, making the only noise I could hear—a noise I would compare to the flapping of a broken venetian blind.

"There was very little wind, and I saw that I would land in, or pretty close to, a bush—this was a whole bunch of trees, not just a bush—so I attempted to slip the chute to take me away from the bush. I hit the ground in an open gully about half a mile from a farmhouse [not far from Uxbridge, Ontario].

"Gathering up my chute and walking to the farmhouse, the aircraft was not to be seen. I telephoned the plant to report the aircraft down and my position. It was flight test engineer Dick Batch that I talked to on the phone, and it was Jack Uffen, director of development engineering, who came up in the truck to pick me up. So that's the story."

FROM VERY EARLY in his career as a pilot, Neal was a pioneer of scientific flight testing (although he would never have used a word like scientific). His approach was very different from taking a prototype up, slicing up the sky, and telling the guys on the ground whether or not you liked the way it flew. Neal sees himself as a transitional figure in the history of Canadian aviation, one of the few who took the test pilot's craft from daredevilry to data acquisition.

"Really, it wasn't until engineering started to put the cuffs on these test pilots that flight testing was done properly," Neal explains. "It was only then that information was gathered that engineering, on the ground, would be able to use in the future, and that other people, other companies could use. The early test pilots, they would take the airplane up, throw it around, and they were looking for things they didn't like about it. Well, to an engineer, you come down and say, 'I don't like the way the controls work.'

"'Well, what don't you like?'

"'Well, I don't know, it's just that I don't like them.' Now, an engineer can't do anything with that kind of information.

"So, eventually, the engineering people said, 'Well, we've got to get this information.' They devised ways and means of recording the information. They set up programs. And eventually they won. They got the information.

"You go up and you do a systematic check on controls, displacements, forces, everything that engineering want to know. And in that way, you work up to it and you find out whether there's any bad control characteristics, or whether you run out of control, or it's unstable, all those sorts of things. You do it gently, and you do it according to a program, so you know where you're at. So the pilot learns to know the airplane by doing that.

"If he just goes up and throws it around, he's not going to learn anything about the airplane! He's just making it look good to people on the ground—what a great guy he is to be doing that. It's a business you're in and, of course, you're always short of money, so you move through the program as fast as you can. If there are problems, engineering will come up with the fixes, you go up and repeat the tests, till you finally get it right.

"I sided with the engineers, because I knew what they were up against. *They* couldn't fly. And it was qualitative, I guess, what the test pilots in the old days were doing. Whereas engineering wanted quantitative testing. How far did the aileron go before it started to snatch? Or how far did the rudder go before it locked over? Where did the forces reverse on the elevator? You know, that kind of thing is what engineering wanted. And at what speed was it? At constant speed? Or was it five miles above the stall? Or was it 50 miles? Those were the definite things engineering wanted to know."

Neal sympathized with engineers because he was one himself. Not that he had an engineering degree, but he had built engines, propellers, and almost everything else that made an airplane fly. He became an engineer and a pilot almost simultaneously, long before test pilots were trained in both of those disciplines as a matter of course.

George Neal presented himself at DHC's engine shop as a fully qualified automobile engine mechanic and licenced pilot at the age of 18, in January 1937. He was something of a prodigy, and he was joining the family firm: the Neal family lived in the Downsview neighbourhood, George's father John Senior worked at DHC, and he was eventually joined by the Neal brothers George and John and all three of their sisters. George worked in every workshop at DHC before he ever became a test pilot. In early 1940, Neal was photographed putting the finishing touches to the starboard Armstrong-Whitworth Cheetah radial engine on a war-weary Avro Anson shipped to Downsview from England. It was being reconditioned for bomber crew training under the British Commonwealth Air Training Plan. A little more than a year later, he was flight testing the same type of aircraft after maintenance at the BCATP's base at Chatham, New Brunswick, where his responsibilities put him as much in the hangar as in the sky. He flew Tiger Moths and Anson Is and Vs at Chatham, adding more than 2,000 hours on Ansons to his logbook. He finished the war as the owner of a surplus twin-engine Cessna Crane. His first postwar test flight at Downsview, on July 14, 1945, was in an Anson V, which was powered with a pair of the same Pratt & Whitney R-985 Wasp Juniors that made the DHC-2 Beaver such a sparkling short-field performer. When he was checked out on the first Beaver, CF-FHB-X, on September 27, 1947, he immediately felt at home in this prototype that only CTP Russ Bannock had flown before him.

Why? "I knew the engine. I'd been flying the engine for years."

Neal has always thought that knowing aircraft from the inside out was the key to his success as a test pilot. He could feel the way the airplane wanted to be flown. This sensation was quite different from flying by the seat of your pants. It was in your hands, your feet, your ears, your eyes, your memory, and in whatever improved instrumentation you could improvise or find. In fact, you could construct a history of Canadian flight test over the critical 15-year period from 1946 to 1961, from the Chipmunk to the Caribou, using nothing more than

George Neal's stories about finding ways to present DHC's flight test engineers with solid quantitative data, airplane by airplane, test program by test program. Bob Fowler, who followed Neal on the DHC flight test career track, says he learned his craft watching Neal and Dave Fairbanks work on the Caribou.

A highlight of the trend toward more rigorous flight test procedures at DHC was the Chipmunk takeoff performance graph. The DHC-1 Chipmunk, which replaced the Tiger Moth as primary trainer for the Royal Air Force from 1949 to 1973, was the program that put DHC on the map as a manufacturer of its own designs. (Actually, the de Havilland plants at Chester and Hatfield, England, assembled 1,000 of the 1,283 Chipmunks built. But aside from Hatfield's Pat Fillingham being brought in to handle the first flight of the Chipmunk prototype, CF-DIO-X, on May 22, 1946—and a few subsequent flights—the Chipmunk's flight test development program was handled by Russ Bannock until March 13, 1947, when Neal took over.) The Chipmunk gave DHC's experimental test flight department its start. Flying it made Neal an experimental test pilot.

One basic task of an experimental test pilot is to establish the performance of a new airplane. It sounds easy: just fly the airplane and read the instruments.

"The early test pilots, well, heh-heh, they had no instrumentation. All they had was an airspeed, altimeter, and a turn-and-skid. Engineering, they knew how the airplane should fly. But they weren't getting the numbers to tell them how close it was coming to their design expectations.

"For instance, when I was doing the Chipmunk, the Beaver, and the Otter, I had a standard airspeed indicator in there and the segments were close together, a quarter of an inch for, say, 10 miles an hour. Well, you had to guess whether it was 61, 62, or 63 mph. And engineering, they want you to fly at 64 mph. It's just about impossible, because the graduations were too small. In one of my reports, I recommended that if they wanted these numbers, they'd have to give us sensitive airspeed indicators. And they gave us sensitive airspeed indicators."

Still, assuming that you could fly with confidence at an exact speed, it was difficult to note down on a clipboard and coordinate separate pieces of information. A simple example was plotting the rising curve of the points where altitude and speed intersect to form a takeoff performance graph. Even if the instruments were readable as you flew, plotting the points where altitude and speed intersected along the curve was difficult. The answer was crude but workable: let the pilot fly the airplane and let something else plot the curve.

"When we were flying the Chipmunk, we had to get landing and takeoff performance. On the Chipmunk, what we did, we had a chap in the back seat, and he was holding an aircraft landing light that was hooked up to an additional battery—it was stuck in the little area that was in that rear cockpit. And we waited till dusk. We had a camera—Reg Corlett made up a special camera—it would take segment pictures"—Neal chops his hand up and down several times along the approximate upward-curving line of a takeoff—"like that, eh?

"And, what we would do is, for the takeoff, the man with the camera [on the ground] would wave his flashlight, and I would say, 'Okay, we're going.' And my fellow in the back would turn on his landing light—Jesus, what a glare!—and I would take off and climb out at the speeds that we were supposed to. And the landing light was shone back at the camera. Well, when the film was developed, here's this bright light tracing the upward curve of a takeoff, like a strobe. You could just put your graph up to it, and there it is." The curve of a takeoff clearing a 50-foot barrier: a thing of beauty and a joy to behold.

DHC's follow-up to the Chipmunk was the most successful Canadian aircraft design in terms of the number sold: nearly 1,700. The de Havilland Beaver was a winner from the moment the decision was made in March 1947 to power it with the P&W R-985, which offers 450hp, instead of a projected engine from Hatfield that never produced the output it was designed for. The Beaver was redesigned, losing the sleek pointed nose made possible by the DH inline engine in favour of the flat, bulky radial that turned the Beaver into a bulldog of an airplane—stronger and brawnier, but not nearly as aerodynamic.

Chief aerodynamicist Dick Hiscocks, who redesigned the Beaver in around the beefy radial in five months flat, often pointed out that, with such a quick redesign, compromises in the Beaver's shape were inevitable. Smoothing out the wrinkles was one objective of the Beaver's test flight program. Another was to give pilots adequate warning when they were pushing the Beaver's impressive low-and-slow STOL performance too far and were in danger of stalling the airplane.

"A stall is where the airflow breaks down all across the wing and there's no more lift," Neal explained in 1995. "When the Beaver stalled, it dropped a wing. The idea is, you don't want the airflow to break down all at once, because if it does, it'll roll either way. And you've got no control, you can't stop it. It might go a full turn." And, after that, into a spin. "And so we had to get stall bars and find a location for them, where they would work properly and yet not cause a lot of drag.

"Stall bars are little wide-angle v-shaped pieces of metal, a strip maybe a foot long, and they're riveted to the leading edge of the wing. You have to find a position for them on that leading edge so that as the wing comes up in angle-of-attack, before the outboard wing section stalls, the stall bar will start turbulence at the inboard section. That's where you put them, near the roots, so the flow behind the stall bar starts to break down before the rest of the wing does. It causes disturbed flow to go back on the tailplane, changes the angle there, and reduces your elevator effectiveness, so the nose pitches, and you don't roll either way.

"The idea is you were able to stall the airplane by reducing the air-speed, come back, and either get this nose-down pitch, or reach the rear stops of the elevators, as far back as you could go. You had to do either one or the other. We couldn't do either when we first started, because it rolled. The stall bars prevent roll-off because the outer wings are still flying. We tailored it with these stall bars so that we could do that.

"With stall bars, you'd get more warning [of the oncoming stall]. It gives you a buffet on the tail that shakes the airplane. Also, the main thing is, it disturbs the flow, stalls the air directly behind those bars. That airflow is now turbulent. It could be in a nice smooth wind, but it's all turbulent [behind the stall bar], and it goes back and changes the angle-of-attack of the tailplane, which reduces the lift of the tailplane. Now the lift on the tailplane is in a downward motion, to balance the nose-down pitching of the wing. As soon as it reduces that lift, although you come back on the stick, the nose will pitch. You're stalled enough so that [the airplane] is telling you you're too slow, get your airspeed up, and unstall this thing. But if you didn't have the stall bars there, well, it's too late. With the stall bars, you can push the nose down, and it will take its time to recover, to get the flow attached to the wing again, to get it nice and smooth.

"So that's the key to the stalls. So that's what we played with, and, we finally, naturally, came up with the fix for it: the right length of bar, and where it was located."

THE CAREFUL PREPARATIONS he made before parachuting from LKI were one signature of George Neal the test pilot. He was not, strictly speaking, abandoning the aircraft—at least, not for long. Neal was merely putting its useful life on hold by leaving it temporarily and saving his own life. He would be back in that cockpit. He would find and reclaim his trademark baseball-style cap. And so Neal had done everything he could think of before jumping to ensure that the crumpled wreck would not explode or burn upon impact. Among other precautions, he braced himself inside the cockpit of the diving prototype and carefully switched off its ignition and fuel-flow controls. He knew that the last minutes of LKI's flight that day would yield a bonanza of information, piece by piece, scattered across the countryside along its flight path. The crash would be an invaluable phase in the Caribou's development; though neither scheduled nor simulated, it needed to be fully exploited. A pilot without an engineering background might not have seen the situation quite that way.

"The next day we began a big investigation," Neal recounts.

"We started looking for parts on the ground. I told [the flight test department] what had happened. They knew roughly where to look and found the spring tab and the actuating rod, and they just kept heading in a straight line to where they knew the wreckage was. And they picked up pieces all the way along.

"So, with that, they were able to piece together what really started it. They confirmed that it was the spring tab that was fluttering, and how it broke, and how pieces of the tailplane came off on the port side. We had some experimental leading edges on the tailplanes, and we had experimental horn balances on the elevators. The fluttering loosened the leading edge on the port side and the tip, and parts of them came away and dropped down. The tailplane shed those from fluttering. It made a picture and a pattern, of all the debris: of the door Walter pushed out first, where it fell, then where he landed; the underside door as well. They found everything! It was fantastic, how they found all these pieces. And they put it all on paper and so on.

"The engineers had a story right there, and they had the answer as to what caused it. The extension of the fuselage necessitated increasing the length of all the control cables by the four feet of the extension. That detuned the cables to a frequency below the flutter range. The frequency at which the cables vibrated matched the frequency of the elevator. And so, instead of dampening the elevator, stopping it from fluttering, it added to it. So the elevator just kept fluttering.

"Now, the elevators broke first at the centre of the torque tube that joined the elevators together, because the spring tab that was fluttering was on the left elevator. The trim tab, connected with the trim wheel up front, was on the right elevator. Now, here was the left tab exciting the left elevator, and the right elevator is resisting the flutter. So you get this torsion on the cross-tube, the tube that joins the main spar of the two elevators. With the constant fluttering, it finally twisted and broke. So that then allowed the right elevator to fly in streamlined position, and the left elevator just kept on fluttering: now it's free, there's nothing to stop it, it kept fluttering at that speed. The tab came off, and the elevator was still fluttering away there. Nothing to stop it.

"What they did was to beef up and change some of the routing, and change the cable dimensions, I believe, to change the frequency of those things so they were well above the frequency of what the tabs or the elevators would be at the Caribou's maximum speed.

"That was how it was overcome. But a simple thing like that . . . To prove the theory that these cables were adding to the tab [oscillations], they built some balsa wood models, just primitive models, they built in the different flutter modes and flutter strengths into these models. Then they put them in the wind tunnel and they were able to reproduce the fluttering. And without a doubt, that's what it was.

"The other thing they did, they put, instead of one big spring tab on the left elevator and one big trim tab on the right elevator, they cut them both in half and made a spring tab and a trim tab on each elevator. So that, if it ever occurred again, the elevators would be in unison. You'd get the flutter-dampening effect from both elevators.

"Bob Fowler did the last dives with the modified elevators and the longer cables. There was no flutter. It went over the 285 mph, I think about 290, and still no sign of flutter. So the Caribou was cleared then."

NEAL HANDLED THE first flight of the DHC-3 Otter December 12, 1951, with chief design engineer Fred Buller's last-minute warning to watch for tail flutter very much in mind. There was no flutter with the Otter, although Neal's instinctive assessment of the size of the fin as inadequate for directional stability proved sound. The fin was enlarged.

He also flew the Otter's subsequent two-year development and certification programs by himself, with the occasional look-in flight by Russ Bannock, flying a textbook regime on an airplane that was such a leap forward as a big single-engine bush plane that it may only now be coming into its own with more powerful turboprop engines. When two production Otters crashed in 1956, Neal and Bob Fowler flew an Otter with strengthened wings and special instrumentation, duplicating the circumstances in which the unfortunate Otters had gone down.

By 1959, George Neal was fully absorbed with the difficult flight test program of the Caribou—a military transport required to be certified under vastly more demanding civil transport rules.

That February late-morning trip for Neal and Walter Gadzos in the third prototype Caribou set off several months of demanding test flying, including an intensive summertime program flown by Fowler and Ted Johnson to cure the Caribou's behaviour at the stall, which Neal had already characterized as "borderline."

That program led to a package of aerodynamic refinements to the Caribou's wing, including stall bars, airstream fences outboard of the engines, drooped outer wing leading edges—all of which enhanced the Caribou's controllability at slow speeds—and the stick-shaker stall-warning device for those unwary pilots who had squandered the hints conferred by the previous modifications and needed a more compelling warning.

"The thing that I didn't think could happen," Neal reflects today, revisiting his decision to bail out of LKI when he did, "was that the fuselage could go in sympathy with a certain frequency of the elevator flutter. And that's what was actually causing the fuselage to snake along its length. It actually hit my seat, and it was hitting my behind, just like riding a horse. That's why I was concerned about trying to land it.

"I talked to [chief aerodynamicist] Dick Hiscocks. And I asked, how long would that structure last with that thing snaking like that?

"He said, 'Well, it would depend on how severe it was or how long it went on.' He said he couldn't tell. He said it might have gone in the next couple of minutes or it might have taken half an hour. But he said that eventually the fuselage would have cracked in half.

"So we were lucky. We were lucky things worked out that we got out of it and it got down reasonably intact so they could troubleshoot what went wrong. Possibly, if I'd tried to take it back home, if the fuselage had parted company, I might not be here to tell the tale. Or it might have—as I slowed it down—it might've really got going and hit the ground and demolished me, too. So, everything works out in the right way . . .

"A lot was learned on that Caribou. The engineering people, it was a new project for them. I mean, no one else had built a STOL twin-engine transport. So they had a real chore on their hands. But the airplane, when we finally finished it, was a darn fine airplane."

GEORGE NEAL WAS ELECTED to the Canadian Aviation Hall of Fame in 1995 for the most versatile career in aircraft engineering and flying ever seen in this country. Nearly 15,000 hours flying more than 100 different types: as impressive as those round numbers are, they only hint at his achievements. Neal also built airplanes—experimental homebuilts—restored First War fighters and replicas, and flew his handiwork on behalf of the National Aviation Museum in Ottawa. He won Canada's most prestigious aviation award, the Trans-Canada

(McKee) Trophy, in 1989, for more reasons than could be outlined in a short citation. He is a member of the DHC Hall of Fame. But his most important credential, all things considered, is his membership in the Caterpillar Club.

The Caterpillar Club, sponsored by the Irvin Parachute Company, refers to the silkworms that produce the basic material for parachutes. The club is the organization of pilots who have saved their lives by taking to their parachutes from crippled aircraft. The credo of the test pilot is to have done anything an average pilot might do in an aircraft in any possible situation. In bailing out of Caribou LKI, George Neal (and Walter Gadzos) can claim to have accomplished the test pilot's task as few others in the modern era have had to.

10

➤ **BOB FOWLER:**

STOL MAN

CHRONOLOGY: Flight Lt. Robert Howden (Bob) Fowler (RCAF ret'd) b. September 19, 1922, Toronto, where he was educated and worked for Maclean-Hunter Publishing Company 1939–41 and for Canadian Fine Chemicals (overlooking Toronto Island Airport) 1941–42. Learned to fly J-3 Cubs with Patterson & Hill at Barker Airfield, near de Havilland Canada, Downsview. Joined RCAF July 1942, graduated with pilot's wings and commission at No. 8 Service Flying Training School, Moncton, August 1943. That December posted to No. 34 RAF Operational Training Unit, Pennfield Ridge, New Brunswick, flying Lockheed Venturas. To England end 1943 as Pilot Officer. Completed 48 missions on B-25 Mitchell medium bombers with RAF 226 Sqn. Second Tactical Air Force (2TAF). Instructed and ferried aircraft at 2TAF Group Support Unit and ferried aircraft late in war before returning to Canada in August 1945.

Postwar Fowler enrolled in law school, but after a year resumed full-time flying, earning Commercial Pilot's Certificate in May 1946. Became chief pilot for Dominion Gulf Co., carrying out magnetic surveys over northern Quebec and Ontario with Grumman Goose and later PBY-5A Canso. In 1949 joined Spartan Air Services of Ottawa: spent next three years flying magnometer-equipped Anson Vs, and, later, modified P-38 Lightning fighters on high-altitude (35,000 feet) photo surveys out of Dawson City, Vancouver, and Ottawa.

Joined de Havilland Canada March 1952. After flying final certification program of DHC-4 Caribou, performed first flights of first five turbine-powered DHC-designed aircraft. Also participated in special test programs, including 1956 Otter crash investigation. Appointed DHC chief experimental test pilot June 2, 1959, charged with resolving Caribou stall and flutter problems.

First flights: Pratt & Whitney Canada PT6A turboprop engine, in nose of RCAF Beech Expeditor HB109, with John Hunt of P&WC, May 30, 1961; General Electric YT64 turbine-powered Caribou prototype (with Mick Saunders, Bob Dingle, Maj. "Doc" Richardson USMC), September 22, 1961; Turbo Beaver prototype, CF-PSM-X (with Jock Aitken), December 31, 1963; DHC-5 Buffalo prototype (with Saunders, Dingle), April 9, 1964; Twin Otter prototype CF-DHC-X (with Saunders and Barry Hubbard), May 20, 1965; Dash 7 prototype C-GNBX-X (with Saunders, Dingle, Aitken), March 27, 1975; Dash 8 prototype C-GDNK (with Saunders, Don Brand, Geoff Pyne), June 20, 1983. Co-pilot on first flight of stretched Dash-8 Series 300, C-GDNK, captained by Wally Warner (engineers Dave Monteith, Lee Fasken).

Flew DHC-Defence Research Board Otter 3682 extreme-STOL research aircraft from 1958 as backup pilot to George Neal, then as project pilot from late 1961, when it flew with a cabin-installed J85 jet engine exhausting through side-mounted modulating valves (December 18, 1961), until project's last flight (July 15, 1965), by which time 3682 sported two wing-mounted PT6 turboprops.

For two years from 1972, worked with National Aeronautics and Space Administration's Ames Flight Research Center, Moffett Field, California, to develop and evaluate Augmentor Wing Jet Research Aircraft, and, later, NASA's Quiet Short-Haul Research Aircraft, both STOL demonstrators.

Retired September 1987 after 35 years of test flying with de Havilland. In 49 years as a professional pilot, flew 15,000 hours as captain of 60 aircraft types. Received Trans-Canada (McKee) Trophy, 1974. Became Officer of Order of Canada, 1975. Inducted into Canada's Aviation Hall of Fame, 1980.

V V V

A MAN'S DEN SAYS A LOT about him. Bob Fowler works out of a small, well-lit, cluttered ground floor room in which he puts together beautifully written memoirs about his flying career for such publications as the Canadian Aviation Historical Society *Journal*. Fowler has made his share of Canadian aviation history: more first flights of new types of aircraft than anyone in Canada. He is the Canadian test pilot's test pilot, still consulted on new or developing projects.

There is a tiny desk with a computer and keyboard—one of three computers, linked to two printers, in the room. Outside the door, in the basement hallway, are skis and golf clubs that look well used. On the wall opposite Fowler's desk are two overflowing bookcases. They hold a Bible and collections of the works of Rudyard Kipling and Shakespeare. Aside from those and some titles on golf, the books on these shelves are about aviation. Nine RCAF logbooks are there, along with one $2.25 logbook from Eaton's department store. Much of the collection appears to be engineering textbooks: physics, advanced math (which Fowler reads but claims not to understand), aerodynamics, propulsion. This is the library of a lifetime student of aero engineering and one of the most technically oriented Canadian test pilots of his time. There are several aviation histories, including Fred Hotson's books on de Havilland of Canada, in which there are many references to Fowler. Borrowed copies of *Aviation Week and Aerospace Technology* keep him current, and copies of *Air International* are open to such meaty, if esoteric, big-picture topics as "Fundamentals of Fighter Design." Small stacks of books, magazines, and papers scattered throughout the room denote ongoing projects.

Most of the pictures in Fowler's office are grouped around his desk. There is an arresting print of a painting showing an RAF Second Tactical Air Force (2TAF) B-25 Mitchell bomber taxiing out in the rain at an RAF base. It has that bird-of-prey look B-25s have on the ground: the gull wings, the sloping glass nose, and the endplate rudders all seeming to droop around its spidery tricycle landing gear. The Mitchell was "a peerless aircraft to fly," Fowler says, having flown 48 missions in them, many of those in the skies over Normandy shortly after D-Day.

In the desk alcove is a sensational photo of Fowler in the polished natural metal, first prototype de Havilland Canada (DHC) Twin Otter, CF-DHC-X, on floats, taken moments after he alighted at Toronto's Island Airport, some time in 1965. Through the windshield of the aircraft you can see Fowler's left hand reaching up to operate the roof-mounted throttles, and an especially foamy roostertail billows off the floats out back. Fowler got that dramatic effect by holding the Twin Otter up on its float steps, nose slightly high, with lots of throttle—even though his view through the windshield was filling up with de Havilland's Toronto Island base hangar "and a whole lot of concrete" getting closer by the second. Fowler knew that with the Twin Otter's reversing propellers, he could stop the airplane "in a second." For DHC photographer Reg Corlett, standing onshore, there was only one chance to get the shot.

There are also photos of three one-off experimental airplanes Fowler flew to explore the limits of STOL technology. DHC's mission through six different aircraft designs, from the single-engine Beaver of 1947 through the four-turboprop Dash-7 airliner, which first flew in

1975, was to bring the benefits of air travel to both remote areas of the globe and the downtown cores of major centres by eliminating the need for mile-long concrete runways. Fowler was chief experimental test pilot at DHC for 29 years of that 35-year period. He kept himself current with the latest developments in STOL by helping develop short-field technology demonstrators that could take off and land a lot like helicopters but operated with the simpler controls of airplanes.

One of those x-planes was the Defence Research Board–DHC STOL Otter. The other two experimentals whose photos grace Fowler's office walls were National Aeronautics and Space Administration (NASA) projects using highly modified twin-turboprop DHC Buffalo battlefield transports converted to jet power. The NASA Augmentor Wing Buffalo and the NASA/Boeing Quiet Short-Haul Research Aircraft (QSRA), both of which flew during the 1970s, established new performance criteria for STOL aircraft, behaving much like big helicopters, flying under control as slowly as 58 mph, making steep landing approaches up to 18 degrees, and, in the case of the QSRA, doing so quietly enough to point the way to a future interurban commuter airplane.

There are also four photographs of the former Margaret Phillips, daughter of George Phillips, 1931 McKee Trophy winner and onetime chief pilot of the Ontario Provincial Air Service, and sister of Jack Phillips, a 418 Squadron–mate of Russ Bannock's. One of those photos shows a very fetching Margaret five minutes after she and Bob Fowler met. This time too, the dashing pilot married the pretty girl. Margaret calls her husband's office "The Swamp." He likes that.

BOB FOWLER NEVER HAD that flyer's basic credential, a private pilot's licence. (He notes that John "Cat's Eyes" Cunningham, night-fighter ace and CTP of DH England, had nothing more than his private licence until well into Comet jet airliner test flying.) A high school dropout whose father died when he was five, Fowler worked as an office boy at a publishing company, where he knew *Canadian Aviation* magazine editor Ron Keith. He made $6 a week, $4 of which went to his mother. Fowler learned to fly J-3 Cubs at Barker Field, near DHC's Downsview facility. He took dual instruction for six hours, 40 minutes before soloing, the first three lessons with Jim Henderson, a wartime Atlantic Ferry Command pilot, at $4.50 a half-hour. His talent was polished by Vi Milstead-Warren in September 1939. She was, he says, "one peach of a pilot. She could fly like a million bucks. She had a real touch. Cute as a button." Warren later joined the RAF's Air Transport Auxiliary at White Waltham, England, and flew all the current fighters and bombers.

Fowler joined the RCAF in 1942. Lacking a logbook as a pilot's credential—"It cost $2.25 at Eaton's"—Fowler presented his Barker Field bills. He attended Toronto's Jarvis Collegiate at night to do algebra and geometry, and he took a course with the RCAF consisting mostly of maths and science. You passed this course, Fowler recalls, "or you became a gunner."

Fowler received his wings at No. 8 Service Flying Training School (SFTS), Moncton, New Brunswick, August 31, 1943. Like so many superior student-pilots, Fowler nearly became an instructor. He was posted to the training base at Trenton, but "I threw a fit." Instead, he was sent to Pennfield Ridge, near St. John, New Brunswick, where No. 34 Operational Training Unit (OTU) turned out four-man Lockheed Ventura crews for the RAF's Second Tactical Air Force (2TAF). No. 34 OTU was, as Fowler remembers it, "a solid little British enclave . . . right down to the batmen."

Fowler thought it a small miracle that the leap from flying the Anson II trainer with its two 300hp engines to the Lockheed Ventura medium bomber, with its twin 2,000hp engines, did not leave "more Venturas lying about the airfield at the end of each day." One reason was that the instruction was good: the instructors at Pennfield, he noted, were all veterans of at least one operational tour: "Some twitchy ones had three." The awful weather at Pennfield was a good preview of what they would encounter over England.

"Sometimes," Fowler wrote in a wartime memoir published in 1999, "we can embark on what seems a perfectly innocuous event without any suspicion that we are walking into an experience we will be able to recall in stark detail for the rest of our lives."

For Fowler, such an event was a ride he took in a Ventura piloted by the most highly regarded student pilot on his course. The feeling of being responsible for a crew of four was new to Fowler. Being mock-intercepted by Hurricanes flown by tour-expired fighter pilots made him wonder what life was like elsewhere than in the left-hand cockpit seat. So he hitched a ride in the mid-upper gun turret of a Ventura with only one good radio transceiver, its compass course needle stuck on 254 degrees, and snow forecast for that afternoon.

With its snags and malfunctions, the Ventura was restricted to takeoffs and landings. After the third or fourth circuit, each of them concluded with a three-point touchdown, the pilot asked the tower for permission to do "one more quick circuit."

The weather front was clearly advancing more quickly than forecast. "I remember thinking," Fowler wrote, "that this pilot was obviously a solid *press on* type."

Of course the Ventura lost the race to land before the airfield was socked in by snow. After a missed approach to an equally whited-out airport at a place called Blissville, the Pennfield tower suggested a 150-mile detour northwest to Caribou, Maine. Folowing an hour's flying on instruments and no sign of clearing anywhere, Fowler moved up to the navigation compartment. From there he saw the pilot looking out his windows for the ground, affecting, Fowler noticed, his directional accuracy. A conversation about parachutes took place. Fowler joined the discussion, saying *he* would not jump until the fuel gauges showed empty tanks.

"I didn't envy our pilot," Fowler recalled in his memoir. "He looked tired and was becoming a bit edgy. Neither of us had likely ever flown on continuous instruments for much more than an hour—or two at most. Every one of us in the aircraft was a rank amateur."

Soon after, the pilot rose from the left seat, asking Fowler to take over. After unsuccessfully encouraging the pilot to stay put, Fowler "slipped into it with an eagerness that surprised me." He began letting down in 1,000-foot intervals in hopes of seeing something on the ground. "It seemed to be at least a start." They circled over each opening, taking care to make a complete 360-degree turn so as not to lose direction. Several such explorations yielded nothing recognizable until they discovered a tidal shoreline.

After close to three hours of flying, presumably northwest into the United States, Fowler recognized that they were over Moncton, home of No. 8 SFTS, his previous base, about 120 miles northeast of Pennfield. It, too, was snowbound. It took four or five approaches for him to land the Ventura in the whiteout. He did each approach flaps-up: with limited visibility until the last moment, he had to plan for an overshoot. In that state, with all the snow, and the flaps still lowering, they used the entire runway getting stopped.

Fowler noticed that once he had three wheels on the ground the fuel gauges' needles stopped moving. With the tail down, there wasn't enough fuel in the tanks to move the indicators. "It would be an understatement," Fowler wrote, "to say I enjoyed parking the Ventura."

Having survived training, Fowler and his crew shipped to England over New Year's 1944 aboard the *Louis Pasteur,* in what they were told was the roughest trans-Atlantic voyage the ship had ever experienced. After a month-long Commando and Escape Course that taught Fowler how to kill with his bare hands, he had his entry to combat further delayed so he could learn the RAF's blind landing system using Airspeed Oxford twin-engine trainers. Within two weeks, pilots like Fowler were making landings in thick fog using the system.

He and his Ventura crew converted to B-25CS, or Mitchell IIs as the RAF referred to the medium bombers, at Finmere, Buckinghamshire. They began flying combat missions July 2, 1944, with RAF 226 Squadron, part of 2TAF's 137 Wing out of Hartford Bridge, Surrey. It was almost two years to the day since Fowler's enlistment. At his first briefing, Fowler remembers thinking, *I have finally made it to the war!* Too true: he and his crew did their 48 missions in three months flat, sometimes two a day, many of them at night.

It was mid-afternoon August 6 when Fowler's Mitchell, Orange Four, was hit by flak at 12,000 feet over the German stronghold of Caen. Within seconds there were 80 holes, each of them big enough to put a half-crown through, scattered around the port side of Fowler's Mitchell II. The left engine was hit and its propeller rendered ungovernable. Reducing power was the only way to keep it from overspeeding. Raw fuel poured into the navigator's compartment from the left wing root, filling it deep enough to burn the navigator's feet inside his shoes. The wireless operator/air gunner leaped across his compartment in the rear when holes appeared inches from his feet, pulling his intercom plug out. Silence from the aft compartment led Fowler to assume he was hit. Another B-25 radioed that Fowler's landing gear were down; the flak had unlocked them. Fowler personally blames the 21st Panzers, who were holding Caen against the Poles and the Canadians.

On one engine, gear down, Fowler's Mitchell began losing altitude. He offered the navigator the option of bailing out, but both decided to ride it down to save the gunner, should he still be alive.

Orange Four found itself left behind by its formation, but it followed two other crippled and descending Mitchells, all three of which made it to a short P-47 fighter strip under construction near Vire, in the American zone. The runway was graded for half its width and temporarily surfaced with four 10-foot-wide strips of half-inch tarpaper. The first Mitchell, with a prop that would not stay feathered, made a normal landing and parked. The second, without landing gear or flaps, bellied in on the relatively smooth tarpaper surface, then slid past the end of the runway, across a field, and into some woods, where it burst into flames and had its ammunition and flares exploded by the intense heat. The pilot, Mac McQueen, escaped, but returned through the flames and exploding flares and ammo to boost his navigator out through the topside hatch, then returned again for his gunner.

Fowler's navigator laboriously hand-pumped the Mitchell's landing gear down and locked it by hand. It was only on final approach Fowler confirmed that, with the hydraulic system shot up, he had no flaps. The moment his Mitchell touched down, he knew his left main wheel had had its tire shot off. The bomber slewed to the left as the bare wheel dug in. Fowler found himself heading directly for the parked Mitchell. Still moving at high speed, he lifted his left wing with aileron and got straightened out for a several-hundred-foot ground run on his right main wheel. Straightened out, Fowler now found himself headed directly for the fireworks display the second Mitchell had become. As speed fell off, letting the left wing back down, surprised to get some braking from the left wheel, Fowler ground-looped the Mitchell and got it stopped.

Fowler and his crew could still have perished. Fuel was pouring out of the airplane, which was listing to the left. The construction gang's reaction to the drama they had just witnessed was to gather around Fowler's Mitchell, some with lighted cigarettes.

WHILE OVERSEAS, Fowler met Russ Bannock, then CO of the RCAF's 418 Squadron. The connection was likely made through Jack Phillips, who was with 418 before and after Bannock. The squadron flew Mosquitoes. Phillips was Fowler's future brother-in-law.

"Russ and I both stayed at an air officer's club for Canadians that was a very lovely place on Cadogan Gardens, very close to Sloan Square. The Sloan Square tube station which took a direct hit . . . is very close to Harrod's.

"I might have met Russ with Jack. I met more of Jack's 418 friends when we were killing time in London. We spent bits of time in London together."

Normal life for Fowler after his return to Canada in August 1945 meant completing high school, compiling marks good enough to get him into law school. He did a year of legal studies, after which he went looking for a summer job. That May, he qualified for his first civil flying credential, his commercial pilot's licence. He found work as a pilot with Dominion Gulf, a Canadian subsidiary of Gulf Oil and Gulf Research and Development, flying a Grumman Goose amphibian at Larder Lake, about 90 miles due north of North Bay, Ontario, and Chibougamau, Quebec, and a Canso at Kapuskasing, Ontario, eventually becoming chief pilot. Fowler hired a friend and wartime Spitfire pilot, Bill Ferderber, who had been flying a Norseman for Arthur Fecteau at Senneterre, Quebec, and checked him out on the Goose.

By 1949 Gulf's Goose bases had been taken over by Ottawa-based Spartan Air Services. While Fowler was with Spartan, the company began flying war-surplus Lockheed P-38 twin-engine fighters on photo survey work. Fowler and the legendary pilot/engineer Weldy Phipps modified one of the P-38s, which, by flying at 35,000 feet, could cover much larger strips of territory than had been possible with such aircraft as Ansons. Fowler flew survey P-38s for two seasons. The work required disciplined flying, holding strictly to headings and altitude—skills applicable to flight testing. Ferderber bought himself a DH.103 Sea Hornet, then a front-line British twin-engine naval fighter, surplused after being tested for cold-weather operations at Edmonton, and used it to fulfill a high-altitude photo-survey contract with Spartan.

By 1951, Ferderber was an engineering/production test pilot with DHC. Russ Bannock asked him if his buddy Fowler, whom Bannock remembered from Cadogan Gardens, would be interested in the work they were doing at DHC. Ferderber thought he might.

"I was very impressed with him," Bannock says of Fowler, who joined DHC in March 1952. Fowler landed at Downsview in the ex-Ferderber Sea Hornet, which was impressive in itself. "Apart from being a good pilot," Bannock thought, "he was a very nice guy." That was an important factor at DHC. "You had to be a salesman first," Fowler remembers. "We had to demonstrate the planes."

Fowler started as a production test pilot, doing whatever needed to be done: flying new Beavers and Chipmunks and testing Lancaster maritime reconnaissance conversions, as well as overhauled North Star transports and the RCAF's Vampire jet fighters after they were uncrated and assembled. He flew the corporate twin-engine Dove and, occasionally, DHC managing director Phil Garratt's personal Hornet Moth. He also did a Middle East tour in 1955, demonstrating a Beaver. Three years later he was chief production test pilot.

In February 1956 Bill Ferderber had been checking out three U.S. Army pilots for an hour in the newly manufactured Number 92 Otter over Downsview when a wing panel was seen to separate from the aircraft. The rest of the machine spun 3,000 feet to earth, killing all four men. A blue-ribbon accident investigative panel was formed, headed by Fred Jones of the Royal Aircraft Establishment (RAE), Farnborough, England, that included company, scientific, and customer representatives.

One of the more dangerous avenues of inquiry was a series of flights undertaken by George Neal and Bob Fowler, who wore parachutes in a strengthened and instrumented Otter to duplicate the pitching behaviour Ferderber's aircraft had been subjected to. Their flights led to a theory about what had happened: with elevator trim selected nose-down, a sudden retraction of the Otter's big double-slotted flaps would cause the Otter to "bunt," that is, to dive past the vertical, imposing negative-G downward loads the wing was not designed to withstand. George Neal, with Fowler in the right seat, proved that a pilot prepared for this situation could take corrective action. But if the pilot were taken by surprise, the scenario would play out too fast to be stopped.

That April, another Otter crashed at Goose Bay, this time an early-production RCAF machine that was having a replacement flap flight tested. As unfortunate as the second accident was, it did supply more evidence, and, thanks in part to Neal and Fowler's bunt flights, the mystery was solved. Fowler later became DHC chief engineering test pilot.

FOWLER CAME INTO HIS OWN during de Havilland Canada's defining crisis, the Caribou's difficult flight test program. The crash of the third prototype Caribou, CF-LKI-X, February 24, 1959, coming as it did only days after Black Friday at Avro, only emphasized how quickly the fortunes of Canadian aircraft manufacturers could plummet. It showed how thin the line was between the profitable mass production of three different types of aircraft—as DHC was doing with the Chipmunk, the Beaver, and the Otter—and having to ask bankers for the money to launch the Caribou, up to then the most expensive new aircraft in the company's history, as DHC was also doing.

Although CTP George Neal had thought the big twin was on the verge of being certified as airworthy, the Caribou's misfortune showed that there were hidden gremlins in the lengthened fuselage, introduced to make it more versatile, that could have been fatal. And those gremlins came on top of the Caribou's wing-drop tendency at the stall in a couple of scenarios specified in Civil Air Regulations 4b, airworthiness standards the Caribou was required to meet. This was behaviour that Neal considered, at best, borderline.

The Caribou's stall problem was handed to Fowler, who was called into Russ Bannock's office June 2, 1959, and invited to choose anyone from the company's flight test staff to take part in the Caribou program. Bannock had hired his old 418 Squadron–mate Ted Johnson to become his right-hand man in military sales. Johnson was supposed to spend six months learning the company's product line as part of the flight test staff. He had been doing so for five months when Fowler tapped him to help with the Caribou. Fowler and Johnson embarked upon what Johnson later called "The Summer of a Thousand Stalls."

It took several aerodynamic fixes, including stall bars, upper-wing fences, a drooped outer leading edge, and other modifications, to civilize the Caribou's entry into the stall. Each fix had to be flight tested for location, degree of change, and size. Sheer effort resolved the problem.

For close to six years thereafter, Fowler, by then DHC's chief experimental test pilot, was kept busy with an impressive series of first flights of prototype aircraft and intensive development of STOL X-planes. Those programs were flown on behalf of DHC, often as joint ventures with other manufacturers such as engine or propeller manufacturers, or in cooperation with scientific bodies such as Canada's Defence Research Board and the U.S. National Aeronautics and Space Administration. Fowler describes himself, accurately enough but in the faintly ironic way test pilots cultivate, as "a frustrated engineer." In truth, he wasn't all that frustrated. He was, rather, a lifetime student of engineering who never got to the point where he thought he knew it all. Fowler did not have the opportunity to study engineering formally, so his quest for an understanding of the principles of aero engineering was his lifetime's calling. The faculty was DHC's engineering department. All in all, his career represented the final victory of the guys on the ground (at DHC, at least) in the ongoing tug-of-war between engineers and test pilots, the conflict George Neal has described. "I had no such conflict that was not open, healthy, and productive," Fowler writes. End of story.

Fowler's initial pair of first flights were of engine testbeds. As Mike Cooper-Slipper of Avro learned, there is an art to flying an airplane with an engine or engines that don't, strictly speaking, belong on it. The first of those was Pratt & Whitney Canada's small PT6 turboprop, which Fowler tested in the nose of an RCAF Beech Expeditor twin beginning May 30, 1961. The PT6 became the most successful small turboprop engine in the world.

Fowler's second engine-testing first flight was General Electric's big T64, which was being developed for the U.S. Navy. Fowler flew two T64s, which replaced the 1,200hp P&W R-2000 radials on the prototype Caribou, loaned to DHC for this purpose by the RCAF. With two untested prototype engines, there was no source of power, as there had been in the Expeditor, if the T64s failed. The T64 was developing around 3,000 shaft horsepower and had the potential for 25 percent more. The Caribou was an appropriate engine testbed for the mighty T64 sizewise, but it had been designed for 50 percent less installed power.

The first flight of the T64 Caribou took place September 22, 1961. With its new T64s, the Caribou could exceed its maximum level flight speed on one engine. It could surpass its maximum design dive speed in level flight. So the T64 Caribou had to be flown carefully and with a constant eye on the airspeed indicator.

The art of flying engine testbeds, as with any unproven aircraft or modification, consists largely of looking for trouble. There was plenty that could go wrong in such an overpowered test vehicle. With all the power on tap, the consequences would only be worse if something went wrong with the mechanisms that had to absorb it all, the propellers. All that power drove wide, square-tipped paddle-type Hamilton Standard propeller blades that could move air in big chunks. But what if those massive props misbehaved?

George Georgas, Fowler's flight test engineer and co-pilot on that particular series of tests, thought it could happen. Georgas was chief of engineering flight test at the time. Fowler respected engineers more than some test pilots did, and he respected Georgas, who was no slouch as a pilot himself: he was a retired RCAF Reserve wing commander who had flown Vampire and Sabre fighter jets. Georgas did a projection from ground testing data and the few flights undertaken so far which predicted that, with the fine pitch stop removed, the propellers could reverse in flight. Normally, safeguards would be in place to prevent such a possibility. But since the engine was new, so was the marriage of engine and propeller.

Georgas thought that as the wide props governed themselves into fine pitch, angling into an almost flat disc, the twist built into each propeller blade would eventually put its outer tip into reverse, with the rest of the blade following. With the fine pitch functionally removed, governor logic could possibly drive the blades into reverse, causing the air to be pushed forward instead of back. Would the fastest-ever Caribou shudder to a halt in mid-air? Would the airplane hold together? It wouldn't take long to find out.

"At one time in the air we had *both* of them go into reverse, at about 95 knots [109 mph]. Yes, at the same time. Right together. Talk about amazing," Fowler remembers.

Amazing is right. Had one gone into reverse and not the other, Fowler and Georgas would have been in a whole different can of worms. With all of their disaster planning, it had never crossed either of their minds that both props might go into reverse at the same time.

"In fact," Fowler explains, "the guys from Ham Standard said, 'Gee whiz, nice to know we made two of them that similar.'

"And the airplane pitched nose-up, then nose-down, and up and down. First it pointed steeply up. Then it pointed what looked to be straight down. Then back upward again. I was curious to see where I'd have to quit.

"Georgas thought I'd forgotten [what we'd agreed to do] about it. But I was just curious as to what these forces were doing, because the elevators were all over the place. And the airplane was doing this *ptee* pitching manoeuvre."

Ptee? At this point in our interview, one hand level in front of his head, bending and unbending all four fingers at the knuckles, Fowler demonstrates how the T64 Caribou's nose was pitching up and down, repeating *ptee, ptee,* which is how the screaming props sounded.

Here was the intrepid test pilot, putting unimaginable strain on a pair of priceless unproven engine prototypes (not to mention abusing the Caribou), living a prop-job driver's nightmare, and actually prolonging the agony as the T64 Caribou fought with itself—just to see if it could be controlled! Out of sheer stupid curiosity!

"Then I hear this voice in the headset saying, 'Let's feather them, Bob.' Georgas didn't say, *The way we had talked about it.*

"And so I put my hand on the feathering button. His was [already] there"—but Georgas hadn't pushed it, professional that he was—"and, we went, just with body English, moving our shoulders, our heads, and then our hands, *euggh!* We held it in.

"So it worked fine. Then we just looked at each other. That was one of the thrills we had with each other over the years."

The T64 Caribou was an important experimental airplane. It was the testbed for the powerful new turbine engine that, as a turboprop, might have powered some U.S. Navy propeller-driven aircraft and, as a turboshaft, the Sikorsky H-53 series of helicopters. In the helicopters, it developed close to 4,000-shaft horsepower. From de Havilland's and Bob Fowler's point of view, the re-engined Caribou led directly to the Buffalo, powered by a pair of the same engines. The Buffalo—and a couple of its jet-powered research derivatives—was one of the loves of Bob Fowler's flying life.

Fowler performed the first flight of the Buffalo in April 1964. The Buffalo was a very impressive tactical hauler which, in time, proved capable of lifting payloads up to five tons from almost any relatively smooth surface three football fields long.

"The Buffalo was a big thing. It had a T-tail"—so named for its horizontal tail being set on the top of its fin—"it had the big double-slotted flaps we'd been using for so long to make it a STOL airplane. Certificating it was kind of a formality; it was mainly to get some kind of a civil certificate so the U.S. Army could buy it off the shelf as a certified airplane. That way, it wasn't an airplane that was being developed for them. The Corps of Aviation of the U.S. Army wasn't allowed to develop airplanes for itself. So we had to get a C of A [certificate of airworthiness] for it. We certificated it up to 42,000 pounds for takeoff, but I think it eventually got up to 49,000 pounds. Later, with a couple of engines that, give or take a horsepower, were about 3,000 apiece. So the Buffalo was a big project to us. And it was a peach of an airplane. It did everything it was supposed to do. It did everything *so* well.

"We were a little spooky about our first T-tail aircraft. But we de-spooked that, through a lot of steady work. We didn't want anything ever becoming a problem that we hadn't encountered. Everything went just that way."

Fowler was up to his neck in Buffalo flight testing when he ran into DHC's managing director, Phil Garratt, one day at the plant.

"The managing director asked me whether we were going to finish the Buffalo on time, and I said, 'Oh yeah, we'll have it finished within the year that we've allocated to it.'

(Which was true: The Buffalo would be certified as airworthy in April 1965.)

"He said, 'It's very important.'

"I said, 'Oh, why?'

"And he said, 'We've decided to do the little twin turboprop.' They weren't calling it the Twin Otter at the time.

"I said, 'Really, you're going ahead with that?'

"And he said, 'The decision's been made. It should be ready to fly about the time you're finished certificating the Buffalo.'

"I said, 'You're going to put twin gas-guzzling turboprops on an Otter-sized airplane to haul 14 passengers through the air at 140 knots with the undercarriage hanging down and the wing held up with struts on both sides ... And we're going to ask 230-some-odd thousand dollars for it?'

"And he said, 'Yes. We have a pretty good market interest.'

"I said, 'I'm amazed that people would pay that kind of money.'

"He said, 'Oh yes, if we could sell a hundred of those—or even a hundred and fifty—that would keep the lights on, could pay for the telephone, the heat, light and power, until we get into the next airplane.'"

"We were selling them," Fowler sums up with a punchline at his own expense, "for a million and a half before we were through. Maybe even more."

Some time later, Fowler recalls, with the Twin Otter on track to sell its eventual 844 copies over 13 years of production, Garratt kidded him by saying, "If we're ever in any doubt about whether to do something or not, ask Fowler, get his opinion, and then do the opposite."

FOWLER HAD, OF COURSE, stayed in touch with engineering as they schemed the project that became the Twin Otter. Few test pilots have ever been as fully prepared to take a specific prototype

196 | THE CHOSEN ONES

aloft as Bob Fowler was to fly the Twin Otter for the first time. He had done the first flight tests of the engine that powered the Twin Otter—indeed, the engine that made the Twin Otter possible—flying the Beech testbed with the prototype P&WC PT6 turboprop installed in its nose.

Nearly a couple of years after taking the PT6 aloft for the first time, Fowler flew a pair of pre-production PT6s on the wing of the Defence Research Board–DHC extreme-STOL experimental Otter, formerly a stock single-engine Otter. The aircraft had been previously modified with high-impact landing gear, a different tail, and a J85 jet in the fuselage exhausting through two thrust-gas modulator valves, one on each side of the fuselage, giving downward thrust that enabled the x-Otter to make landing approaches at very steep angles. These changes, made over a five-year developmental period ending in 1964, turned an ordinary RCAF Search-and-Rescue single-engine Otter, RCAF serial 3682, into a STOL research aircraft that Fowler first flew with the two PT6s running March 7, 1963. Flying the x-Otter with its PT6s was one more way Fowler inadvertently prepared for the first flight of the design that became the Twin Otter.

Yet another preparation to fly a PT6-powered aircraft was the first flight of the Turbo Beaver prototype on the last day of 1963. It was the first DHC production aircraft to be powered by the PT6.

All that previous experience flying the engine that made the Twin Otter possible may be why, among all of Fowler's first flights, the one in the "little twin turboprop" that turned out to be a best-seller was, as he puts it, "anti-climactic."

"It was called the twin-engine Otter. The only thing that surprised me was the fuss everybody was making on about this Twin Otter. I was full up to my ears with the Buffalo, which I'd put in a solid year on. What's all this fuss about a little airplane?

"It seemed like a nice little airplane to be going flying on the first flight. An interesting little airplane. The Buffalo had been kind of big-league."

It was customary for de Havilland Canada prototypes to be registered with letters that honoured, for example, their chief designers. The first Twin Otter was instead registered CF-DHC-X, in honour of the entire company, in accord with DHC's assessment of the new design's potential. Good customers such as Max Ward and the U.S. Army had been begging for something like the Twin Otter for close to 15 years. The Twin Otter inspired a new aviation industry term: the commuter, or air taxi, business. Dick Hiscocks, who during the Twin Otter's gestation was DHC's vice-president, engineering, pointed out in 1993 that, for many years, the Twin Otter represented 10 to 20 percent of all scheduled aircraft in service worldwide. It was the most numerous propeller-driven aircraft in scheduled passenger service for much of that time.

The Twin Otter had the second-longest production run of any Canadian-designed aircraft. You can understand why Fowler remembers it as "an interesting little airplane." After what he'd been through from 1959 to 1965—the Otter bunt tests, the Caribou stalls, having the T64's props reverse in the air, and numberless other adventures in flight testing—the Twin Otter was a piece of cake. Almost everything went according to plan. And Fowler, trusted by the engineers, wrote the plan.

Fowler, with test pilot A. M. "Mick" Saunders and flight test engineer Barry Hubbard, did the Twin Otter's initial flight May 20, 1965. It was uneventful by first-flight standards.

Actually, Fowler regrets to this day missing an opportunity to make it more of an historic event. Martin Sharp, historian of DH England, was there for the Twin Otter's first flight, which coincided with some important changes in the Canadian company. (News of the death of Sir Geoffrey de Havilland came a day later, and the takeover later that summer of DHC's board by nominees of Hawker-Siddeley, including Phil Garratt's replacement by H-S's Bill Boggs, made the summer of 1965 momentous for the company. Sir Roy Dobson, founder of Avro Canada and DHC's new master, also appeared for the Twin Otter rollout.)

Fowler remembers Sharp waving at him from the left side of CF-DHC-X after he, Saunders, and Hubbard had buckled in but not yet started the engines. Fowler pulled down the window, lifted his earphone from his left ear, and asked what the problem was. Sharp asked "if I could tell him what I was going to do on the flight." It was a chance for Fowler to say something memorable and have it recorded for posterity. Put on the spot, the only reply he could think of was to hold up his clipboard and the thick flight plan and say, "I hope we are going to do everything on this board, Martin."

However prosaic he sounded, Fowler was telling the truth. He replaced his headphones, fired up the Twin Otter's PT6s, and began a conversation with his crew, the engineers—led by Dick Batch, director of technical design—and, in all likelihood, "the president in his office listening in too.

"If you're going to make a fool of yourself, you're going to do it in front of an audience that will simplify things for you from then on. The big thing is, do all the planning you possibly can beforehand. Batch said to me, 'Why don't you write the scenario for the first flight?' I thought that was incredible. That's the way it was with Dick Batch. I was used to what they liked, but I had put in a few things I wanted to do in a certain order."

It all went so smoothly that Fowler remembers nothing of the first flight. "There was a lot more to this airplane than we thought. It flew like a million bucks."

The crisis in Twin Otter development appeared not in the air but in the static test rig. The new DHC president, Bill Boggs, happened to be in the static test area, where weights and jacks simulate the stresses of flight and landing, November 25, 1965, when future vice-president, engineering John Thompson explained that the Twin Otter fuselage was being tested to see how it withstood heavy landings on one main gear.

Soon after Boggs left, the test fuselage buckled at the point where the main gear strut and the wing strut loads fed into a sheet-metal frame member. This happened at half the design load. Wrinkles appeared aft along the fuselage.

The solution was to cut each of the five prototypes and 10 production Twin Otters on the assembly line in half at the frame, replace the sheet-metal frame member with a costly machined aluminum one, and then reunite each airframe. It was nice to have a failure occur with no test pilot involved.

Because the Twin Otter was designed to be operated on wheels, skis, and floats, some of the most critical flight testing did not involve flying at all. Fowler did fairly hair-raising tests on the ground, such as taxiing on one main landing gear wheel at a time. Or, on the water, doing porpoising tests to see how easy it was to dig the forward float tips into the water. Digging the tips leads to the airplane flipping nose over teakettle to rest floats-up. These tests made Fowler look like something of a hot dog, but he had his reasons.

"I liked to kid the engineers about different things. I used to talk about the wheels being not terribly wide-track, you know. But it didn't seem to matter a darn. The undercarriage was soft enough on the rubber shock absorbers that, once you were on the ground in a crosswind, you could apply and hold a bank angle much easier than you could with a wide-track undercarriage, because it was a non-hydraulic undercarriage. That's strictly in the shock absorber sense. These were big blocks of highly sophisticated rubber material. These blocks had none of the rate sensitivity [of a hydraulic shock absorber]. That is, if you move fast, a hydraulic thing will resist. But if you moved these things fast, they didn't react in the same way at all.

"As a result, you could put on aileron and rock the airplane and hold a little bit of bank on while you were rolling down the runway on either takeoff or landing in a crosswind. You could compress the [rubber] on one side and hold it there. If you took the aileron off, it would put itself back level. Both wheels would be in contact. You can do the same stuff with a hydraulic system too, but not in the same sense; it will tend to resist you a bit as a function of rate of closure. And that's done in just the same way as a hydraulic door closer, which keeps the door from slamming.

"Certificating the Twin Otter wasn't dead easy; we had stall troubles with it. We had stall problems with the second aircraft once we put de-icing boots on its leading edge. They held us up; they had funny little sensitivities about it. The stretched Series 300 [which appeared in 1969] had a more powerful PT6 and larger propeller blades; it had to be certificated to the air taxi requirement, which updated the U.S. Civil Air Regulations [CAR] 3 quite a bit."

Fowler's porpoising tests on floats, which involved pitching the Twin Otter prototypes nose-up, then nose-down, are more important to Twin Otter users today than they might have been at the time. Most new Twin Otters were used as intercity commuter aircraft, but more are on floats today than ever before. Of course, in port cities such as Vancouver and Victoria, British Columbia, most intercity commuter aircraft *are* floatplanes. On floats, a Twin Otter is the ultimate seaplane.

The Twin Otter is unique in any number of ways, one of which is its configuration on floats. A floatplane Twin Otter looks different from almost any other floatplane. The floats are more integrated with the rest of the airplane. They are better streamlined and bigger than most, and they are set closer to the fuselage. The Twin Otter's nose extends forward past the bow tips of its floats. Most aircraft floats have their bow tips set well ahead of the nose of the aircraft they are mounted on, especially floatplane Beavers and Otters, which have heavy nose-mounted engines and therefore a higher concentration of weight up front. But the Twin Otter's nose, reaching farther forward, looks as if the airplane might be easy to trip up.

This raises a question that Fowler spent months' worth of mornings skimming around Toronto Harbour trying to answer: how easy was it to dig those front tips into the water? In certain situations, rogue waves can cause upsets. What were the margins?

"It's a completely different airplane with those great big 30-foot floats," Fowler explains. "They are much more streamlined than the traditional Edo floats [the standard aircraft float, manufactured by the Edo Aircraft Corporation, College Point, Long Island, or its licensees]. They were built by Canadian Aircraft Products (CAP) in Vancouver. They were designed from both a hydrodynamic and an aerodynamic standpoint. They were designed for minimal aerodynamic drag, even maybe lift effects, too.

"They are much smoother. The CAP float has a turtle deck on top, instead of a flat deck. Much more effective dragwise. What especially interested us, in the float, was its hydrodynamic qualities. Because it was designed from a completely different standpoint to an Edo float. And they behave very differently. People that had thousands of hours flying Edo floats who thought they'd just jump in this thing and fly it . . . found that it wasn't flying quite the same off the water. It does different things.

"And we had to do things I don't think they ever did with Edo floats. We had porpoising modes that we had to check. You'd go out with the airplane loaded at the aft limit, at high weight, down in that big bay off the airport at Toronto Island.

"I usually had the bay all to myself; I had to wait until after the ships went away and their wakes had gone. Then I would hold the stick all the way forward and put the power up to takeoff power. Just keep holding the stick forward. And that's very thrilling. Keeps you wide awake, I'll tell you. It feels like it starts to dig in, you wonder how far this thing is gonna go . . .

"Probably the most critical porpoising test case is with a forward centre-of-gravity at light weight, the C of G–forward low-angle por-poising mode. That's where the C of G is forward, and the airplane is light. You hold the stick forward and put takeoff power on. You do this with flaps-up, flaps-down. If it *won't* do all the flap cases with forward C of G safely, you might have to write quite a story in the manual about how to do it. We never had that problem. If the forward yoke pressure is released, or power is reduced, the porpoising must auto-arrest. These are all the things that you've got to think of and keep records of. Somebody would say, 'We thought of another one last night,' and I'd say, 'Why didn't you go to bed?'

"I spent weeks in 1965 going back and forth across that bay. The bay is more than two miles long. You've got to do downwind takeoffs, upwind takeoffs, every combination you can think of that could upset the handling of the thing. But the porpoising modes are a real mittful.

"It'd surprise you how far nose-down you can go without them digging in. I never dug in a float or got the props in the water—ever."

FOR FOWLER, THE TWIN OTTER porpoising tests more or less summed up his philosophy of flight test procedures.

"The thing you want to keep telling yourself all the time is that some guy, ham-fisted as hell, who's going to check himself out in this thing and thinks he knows a whole lot about floats, might kill himself if he tries to do what he got away with in something else. I don't want him doing something that I haven't done. I want to make all his mistakes. And if I bust the airplane, that's what I'm there for. We've found something out. As long as I don't carve myself up and I can get out of it.

"We're doing it all on purpose. You must find where the edges are. That's the big problem. That's where the darn judgement thing comes in. You just don't know where the edges are when you get into a dynamic thing like that. You can have somebody look at it from the outside, but he doesn't know how close to the edge of digging in the tips were."

Fowler knows. As for the rest of us, he suggests we don't try it at home.

ENDNOTES

CHAPTER 1: DON ROGERS

Chronology: The best short account of Don Rogers' career appears in Mary E. Oswald, ed., *They Led the Way: Members of Canada's Aviation Hall of Fame* (Wetaskiwin, Alberta: Canada's Aviation Hall of Fame, 1999), pp. 174–75. Larry Milberry's *The Avro CF-100* (Toronto: CANAV Books, 1981) has a useful account of the hirings and exploits of Avro Canada's flight test team, pp. 45–47. I also interviewed Rogers at length at his home in Toronto, May 17, 1999.

There's a photograph in Jim Floyd's book The Avro Jetliner: Jim Floyd, *The Avro Jetliner* (Erin, Ontario: Boston Mills Press, 1986), p. 68.

[The Jetliner] was the first North American jet-powered airliner ever to fly: Boeing's Model 367-80, known within the company as the Dash-80 and the direct lineal ancestor of both the military KC-135 Stratotanker and the revolutionary 707 airliner, first flew in the hands of Tex Johnston, July 15, 1954, nearly five years after the Jetliner. The Dash-80 was far more advanced aerodynamically and yet more proven because of Boeing's experience with its B-47 and B-52 bombers. The Dash-80 was powered with four Pratt & Whitney JT3 engines (civil derivatives of the B-52's J57s), each of which developed the same 10,000-pound thrust then available from each of the two Rolls-Royce Avons the Jetliner was designed around. Many 707/KC-135 variants are still active with military air arms worldwide.

More speed and altitude milestones than any other Canadian: Don Rogers was Avro Canada CTP on the Jetliner project, which set many city-to-city speed records. He was co-pilot on the Jetliner's first flight. Rogers oversaw the first flight (by Bill Waterton) of the CF-100, Canada's first and still only fighter to reach production, and assigned the test pilots (notably Peter Cope and Jan Zurakowski) who flew a long and difficult development program—a program that cost lives—to make the CF-100 useful operationally. And, of course, he supervised the flight test programs of the 1,000-mph Avro Arrow and its engine, the Orenda Iroquois. The Arrow set Canadian records for speed and altitude that will not be broken.

Rogers looked the test-pilot part: The question was taken seriously by aviation reporters in Toronto at the time, where by 1950 de Havilland Canada and Avro were involved in intensive flight test programs of the aircraft they designed, prototyped, and manufactured. Toronto's three daily newspapers employed beat reporters to cover aviation full time, and one of their recurring themes was what a test pilot should look like and whether any given test pilot met the flyboy standard. This critical issue reached its zenith in 1950, when Jan Zurakowski was hired for Avro by Rogers. Zurakowski, a wiry, balding man who with his Polish accent sounded anything but a hero, was adjudged by one newspaper on his arrival from Britain *not* to look like a test pilot. In an article published during the fall of 1953, the knowledgeable Bill Stevenson of the *Toronto Star* (future author of the best-selling *A Man Called Intrepid*), recounted his ride with Zurakowski during the test pilot's rehearsal in a CF-100 for the Canadian National Exhibition airshow, noting, "He was short, soft-spoken, with nothing in his face to record 24 years of continuous arduous flying." Stevenson made an important point about test pilots: the best of them don't show the strain.

Companies working simultaneously on fighter and airliner prototypes were even fewer in number: The only other one that comes to mind is the de Havilland Aircraft Company of Hatfield, England, which was working on the Comet jet airliner that barely beat the Avro Jetliner off the ground, thus becoming the world's first jet airliner. The Comet was powered by engines designed and built by de Havilland. The company was also developing more capable versions of its Vampire jet fighter, the second Allied operational jet fighter of the war.

Bristol, also in the United Kingdom, was working on unsuccessful fighter and airliner prototypes. Its engine division survived the closing of its airframe business and was eventually absorbed by Rolls-Royce. The engine that powers the British Aerospace and Boeing versions of the Harrier jump-jet originated with Bristol Engines.

There was no flying work available, even for a Battle of Britain ace: Ace, an often misused term, denotes a fighter pilot who destroys five or more enemy aircraft during a given conflict. Cooper-Slipper had seven confirmed victories during the Battle of Britain alone.

Warren and his twin brother, Douglas, both nicknamed "Duke," had served together on Spitfires: The most complete profile I have seen of the Warren twins appears in Philip Kaplan's *Fighter Pilot: A History and a Celebration* (London: Aurum Press, 1999), pp. 194–207.

Zurakowski, Duke said at the time, was "the finest test pilot flying": Quoted in Bill Stevenson's story in the *Toronto Star,* "Zura Takes Star Man on 'Zero-Speed Climb,' 'Rainbow' in New Jet." The copy I have is undated, but it was written only days before the airshow at the 1953 Canadian National Exhibition, for which Zurakowski and his CF-100 were practising. That would place it as concurrent with Duke's speed record of that September. Duke's record, set September 7, was broken 17 days later by another British aircraft, a Supermarine Swift piloted by Mike Lithgow, who raised Duke's mark of 727 mph by 10 mph September 24. That record lasted only nine days; it was broken by a U.S. Navy Douglas F4D Skyray, which raised the record to 753.4 mph (Mach .964 100–200 feet above sea level) October 3, 1953. Those were golden years for high-speed test flying. By the early 1960s, world speed records had become military secrets. Source: David W. Wragg, *Speed in the Air* (New York: Frederick Fell Publishers, 1974), especially pp. 113–15 and 121–22.

They often did what Pike regarded as more thrilling work: Author interview with Chris Pike at Victoria, B.C., November 13, 1999.

Pike had his ailerons lock: This story and the following one are from Milberry, *The Avro CF-100,* op. cit., p. 47.

Stan Haswell remembers his first hairy flights: Author interview with Stan Haswell, Toronto, June 17, 1999. See also "Testing the CF-100," a talk by Haswell to a meeting of the Toronto chapter of the Canadian Aviation Historical Society (undated), reprinted in the *CAHS Journal,* Fall 1983, pp. 86–93.

"Who got laid off at 40,000 feet?": Haswell, *CAHS Journal,* op. cit., p. 88.

The Jetliner prototype was not the article those meetings produced: Avro's Jetliner and Arrow were such advances over contemporary aircraft that the technical problems that came with their leaps forward are given the back of the hand by their fans. As William Mellberg puts it in *Air Enthusiast 46* (Summer 1992, p. 59), "It was politics, not any technical troubles, that cost Canada its brief, though tremendous, lead in aviation."

Gordon McGregor, who became president of TCA in 1948, tells us in his memoir *The Adolescence of an Airline* (Montreal: Air Canada, 1980, pp. 39–40) why Trans-Canada Air Lines did not buy the Jetliner: "An unfortunate event occurred during the development of this Canadian prototype which was largely responsible for the eventual abandonment of the enterprise. The airframe was originally designed on the basis that propulsion would be derived from two Rolls-Royce Avon engines. In 1947, with construction of the airframe and wing structure nearly completed, it was ruled by the U.K. government that development of the Avon must be a military proposition, and that it could not be released for civilian use. Quite surprisingly, Avro then decided to increase the span of the wing and to power the aircraft with four of the lower thrust Derwent engines. This very major design modification, coupled with perhaps some original faults in the basic design, left the aircraft with a short range, and, among other things, a very critical centre-of-gravity problem—to the point where one check pilot commented wryly that it made a difference on which side you parted your hair ...

"The airline was never committed to the purchase of any of these aircraft, and after the substitution of engines, withdrew completely from any participation in development cost, and allowed the letter of intent to lapse. This was a wise move, considering the aircraft's unsuitability for TCA's use in almost every respect including cost, fuel consumption, range, payload, flying characteristics and delay in its delivery date. This did not stop the manufacturer from periodically intimating that TCA was buying the Jetliner, in its efforts to make sales elsewhere, and any testing or evaluation the airline was persuaded to undertake at various stages of development was grist to their mill."

No airline flies four-engine equipment when a twin can do the job: The fact that the four-engine Vickers Viscount became TCA's short-haul workhorse (replacing the DC-3) is reflective of the same phases of aero-engine development that victimized the Jetliner. The Viscount's Rolls-Royce Dart turboprop was the West's finest big turboprop engine by the time it was installed in Viscounts in 1952 and for 30 years afterward. Its success (more than 7,100 engines; 114 million hours; still in production) lulled its manufacturer into the mistake of not designing a replacement. On a Viscount demonstration flight, TCA's Gordon McGregor, who had flown only pistons, was astounded to see a coin balanced on its edge on a cabin table stay upright. Not only were the Darts almost as smooth as pure jets: being turboprops, they were far less thirsty than the four Derwents that powered Avro's Jetliner entry.

As soon as the DC-9 presented itself during the late 1960s, the renamed TCA, Air Canada, reintroduced twin-engine equipment on its short-haul routes. Some DC-9s were still operated by Air Canada in 1999.

Production figures for the R-R Dart are from Bill Gunston's *World Encyclopedia of Aero Engines,* 3rd ed. (Yeovil: Patrick Stephens, 1996), p. 152.

CHAPTER 2: JIMMY ORRELL

Chronology: My incomplete summary of Orrell's career before his arrival in Canada to test the Jetliner depends heavily upon Don Middleton's short profile in *Test Pilots: The Story of British Test Flying, 1903–1984* (London: Collins, 1985), pp. 175–76. Additional early-life detail is from a profile of Orrell by Middleton, "Test Pilot Profile No. 1: J. H. 'Jimmy' Orrell," in the October 1980 *Aeroplane Monthly,* pp. 512–14, excerpted on the Aerospace Heritage Foundation of Canada website, ahfc.org. Also helpful was the obituary of Orrell by Harry Holmes published in the October 1988 *Aeroplane,* p. 611.

A small man with a gracious manner: My assessment of Jimmy Orrell's personality reflects the opinions of Don Rogers and of Mike Cooper-Slipper and his wife, Rita. Cooper-Slipper flew chase in a B-25 on the Jetliner's first flight. All three stayed in touch with Orrell once he left for England after the first series of Jetliner flights. Author interview with Don Rogers, op. cit. Interview with Mike and Rita Cooper-Slipper, June 5, 1999.

"In the 1930s we were very decent to our customers": Orrell quoted in Middleton, *Test Pilots,* op. cit., p. 176. Because, as in this quote, much material about Orrell is common to both *Test Pilots* and the October 1980 *Aeroplane Monthly* profile, subsequent references are to *Test Pilots* unless otherwise noted.

"Running the gauntlet of the Luftwaffe": Middleton, op. cit., p. 176.

[Orrell] attended the No. 2 course of the newly created Empire Test Pilots' School: Of 28 graduates of No. 2 ETPS course, seven eventually died in flying accidents. The commandant-appointee of the course, RAF Group Captain J. F. X. "Sam" McKenna, was killed in a Mustang when, it is believed, one of its gun access panels flew off in a high-speed dive. Tuition for the course was £10,000, a huge sum in those days, and one likely index of Avro's regard for Orrell. Among the graduates of the following course, No. 3, was Peter Twiss, the first British pilot to exceed 1,000 mph, flying the experimental delta-wing Fairey Delta 2, March 10, 1956.

Information on ETPS comes from Middleton, op. cit., and from John Rawlings and Hilary Sedgewick, *Learn to Test, Test to Learn* (Shrewsbury: Airlife Publishing, 1991), a history of ETPS that includes Orrell's anecdote about landing an Airspeed Oxford in a ploughed field with Mike Lithgow, pp. 11–12.

Useful insights into what a course at ETPS consists of today are available in Brian Johnson's brightly written memoir of the 44/23 Course (1985; 44th fixed-wing course, 23rd rotary-wing course), *Test Pilot* (London: BBC Publications, 1986), written to accompany a British Broadcasting Corporation documentary series of the same name. Johnson shows how students taking that course grappled with learning difficult test flying skills. His account of G/C McKenna's fatal crash appears on p. 34.

The Tudor 2 . . . crashed August 23, 1947: The crash would also have killed Sir Roy Dobson, managing director of the Hawker-Siddeley Group, of which Avro U.K. and Avro Canada were part, had he not been summoned by the control tower to answer a telephone call.

The aircraft was designated the Tudor Mk.8: For a well-written history of the Tudor 8/Ashton, see "Avro's Flying Lab" by Barry Jones, *Aeroplane Monthly,* September 1995, pp. 34–42.

The Jetliner had a similar layout to the Ashton, except for the Jetliner having its paired Rolls-Royce Derwent engines buried in the wing roots where the Ashton's podded R-R Nene pairs hung from the wing at about mid-span. The Derwent V was a downsized Nene. Versions of the Nene, Rolls-Royce's early jet-age masterpiece, powered the American Lockheed P-80 and Soviet MiG-15 and MiG-17 fighters (and still fly today in Lockheed T-33 trainers). Though a significant leap in power over other late-1940s jets, they found only limited use in British combat aircraft. The Tudor 8/Ashton was an attempt to showcase and develop the Nene.

For an inside account of the development of the Derwent and Nene turbojets, see their chief designer Sir Stanley Hooker's highly readable autobiography *Not Much of an Engineer* (Shrewsbury: Airlife Publishing, 1984), written with Bill Gunston, especially Chapter 4.

Making . . . Orrell the second pilot of a jet-propelled civil transport: Second to, as far as I can tell, Vickers CTP John "Mutt" Summers, who first flew Vickers-Armstrong Viking G-AJPH/VX856, re-engined with two Nenes, April 6, 1948, exactly four months before the four-engine Tudor Mk.8 prototype flew. The Nene Viking can be called the first jet-propelled airliner, although, with only one such conversion, AJPH, it may be better characterized as a research aircraft. Source: John Stroud, "Post-War Propliners," *Aeroplane Monthly,* October 1992, pp. 56–63.

"Jimmy Orrell recalled the fascination of the first [jet] flights": Middleton, op. cit., p. 176.

By July 25, 1949, the Jetliner appeared ready for rollout at Malton: It has been said that the Jetliner could have been the first jet airliner into the air. Jim Floyd, Avro's chief technical engineer on the Jetliner project—who was working seven-day weeks, 15 hours a day, at the time, according to a colleague—thinks that the Jetliner could have flown two weeks ahead of the de Havilland Comet, but doing so would have been risky. Source: Greig Stewart, *Shutting down the National Dream* (Toronto: McGraw-Hill Ryerson, 1988), p. 112.

Orrell credited Rogers and Baker with . . . "watching the aircraft grow, [and] learning all about it": This and the six subsequent paragraphs of quotes are from a two-page article by Orrell in the *Avro News* employee publication of September 1949 entitled "1st Flight," reproduced on pp. 173–74 of Jim Floyd, *The Avro Jetliner,* op. cit. My account of the first flight of the Jetliner combines information from two separate parts of Floyd's book, Orrell's memoir of the flight as seen from the cockpit (originally published in the *Avro News*), and Floyd's eyewitness observations from the ground, pp. 63–71. In *The Avro Jetliner,* we are fortunate to have so much first-hand information from its designer about an important Canadian prototype.

Orrell, faced with this dire emergency, had the presence of mind: Middleton, *Aeroplane,* op. cit., p. 514.

To Don Rogers, Jimmy Orrell seemed no different in the midst of this crisis: Author interview with Don Rogers, op. cit.

"The next few weeks saw an intensive program of flight tests": Floyd, *Avro Jetliner,* op. cit., p. 70.

"[Orrell] was a role model": Author interview with Mike Cooper-Slipper, June 5, 1999.

Jimmy Orrell returned to England late in October: He took with him his wife, Nan, and a set of plans for a Canadian-style bungalow to be built on land he had bought on the perimeter of Woodford Aerodrome, A.V. Roe's test facility. The English authorities made Orrell flatten the roof pitch, but soon afterward one of the pioneers of Canadian test flying had a house with an open plan and central heating, with runways in its very large back yard.

Rita Cooper-Slipper recalls Jimmy Orrell and his wife, both of whom were the same diminutive height, as "sweethearts. Unassuming, gracious, dear people. He showed great courtesy toward everyone around him. He did it with grace and charm. 'I' was not one of his words." Author interview with Rita Cooper-Slipper, op. cit.

CHAPTER 3: MIKE COOPER-SLIPPER

Chronology: The specifics of Mike Cooper-Slipper's postings during the Second World War come from my interview with him June 5, 1999, and 11 days later with son Chris Cooper-Slipper, who has prepared a chronology of his father's career. Cooper-Slipper Sr. also made available Chapter 9, "Avro Canada," of his memoir, *Tiger Moth to Aerospace,* as told to Pattie Whitehouse (Victoria, B.C.: Personal History Service, 2001). I further benefited from the exemplary study of each Commonwealth ace's service career in *Aces High* by Christopher Shores and Clive Williams (London: Grub Street, 1994).

Wartime score calculated by Aces High: Mike Cooper-Slipper's modesty may be his defining characteristic. The memorabilia of his wartime RAF career arranged on the walls of his Victoria, British Columbia, home made it irresistible to ask him how many victories he was credited with. He didn't answer my question. Instead, he rose from his easy chair and stepped to his bookshelf, where he reached for his five-inch-thick copy of *Aces High,* op. cit. He opened it to page 191 and pointed to the bottom line of the statistical summary of his WW2 career. There, the hazards of using hard figures to denote aerial combat scores, even in as authoritative an account as this one, are made clear: "TOTAL: Estimated to be approximately 8–10 victories and 2–4 shared destroyed (total 12), 4 damaged."

The Blitz was on: My quick source for Battle of Britain statistics is Len Deighton's *Battle of Britain* (London: George Rainbird, 1980), specifically p. 169 (September 7–11) and pp. 174–75 (September 15).

"The sky was black with [the Dorniers]": Author interview with Mike Cooper-Slipper, op. cit. Cooper-Slipper has also been quoted elsewhere about his exploit. In "The Day the Iroquois Flew," journalist June Callwood's excellent account of the first flight of the Orenda Iroquois on a B-47 engine testbed (*Maclean's,* February 1, 1958), pp. 11–13, 43–46, Cooper-Slipper implies that he rammed the Dornier because he was out of ammunition—the usual reason fighter planes rammed bombers.

In my interview with him, Chris Cooper-Slipper added such details as Mike's close-in gun harmonization and his aileron controls being shot away, which help explain why the ramming tactic sounds less deliberate when Mike tells the story. Chris has seen firsthand evidence of the encounter: he and his father excavated the wreckage of both Hurricane and Dornier during a visit to England on September 15, 1986, the forty-sixth anniversary of Mike's eighth aerial victory.

Chris also told me that, after landing in his parachute, Mike lapsed again into unconsciousness. He awoke to find himself being prodded by the pitchforks of hop pickers: he was wearing a German Mae West, which fit him better than the RAF-issue item, and he was released only after the police arrived and identified him.

"In a slit trench in Singapore he got a good look at courage": Callwood, op. cit., p. 45.

[Cooper-Slipper] test-flew ... "anything odd that had to be done with a Spitfire or Hurricane": Author interview with Mike Cooper-Slipper, op. cit.

"I was fed up with England": Author interview with Mike Cooper-Slipper, op. cit.

In November 1947 ... Tom was ... the most experienced test pilot in the country: A difficult assertion to prove. There were Canadians in the early classes at the Empire Test Pilots' School, including E. L. "Shan" Baudoux, R. M. Mace, and I. Somerville, all of the Royal Canadian Air Force, who attended No. 2 course (1944–45) along with Jimmy Orrell and Jan Zurakowski. There were many Canadians with experience in a wide range of aircraft types—especially those who instructed in the British Commonwealth Air Training Plan or flew with the Trans-Atlantic Ferry Command. But the only name that comes to mind as a comparable test pilot in Canada during the late 1940s is that of Russ Bannock, like Cooper-Slipper a wartime fighter ace.

By the time Cooper-Slipper returned to test flying with Avro Canada in September 1948, Bannock, former commander of 418 (City of Edmonton) Squadron and Mosquito night intruder pilot, was fully involved in flight trials and development of the de Havilland Canada Beaver, which flew for the first time in his hands August 16, 1947. Bannock had flown many aircraft types as a BCATP instructor, some of them after repairs or modifications at Leigh Brintnell's Aircraft Repair shops in Edmonton, before being posted overseas. On his return to Canada, he did development flight testing of the DHC Chipmunk.

The Sea Furys were navalized Hawker Tempests: Alas, the Sea Fury's Bristol Centaurus sleeve-valve radial engine was never reliable. "The engines kept stopping. We had no idea why. The engine went bang," Cooper-Slipper recalled in our interview, op. cit. Most of those Sea Furys still airworthy are powered by American radials.

"It was a very nice aeroplane": Author interview with Mike Cooper-Slipper, op. cit.

"It used to howl and wail at Mach .75": Author interview with Mike Cooper-Slipper, op. cit.

"Something went afoul in the shuffle": Anecdotes about the Orenda Lancaster are found in Larry Milberry, *The Avro CF-100* (Toronto: CANAV Books, 1981), pp. 45–46. It would be instructive to have dates for these incidents, but Cooper-Slipper's logbooks were lost in the hangar fire at Avro that also destroyed the Orenda Lancaster. In *Avro CF-100*, Milberry offers brief, crisp, detailed biographies of the seven pilots hired by Don Rogers for the Avro flight test staff: Cooper-Slipper, Peter Cope, Jan Zurakowski, W. O. "Spud" Potocki, Chris Pike, and Stan Haswell. The seventh, Glen Lynes, died in a CF-100 crash at Malton while doing aerobatics at low altitude.

The Orenda-powered Sabres, one of which failed to relight in the air: Stan Haswell, CAHS *Journal,* op. cit., p. 90.

"Perhaps the greatest turbojet of the 1950s": Bill Gunston, *World Encyclopedia of Aero Engines,* op. cit., pp. 115–16.

Enough B-47s to equip 28 Strategic Air Command Bombardment Wings: Bill Gunston, *American Warplanes* (New York: Crescent Books, 1986), pp. 128–29. For a more complete summary of the engineering effort that went into designing, redesigning, and further redesigning the project that became the B-47, see the chapter on the Seattle Museum of Flight's B-47E Stratojet in Sean Rossiter, *Legends of the Air* (Seattle: Sasquatch Books, 1990), pp. 96–105.

"It was relatively difficult to land": "I think it tended to separate the men from the boys!" wrote Earl G. Peck in his profile "B-47 Stratojet" in Robin Higham and Carol Williams, eds., *Flying Combat Aircraft of the USAAF-USAF,* Vol. 2 (Ames, Iowa: Iowa State University Press, 1978), pp. 82–88. Brig. Gen. Peck accumulated 6,000 flying hours, equally divided between jet fighters and bombers (B-47, B-52). He notes that the B-47 "was one of those airplanes that never seemed to acquire any affectionate nickname . . . This probably stems from the fact that although it was often admired, respected, cursed or even feared, it was almost never loved."

Orenda proposed to use this twitchy craft as the testbed: Many questions about the B-47 testbed remain unanswered, but an informative account of the conversion appears in Ron Pickler and Larry Milberry's *Canadair: The First 50 Years* (Toronto: CANAV Books, 1995), pp. 241–42. A description of the test engine nacelle that includes its dimensions appears in Richard Organ, Ron Page, Don Watson, and Les Wilkinson's *Avro Arrow* (Erin, Ontario: Boston Mills Press, 1980), pp. 125–27. The Arrowheads, as the co-authors of the book style themselves, devote a well-illustrated chapter to the Iroquois flight test program.

In addition to those modifications that affected the B-47 testbed's aerodynamics, strengthening of the aircraft's rear fuselage was done to accommodate the weight and thrust loads of the Iroquois, and a second set of instrumentation and engine controls for the co-pilot was installed. The Iroquois itself, aside from being mounted with its intake toed out from the aircraft centreline, was also set at a higher angle-of-attack (to put it crudely, even more nose-up) than the aircraft itself. There were good reasons for that: the engine's thrust, directed slightly downward, would better help support its own weight.

After all those modifications that made a tricky airplane trickier: In fairness to the Orenda project managers, the B-47 was a big airplane—perhaps the biggest available during the mid-1950s—with installed power slightly higher than the engine to be tested. It may have been the only aircraft with those qualities that the USAF was willing to loan to a foreign power.

Cooper-Slipper's crew consisted of co-pilot Len Hobbs and engineer John McLachlan. Hobbs, like Cooper-Slipper from England and aged 37 at the time, had instructed in Canada during the war and later flew combat in Sumatra and Malaysia. The crew's ages and experience were not necessarily advantages on the B-47 conversion course at McConnell AFB. Older pilots were often chewed out for doing what came naturally with piston engines; with early jets, abrupt throttle movements that piston engines took in stride could cause flameouts. By then, of course, Cooper-Slipper had been flying the Avro Jetliner for five years or so.

Cooper-Slipper and his crew flew the B-47/CL-52 from Canadair's Cartierville plant to Malton April 15, 1957. Takeoff was made even more thrilling than usual by the trio's realization that the Cartierville runway was too short for an abort. The landing at Malton was "very rough," Cooper-Slipper remembers, because of the lift generated by the Orenda installation at the tail as it passed into the ground-effect layer close to the runway. The B-47 had to be touched down nose-up, rear landing gear truck first, to avoid a huge, potentially uncontrollable bounce on impact.

"Do you mean," asked the Texan, "that you little old Canadians": Callwood, op. cit., p. 13.

"The B-47 just wasn't the right airplane for the job": Stewart quoting Mike Cooper-Slipper, op. cit., p. 221.

"When the B-47 was in flight": Organ et al., *Avro Arrow,* op. cit., p. 131.

"The B-47 pilot was able on one occasion to . . . fly on the single Iroquois": Pickler and Milberry, *Canadair,* op. cit., p. 241.

"The acceleration was nothing short of fantastic": Organ et al., *Avro Arrow,* op. cit., p. 125.

The Iroquois had exploded "more than once" in its test cell: This and the subsequent quote are taken from Callwood's text, op. cit., p. 44, which summarizes Avery's remarks. The quotes are thus Callwood's, not Avery's, but they do reflect his concerns.

"What's there to worry about?": Callwood, op. cit., p. 44. Actually, only the pilot and co-pilot had ejection seats. McLachlan would have had to open a hatch and get himself out without striking any of the B-47's flight surfaces before pulling his own ripcord, all at an altitude where he would find it difficult to breathe.

"[Engine] testing at Orenda was not a very happy experience": Author interview with Mike Cooper-Slipper, op. cit. Without naming names, Cooper-Slipper said his experience at Orenda was made unhappy by the inclination of recent University of Toronto graduate engineers to resist being told what they did not want to hear.

"The time was reached when the Iroquois had to be flown": Callwood, op. cit., p. 13. She notes that there were two oil leaks in the test engine and that the crew had agreed to run it at only idle speed.

"Over 125 hours of air flight testing was carried out": Peter M. Bowers, *Boeing Aircraft since 1916* (Annapolis: Naval Institute Press, 1989), p. 390. Total hours with Orenda lit: Organ et al., *Avro Arrow,* op. cit., p. 131.

Program cost for the Iroquois to that point was $90 million: Organ et al., *Avro Arrow,* op. cit., p. 127. The *Avro Arrow* authors have their own axe to grind, i.e., that the Arrow program was not overly expensive when the capabilities of the aircraft are fully appreciated, and, in particular, that the Iroquois figures were "not unreasonable." They make a comparison between the Iroquois' cost by its 50-hour test of $90 million and the cost of the Pratt & Whitney J75 at the same developmental stage: $278 million. (The civil J75 or JT4 powered DC-8s and 707s.) Maybe, considering the success of the JT4, Pratt & Whitney could have afforded developmental costs three times those of the Iroquois.

"Suddenly there was an enormous bang": Organ et al., *Avro Arrow*, op. cit., p. 127. In no published account of this mishap I am aware of is it dated. In his interview with me, Mike Cooper-Slipper guessed it occurred in 1957. The event may well have been classified at the time, of course. The Iroquois was first lit aloft on November 13, 1957, and the Arrow program was cancelled February 20, 1959.

The explosion ... "popped rivets all over the aeroplane": Author interview with Mike Cooper-Slipper, op. cit.

"Stop, no more work, finished": Cooper-Slipper memoir, op. cit., p. 82. Other accounts, notably Stewart, *Shutting Down*, op. cit., p. 266, have Cooper-Slipper recalled to the ground from the air.

"The Iroquois ... wasn't a good engine": Stewart, op. cit., quoting Cooper-Slipper, p. 253.

"We just didn't do enough flight-testing": The Orenda Iroquois recorded a total of 31 hours in flight on the B-47 testbed, according to the authors of *Avro Arrow*, op. cit., pp. 127, 131. Photos in Organ et al., *Avro Arrow*, p. 142, show Iroquois engines being fitted into Arrow 25206.

CHAPTER 4: BILL WATERTON

Chronology: W. A. Waterton declined my request for an interview. I turned instead to his autobiography, *The Quick and the Dead* (London: Frederick Muller, 1956), especially chapter 11, "Canada and the U.S.A.," pp. 162–79, for accounts of his activities on flight testing the CF-100. A useful source for Waterton's early RAF career is Hugh Halliday's *242 Squadron: The Canadian Years* (Stittsville, Ontario: Canada's Wings, 1981). In addition, details of Waterton's decoration citations come via Jerrold Vernon, aviation historian and chairman of the Canadian Aviation Historical Society, Vancouver branch.

[Waterton] had 600 students pass safely through his hands: The context for this claim is Waterton's experience training the first dozen pilots of the 100 Meteor 4s sold by Gloster Aircraft Company to Argentina in 1947. The assignment

reminded him of his wartime service as an instructor. In his autobiography, Waterton writes that he "did not agree with many official training methods, and [training the Argentinian pilots] provided an opportunity for employing my own ideas." From Waterton's autobiography, henceforth cited as Q&D, op. cit., pp. 135–36. It's a pity that he doesn't elaborate on what those ideas were.

The ... Gloster Meteor was still the fastest airplane in the world in early 1947: A Meteor set the first postwar absolute air speed record, averaging 606.38 mph November 7, 1945, flown by Group Captain H. J. "Willie" Wilson, then CO of the Empire Test Pilots' School, over a course at Herne Bay, Kent. Recognizing the likelihood that the U.S. Lockheed P-80 could exceed that mark, the RAF formed a High Speed Flight to raise it. Meteor F.4 EE549 raised the record to 616 mph September 7, 1946, flown by Flight CO G/C Teddy Donaldson back and forth over a 1.8-mile course from Littlehampton to Worthing on the Sussex coast. Flying Meteor sister ship EE550, Bill Waterton also broke the existing record, averaging two miles per hour less than Donaldson in an aircraft that wanted to roll to port at anything over 580 mph. Waterton fought this tendency with right rudder and stick, which cost him speed, making his overall average of 614 mph noteworthy under the circumstances.

Waterton's account of his flights that day make gripping reading. Chapter 2 of his autobiography, op. cit., pp. 37–38, is about the speed record attempt, and it explains how Waterton decided he could make his runs despite EE550's "damnable port wing. I found that I could jam my left arm like a rod between the side of the cockpit and the stick. As long as my palm (against which the stick was resting), wrist and arm held out, the plane could not alter course to the left. To ease the strain I would pull at the stick with my right hand, and to further help out the left wing lowness I could put on some right rudder trim. When we reached very high speed the stick would have to crush my palm, wrist and arm in order to take charge of the aircraft.

"I tore westwards with the throttles fully opened. A glance at the instruments showed everything to be in order. My speed crept up to 590 ... 595 ... 600. At 605 miles an hour the agony was indescribable. It seemed as though every bone from the tip of my elbow to the palm of my hand was in the grip of a giant, remorseless nutcracker: this in addition to the spine-jarring bounce of the bucking aircraft."

Waterton made four more runs in the same painful fashion, "but I have never been so grateful for anything in my life as I was when I passed [the course marker] balloons for the last time."

The third member of the RAF's 1946 High Speed Flight was the great S/L Neville Duke, posted in late June to the flight direct from the ETPS Course No. 4, where he resumed his studies after the record attempts. Duke had joined the RAF in 1940 and finished the war with 28 confirmed victories. Flying after the 1946 record was set, he was unable to improve upon Waterton's times in EE550. Duke did his first test flying as a detached RAF pilot at the Hawker works, joining the company's flight test staff in August 1948 and replacing S/L T. S. "Wimpy" Wade as CTP upon Wade's mysterious death in Hawker's first all-swept flight surface experimental aircraft, the P.1081 prototype. Duke took the P.1067 fighter prototype's first flight on July 20, 1951. It was named the Hunter the following year. Duke set a world airspeed record of 727.6 mph in the Hunter on September 7, 1953. See Neville Duke with Alan W. Mitchell, *Test Pilot* (London: Grub Street, 1997).

EE549's record was broken by U.S. Army Air Force Col. Albert Boyd, who recorded a 623.8 mph average on the best four of his five runs over Muroc Dry Lake (now Edwards AFB, California) in a Lockheed P-80 on June 19, 1947. The X-1 rocket aircraft, piloted by Chuck Yeager, attained 668 mph (Mach .997 at 41,000 feet) October 10, 1947, and went supersonic four days later.

Gloster's French agent . . . arranged for one final low-level fly-past: The accounts of Waterton's Paris beatup and his Paris-London speed record are taken from Q&D, op. cit., pp. 49–55. Q&D, along with various Canadian sources as further noted, form the basis for this chapter. Q&D is riveting reading, its descriptions of Waterton's adventures in the air as atmospheric as those of Antoine de Ste.-Exupery.

Waterton set a new Paris-to-London speed record, [averaging] 618.4 mph: Waterton points out in Q&D, op. cit., pp. 54–55, that his 618.4 mph average speed was "faster than the world's absolute speed record" set by G/C Donaldson. But the two records are not, strictly speaking, comparable. World records for aircraft performance are governed by rules set by the Fédération Aéronautique Internationale. Airspeed attempts at the time involved averaging the best four of five timed runs back and forth over a 3-km (1.8-mile) interval (within an overall 72-km [45-mile] course) at no more than 75 m (246 feet) altitude. Waterton's Paris-London record was a 208-mile straight-line sprint, as much as possible downhill from 12,000 feet. As for Waterton's estimate of a peak speed of 625 mph, Neville Duke's memoir states that the Meteor airframe was capable of little more than 626 (op. cit., p. 113), which Donaldson reached on one pass at 3,000 feet in setting his 1946 record. In 1953, when *Test Pilot* was first published, Duke regarded Waterton as "steady, conscientious . . . a first-class pilot" (Duke, op. cit., p. 115).

"The most experienced jet pilot in the [Hawker-Siddeley] Group at the time": Waterton, Q&D, op. cit., p. 162. The same passage is quoted with minor deletions in Stewart, *Shutting down the National Dream*, op. cit., p. 122. This is the core of

Waterton's argument that he was the best-qualified pilot to do the CF-100's early flight testing in the organization of which Avro Canada was part.

I retell Waterton's account of his low-level Champs Élysées beatup not to portray him as a daredevil but to add some insight into a man whose life before and after his CF-100 period deserves to be retold. Whatever we think about his judgement in buzzing the Champs Élysées, he was unquestionably a fine demonstration pilot. *Q&D*, op. cit., pp. 49–55.

Judged "on appearance alone, Bill Waterton was the ideal test pilot," Stewart writes, "slicked-down, close-cropped hair, parted ever so straightly to one side, predictable handle-bar mustache decorating a square, dark-eyed face resting atop a 6-foot frame that never moved except in a swagger."

Stewart does judge him on appearance alone.

"He rubbed some people the wrong way": Author interview with Don Rogers, op. cit.

"He acted as if he was a white knight": Mike Cooper-Slipper as quoted by Stewart, op. cit., p. 122.

Although Stewart's book is mainly about the Avro CF-105 Arrow program, the first 11 chapters constitute a valuable preamble to that saga. They detail the formation of Avro Canada and the development and testing of the Jetliner and the CF-100. The book contains insights into the operations of Avro and Orenda Engines available nowhere else.

Chapter 9 is about the flight test program of the CF-100 prototypes. Most of that information comes from *Q&D*. Indeed, the title of Stewart's CF-100 flight test chapter is "The Quick and the Dead." Its introduction (pp. 121–22) includes Stewart's rewrite of the charming story of Waterton's offhand, oh-so-English recruitment by Hawker-Siddeley chairman Sir Roy Dobson to test-fly the CF-100 (*Q&D*, pp. 162–63). Stewart's Chapter 9 includes 22 paragraphs, some quite long, of direct quotes from the same book. Stewart also uses material from an interview with Waterton, in one case combining it with text from *Q&D* to Waterton's detriment. Not until p. 298, in Stewart's chapter notes, does the careful reader learn that much of the chapter's material came from *Q&D*. Waterton is listed among Stewart's many interviewees; his book is listed in the bibliography. That is the full extent of credit given.

Ron Page, author of *Canuck CF-100 All-Weather Fighter* (Erin, Ontario: Boston Mills Press, 1981), rewrites page after page of *Q&D* with no attribution or acknowledgement except for a lone "in Bill's own words," after which he quotes "Bill" describing his third wing-root fairing failure. And that's it for an acknowledgement of pages worth of material. On a 46-name Acknowledgements page, Waterton's is notably absent.

An embittered Waterton has refused every interview request (including mine) since Stewart spoke with him in 1978. Can't say I blame him.

"He told me that the Canadians were keen, eager to get on with it, and the most ignorant lot you'll find anywhere": Stewart, op. cit., p. 122. This is one of exactly two passages from his interview with Waterton that Stewart used as direct quotes and identified as such. This quote was inserted after the Dorchester Hotel story, making it seem part of that conversation. But no such quote appears in Waterton's account, Q&D, op. cit., p. 162. Standing as it does alone and out of context in Stewart's book, it makes both Sir Roy Dobson and Waterton seem ungracious.

Advised by Sir Roy that Canadians were somewhat backward—presumably in the flight test department—and aware that landing gear problems had bedevilled the Jetliner's second flight, Dobson can perhaps be pardoned for his sentiment. That Dobson made available such British engineering mainstays as Edgar Atkin, Jim Floyd, and John Frost to head up the CF-100 and Jetliner programs bespeaks his thoughts about aero engineering in Canada, where the sources of talent, such as the University of Toronto's Engineering Physics course under Prof. Tommy Louden, were just beginning to produce homegrown engineers in numbers. The early postwar history of Canadian flight testing is shot through with straightforward mechanical glitches that aborted or hampered first or second flights.

The de Havilland Beaver prototype CF-FHB (first flight August 16, 1947), the most successful Canadian aircraft design ever, had its oil scavenging valve installed upside down, emptying its engine of oil within minutes of its first takeoff. The Jetliner failed to lower its main landing gear after its second flight (August 16, 1949). Waterton exercised his judgement in not overriding the CF-100 prototype's landing gear position selector on its first flight. Nevertheless, he repeatedly enthuses in his autobiography about how superior his flight test experiences in Canada were to those in the U.K.

"I liked the new plane": This, and following quote, from Q&D, op. cit., p. 163.

"The atmosphere was tense ... not only at Avro's, but throughout the country": Three paragraphs from pp. 164–65 of Q&D are slightly reorganized here to rearrange Waterton's thoughts for a smoother flow. There was no question that the CF-100 first took to the air about a year late, as were deliveries of aircraft to the RCAF through most of the production run. Avro did finally catch up to its production schedule.

When detailed engineering of the CF-100 got underway in January 1947, Larry Milberry points out in *Avro CF-100,* op. cit., p. 16, "about 1,000 were on the payroll at Avro and its gas turbine division. Three years later there were almost

4,000 employees." By 1954, Ron Page writes in *Canuck CF-100*, op. cit., p. 37, there were 10,000 workers at Avro among a total of 40,000 involved with CF-100 production nationwide, in a program that absorbed nearly 55 percent of Canada's defence budget that year. Most of the new workers were ascending the steep learning curve of what was then regarded as the world's most advanced all-weather fighter interceptor.

Bill Waterton implied unrealistic production schedules and capacity when he referred to Avro's "sausage-machine production setup" (*Q&D*, p. 165). The first CF-100 for actual use by the RCAF, 18108, was delivered July 22, 1952 (Milberry, *Avro CF-100*, op. cit., p. 32).

"The taxiing trials on 18101 went off better than those of any prototype I handled": Waterton outlines only the procedures he followed in his ground testing of the CF-100, but he says he was satisfied after a single 45-minute outing—"most unusual for me"—which would have taken place in mid-afternoon on January 17, as "the brake plates glowed red in the gathering dusk, due to stopping from high speed." That would leave the next day for resulting adjustments and inspections (*Q&D*, op. cit., pp. 165–66).

Then Waterton tried to retract the landing gear: The problem was a device designed to prevent pilots and ground crew from retracting the CF-100's landing gear on the ground. The retraction button required more pressure—40 pounds—to activate on the ground than in the air, where it took only three to five pounds. But the switch did not release when the aircraft's weight left its landing gear the first time it was called upon to do so. The switch was designed to be activated when the hydraulic shock-absorbing strut returned to its longer, unweighted length upon takeoff, but on this bitter January afternoon the strut contracted with the cold and did not rebound to its unweighted length. It was an easy fix and did not give trouble thereafter.

This may be one point in *Q&D* where Waterton upset Avro people without intending to. He did not push harder on the retraction button because "to override the switch was to ignore that something was wrong," as he recalls (*Q&D*, op. cit., p. 168). "This, I knew, had been done on another aeroplane, resulting in a belly landing. So I left things as they were." That other airplane was, of course, the Jetliner, on its second flight. The test pilot Waterton was implying had made a mistake was Jimmy Orrell, who is celebrated in Avro lore for having made his smooth, minimum-damage, mainwheels-up landing on the grass at Malton.

"For once I was able to be cautiously optimistic": What did Bill Waterton actually say after the first flight of the CF-100? He wrote in *Q&D*, op. cit., p. 168, that "For a

first flight I was well satisfied." The "cautiously optimistic" quote appears at the end of the following paragraph.

In Stewart's account of this historic moment in Canadian aviation (op. cit., p. 126) he follows the "well satisfied" quote with a quote that does not appear in Waterton's memoir but is made in Stewart's narrative to look as if it does.

From the Q&D text: "The brass, sweating it out on the ground, is always rather pathetic at such times, looking at you with spaniel eyes, pleading to be told the best, terrified they'll hear the worst. For once I was able to be cautiously optimistic" (Q&D, op. cit., p. 168).

Stewart picks up after "... terrified they'll hear the worst" and adds, "They were all standing around with their mouths open waiting to hear the good news. 'Well,' I said calmly, 'it flies.'"

We have to suppose that Stewart's insertion in the above paragraph came from his interview with Waterton. Let's compare the two versions. Waterton writes that he was "well satisfied," or, at least "cautiously optimistic," after the first flight of the CF-100. Stewart leaves out Waterton's cautious optimism, writing that the test pilot said only, "Well, it flies."

"This greatly reduced the frontal area of the aircraft," Frost recalled: Stewart, op. cit., p. 95. Stewart's is the first account I am aware of that outlines the preliminary design of the CF-100 and the changes Frost made after he became project engineer, setting the stage for the fateful changes made at the wind-tunnel stage, in Frost's absence, six months or so later.

John Frost joined de Havilland U.K. in 1942, becoming, Stewart writes, "one of the senior members of the Hatfield design team, and probably its youngest" (op. cit., p. 94). Given eight months to modify a Vampire fighter into a swept-wing tailless research aircraft to test that configuration before the projected Comet jet airliner would be designed with those characteristics, Frost produced the DH.108, of which three were built. It was so fast the company prepared for an assault on the world speed record. Geoffrey de Havilland Jr. was killed during a practice run September 21, 1946, at or near the speed of sound.

While that modification had the aerodynamic effect... it also had a structural effect: My account of this vital episode in the design of the CF-100 comes mainly from two sources, Stewart (op. cit., pp. 94–96 and 102–4), which has informative interview quotes from John Frost, and Larry Milberry's *Avro CF-100,* op. cit., which presents invaluable cutaway drawings (p. 19) along with its condensed textual treatment of the problem (pp. 16–20). The cutaway drawings, done by engineer Waclaw Czerwinski himself, clearly illustrate the problem and Czerwinski's eventual fix.

"The ridiculous thing about it," Frost told Stewart (op. cit., p. 104), "was that by moving the engines back, you certainly moved the centre of lift back by a small amount, but the weight of the engines being moved aft moved the centre of gravity back as well—in the wrong direction—and it was doubtful whether the final result altered matters at all."

"As Warren described the CF-100*'s incredible climb rate," Larry Milberry tells us, "Waterton was staggering along above the runway"*: Milberry, *Avro* CF-100, op. cit., p. 20.

"The skin of the wing and centre section had again split": It is at this point that Greig Stewart dismisses Bill Waterton from his history of Avro Canada with the back of his hand.

"Like a cold, bitter winter," Stewart sneers, "Bill Waterton had been around too long. As dedicated as he was to the aircraft itself, there were many people anxious to see him go. [Engineer and CF-100 ground crewman] Bob Johnson and test pilot Mike Cooper-Slipper felt that Waterton was far too protective of the flawed aircraft, like an anxious parent of a disabled child, reluctant to let anyone else near it, and that this slowed up development" (op. cit., p. 129).

What *was* the problem? Was Waterton flying the CF-100 too hard for the wing spars? Or was he "far too protective"? Which was it?

But Stewart is not quite finished with Bill Waterton.

"On February 7, 1951, Waterton shook John Frost's hand, climbed on a plane in the middle of the night, and returned to England. Other than Frost, nobody from A.V. Roe went to the airport to see him off. And, like the dashing hero leaving behind a broken heart, Waterton left behind a broken airplane" (op. cit., pp. 129–30).

Ron Page in *Canuck* CF-100, op. cit., p. 25, does his part to bury Waterton's reputation. "Some of the design and flight test crews had mixed emotions when he [Waterton] left, as his personality and behaviour sometimes held up the program. This was demonstrated one day, when the Air Force test pilots on attachment to Avro, Chan Badeau [sic] and Paul Hartman, known affectionately as Mutt and Jeff, got in ten test flights in one day, compared to the one or two that B.W. was likely to make."

Page doesn't bother to tell us what RCAF Squadron Leaders E. L. (Shan) Baudoux and Paul Hartman did on their 10-flight day that could possibly validate the comparison. Baudoux, by the way, was one of the RCAF's first trio of jet pilots and a graduate, with Orrell and Jan Zurakowski, of the No. 2 Course (1944–45) of the Empire Test Pilots' School.

Today . . . Waterton is forgotten: Waterton lives with his wife, Marjorie, in a charming pioneer log cabin with modern additions. His forebears going back two generations were settlers in the area, known as the Bruce Peninsula. Although Bill declined my request for an interview, he and Marjorie were good hosts during a visit my wife and I made accompanied by a mutual friend.

When Waterton's flight test career was effectively ended by his heroic landing and escape from a burning Gloster Javelin prototype, he became an aviation correspondent on Fleet Street. Piles of old newspaper clippings testify to his published criticisms of Gloster Aircraft Co. He co-wrote an exposé of the Comet tragedies as symptomatic of the state of the British aircraft industry, and his autobiography sold well. But neither book was warmly greeted by an industrial sector that in some ways still led the world but was being run as a loose collection of cottage industries. Bill and Marjorie bought a trailer and toured North Africa with their children, and eventually moved to Ontario, where Bill supported the family by working in a warehouse.

Waterton's neighbours seem to have no idea what he has accomplished, and Waterton seems to prefer it that way. He was scheduled to appear at the annual meeting of the Canadian Aviation Historical Society at Camp Borden during the summer of 1999, but he cancelled his talk about the CF-100 test program when he learned that one of his critics had arranged to speak after him.

Waterton was "proud to have played some part in the birth of Canada's jet aircraft industry": This and following quotes from Waterton, Q&D, op. cit., pp. 178–79.

CHAPTER 5: PETER COPE

Chronology: In addition to an interview with the present author at Seattle November 22, 1999, Peter Cope supplied complete lists of postings, aircraft flown, photos, and other supporting documents and marked up a chronology of his career. He and his wife, Anabel, are impressively well organized. My most important additional source for dates of specific flights by Cope was Larry Milberry's *Avro CF-100*, op. cit., which would be the best monograph on a Canadian aircraft type were it not for the same author's *The Canadair Sabre*.

"The one thing that might have happened": Author interview with Peter Cope, op. cit.

The CF-100 all-weather interceptor was as fast and almost as heavily armed as any aircraft of its kind in the world: On p. 192 of *Avro CF-100*, op. cit., the ever-helpful Larry Milberry supplies a comparison between the CF-100 and seven of its contemporaries from the U.S., Britain, France, and the Soviet Union. The CF-100 was fourth fastest and carried both FFARS and machine guns. The

American F-89 and F-94 carried only the rockets; the Europeans all had cannon armament. The Soviet Yak-25 was second fastest and second most heavily armed, behind the French Vautour IIN in both respects.

The four cannons were installed in the ventral gun bay: The T160 was adapted by the Ford Motor Co. from a German wartime design, the Mauser MG213. The Mauser innovation that—in aviation historian Bill Gunston's words—"can be considered to have made virtually all other aircraft guns obsolete overnight" was its revolver-type cylinder, with five chambers and the barrel aligned with the top, or 12 o'clock, chamber. The most successful American application of this principle was the General Electric M39 series of aircraft guns, in production during the late 1980s for Northrop F-5 fighters still in service, mostly in countries like Chile. But Mauser's better idea was not widely adopted in the U.S., notwithstanding the M39, or for that matter, the T160. Most American aircraft guns of today use multiple barrels, revolving like the Gatling gun of the American Civil War.

As tested in the CF-100, the T160 demonstrated "a very low reliability rate," Larry Milberry reports in *Avro CF-100,* op. cit., p. 50. "There were numerous gun breakages, stoppages due to electrical failures, low-life firing pins, loose components, etc."

Gunston notes that derivatives of the Mauser made up most cannon installations in the Soviet Union up to 1988, and all such aircraft guns in France and Britain were developed from the Mauser design, 40-odd years after the war—a tribute to German engineering. Bill Gunston, *The Illustrated Encyclopedia of Aircraft Armament* (New York: Orion Books, 1988), p. 36.

The observer had to have his hands pried from the ejection seat firing handle: This part of Cope's T160 firing test story is rewritten from Milberry, *Avro CF-100,* op. cit., p. 50. In Cope's retelling during his interview with me, op. cit., he left out the observer's hands having to be pried off the firing handle and the observer being lifted from the cockpit, as Milberry puts it, "literally frozen with fear." I added those details to Cope's account.

By 1956 [Cope] would have accumulated 1,000 hours of experimental test flying on CF-100s: To this day Cope treasures a congratulatory note from the man who hired him for Avro Canada, general manager Fred T. Smye. Dated May 10, 1956, the note credits Cope with having "contributed substantially to the development of the aircraft, and particularly to the development of its armament systems."

In total, "[Cope] spent over 1,600 hours on the CF-100," Larry Milberry writes in *Avro CF-100,* op. cit., p. 46, "making some 1,900 experimental flights on over 200

CF-100s, including the first and last aircraft built." Interviewed by Milberry, Cope referred to his eight years of test flying at Avro as a "paid hobby."

"A course old Screwball Beurling . . . was on too": Flight Lieutenant George Frederick Beurling of Verdun, Quebec, was "the highest-scoring Canadian of them all," according to Brereton Greenhous, Stephen J. Harris, William C. Johnston, and William G. P. Rawling, authors of *The Crucible of War, 1939–45: The Official History of the Royal Canadian Air Force,* Vol. 3 (Toronto: University of Toronto Press, 1994), p. 268, at 31 victories. He was, as *Aces High,* op. cit., puts it, "totally dedicated to aerial fighting," pp. 126–27.

He saw Jan Zurakowski's legendary demonstration: It was also at Farnborough that Cope made the acquaintance of the early-production Bristol Brigand with its two notoriously unreliable Centaurus radial engines. Cope was testing the Brigand when one of its 2,500hp Centaurus piston radials failed on each of three consecutive takeoffs.

An engine failure on a piston twin presents an immediate threat. The airplane wants to swing violently because of the unbalanced torque cranked out by the operating engine at maximum power. The pilot must control the swing and tendency to roll while throttling back the good engine, rudder, and throttle. About the only saving grace in having it happen three times in a row is that by the third time, the drill is pretty much mastered.

"I liked his demonstration better than mine": Cope's recollection of his response to Zurakowski's legendary flying display technique echoes that of Chris Pike, an Avro Canada production test pilot when Cope and Zurakowski were there. Both Cope and Pike thought Zurakowski was harder on the airplane than they were, but they believed that the effects he achieved were worth whatever additional strain these imposed. Cope attributes Zurakowski's more abrupt style to his wartime dogfighting role, as opposed to the smoothness required for photo-recon work.

Cope and Zurakowski worked together on a demonstration routine in a CF-100, and Cope was able to see firsthand what the differences in their display flying techniques were. "Whereas I would fly the aeroplane through the manoeuvres, Jan more or less kicked it through the manoeuvres by brute force. Where I would move the stick gently, he rammed it. Where I would apply gentle rudder, he'd go ram rudder. And this produced a much crisper demonstration. Which I used for myself as well, later on." Author interviews with Chris Pike and Peter Cope, op. cit.

"[Davidson] backed me up on 18 of the 19": "The only one I lost out on was, with the CF-100, you could go from your power-assisted controls to manual control, [but]

you could not get back from manual to power-assisted," Cope says today. "I considered that the air force boys who flew it needed to *know* what it was like flying it manually, but you did not have the capability to put it back into the automatic or the hydraulic modes. I tell you, when that thing was in the manual mode and you were landing, you had about a 35-pound pull on the stick to round it out—it was heavy, real heavy—because the ailerons were loaded and the elevator was loaded. I figured that, hey, the air force boys are going to have problems with this if they try to practise non–power-assisted control.

"Sure enough, one did. One ploughed in, didn't make it on landing. And we got it sorted out."

Peter Cope's definition of a snag was a feature of the aircraft that was "not satisfactory for normal operations," as Cope put it. Thus, his snag list, provided to me by phone June 21, 2000, did not include manufacturing deficiencies.

Besides lack of reversion to powered control from manual control, and the canopy, which Cope considers the most important items on his list, there were such items as:

- The CF-100's overly complicated fuel management system. "Pilots joked," writes Larry Milberry in *Avro CF-100*, op. cit., p. 34, "that the . . . system, with dials all across the [instrument] panel, made an engineering degree mandatory before checking out on the CF-100";
- The unreliability of the hydraulic pump, which powered such features as the flaps and air brakes, the landing gear retraction, and the power-assisted flight control systems;
- Poor cockpit lighting for night fighting (in an all-weather, day-and-night fighter);
- An unreliable radio;
- The absence of anti-skid brakes on an aircraft intended to operate from icy runways;
- Windscreen and canopy prone to misting and icing over, in addition to the above-mentioned canopy operation and locking system, which was prone to catastrophic malfunction.

In fairness to Waterton, he knew about the canopy: Waterton's dive-brake fix, Milberry, *Avro CF-100*, op. cit., p. 20. Canopy blown off, Milberry, op. cit., p. 42, entry from Rogers' logbook quoted: "Started climb test. Hood blew off at 7000 feet at 340 knots [391 mph]."

Cope made 36 flights to evaluate the T160's suitability for use in CF-100s: Milberry, *Avro CF-100*, op. cit., p. 47. Milberry gives a useful list of Cope's milestone experimental flights in CF-100s, testing, among other armament options, the T160, a

48-rocket FFAR belly pack, and various configurations of radar-guided Sparrow air-to-air missiles, none of which were adopted for operational use by the RCAF on CF-100s.

Soon after Jan Zurakowski joined Avro: "When I was helpful in getting Jan over to Canada, I knew perfectly well he wouldn't answer to me. I would answer to him, because he was a far more experienced pilot than I was. We reckoned Jan was the best there was in England. I didn't care whether I worked for him or he worked for me. But we worked together, that was the main thing, developing a good aeroplane. And that's how it worked out." Author interview with Peter Cope, op. cit.

After much careful training and preparation: Cope, of course, had introduced himself to flight at the threshold of the speed of sound in a diving CF-100. He also flew the F-86 Sabre, which could do Mach 1 more reliably in a dive. Like the other CF-105 test pilots, Cope got his supersonic baptism, though, in a Convair F-102 at Palmdale, California, with delta wings similar to the CF-105's. All Cope had to do was keep the F-102 between 50,000 and 55,000 feet. Within that altitude range it would go supersonic in level flight. Just as important, his F-102 experience gave Cope insights into the behaviour of delta-wing aircraft, especially in their nose-up landing attitude.

On "Black Friday," the Arrow program was cancelled: "We saw this thing going on for a very long time," Cope says, explaining what a shock the Arrow cancellation was, "because we had an initial build of 17 aircraft, prior to a production build of 200. And that 17 was basically allowing four for Avro, four for Orenda, four for the air force, four for Hughes Aircraft on the fire-control systems—that was 16— and one for attrition. We figured we'd lose one somewhere. That gave us the 17. And we had a tentative production order for 200.

"That aeroplane would still be no slouch today, you know. Except it would be a lot faster; it'd be up to [Mach] 2.3, 2.4 at least. Had the number six aeroplane flown with the Iroquois engines, our performance analysts thought we would have a Mach 2.3 aeroplane as the Iroquois was a lighter engine with more power than the P&W J75." Author interview with Peter Cope, op. cit.

CHAPTER 6: JAN ZURAKOWSKI

Chronology: My account of Jan Zurakowski's early years and war service is stitched together from many sources. The first is my interview with Zurakowski March 7 and 8, 2000. Another is a copy of a questionnaire fellow Avro Canada test pilot Peter Cope had Zurakowski complete as part of Cope's research for his

May 1966 *Flying* magazine article "The Zurabatic Cartwheel" (p. 69), both of which Cope was kind enough to share with me. The questionnaire includes Zurakowski's handwritten summary of his postings in Poland and with the RAF's mainly Polish Northolt Wing.

Canada's History Channel has several times presented a documentary of Zurakowski's life, entitled *Straight Arrow: The Jan Zurakowski Story*, made by White Pine Pictures in 1998. Peter Cope kindly supplied me with a copy. It is from that source that the outline of the Zurakowski family's flight from Russian-occupied East Poland is taken, augmented by Zurakowski's personal recollections in interviews with me (op. cit.) and his corrections to the draft manuscript.

I am again indebted to the authors of *Aces High* (op. cit., p. 656) for the most accurate of the many short summaries I have seen of Jan Zurakowski's early years and wartime career, with only this reservation: Zurakowski claims not to be an ace.

"Possibly the finest all-round single-seat piston-engine fighter ever designed": My summary of the MB.5's detail engineering and flying qualities comes from several sources, including Don Middleton, who in *Test Pilots* (op. cit., p. 119) describes the MB.5 and cites the A&AEE test reports that unanimously praised its handling qualities. Middleton uses the word "breathtaking" to describe Zurakowski's demonstration of the airplane at Farnborough. A good account of the Martin-Baker series of fighter prototypes, written by Ian Huntley, appears in the April 1992 issue of *Scale Aircraft Modelling* (pp. 310–13). Huntley calls Zurakowski's 1946 demonstration "brilliant and sparkling." The quote in italics above is from Peter Lewis' *The British Fighter since 1912* (London: Putnam, 1965), which has separate and authoritative accounts of each of the Martin-Baker prototypes, with the MB.5's on pp. 302–3. In his caption under the photograph of the MB.5 (p. 302), Lewis calls it "the magnificent Martin-Baker MB5." Zurakowski characteristically called his Farnborough 1946 demonstration "nothing special" in conversation with me, op. cit. The quote from the July 4, 1946, issue of *Flight* was hand-copied by the author from Zurakowski's copy of the magazine.

Coincidentally, the engineers of the MB.5 were called upon to lay out the cockpit of the CF-105, and, in the opinion of Peter Cope, did an equally outstanding job on it. In addition, Martin-Baker ejection seats were installed in the Arrow. Zurakowski notes that the number of switches and instruments in the CF-105 cockpit was 70 percent of those in the CF-100. Both were two-seat cockpits.

Canada's willingness to . . . "shut down the national dream": Zurakowski is quoted in, among many other places, "Janusz Zurakowski: Portrait of a World-Famous Pilot" by W. L. Bialkowski, an Internet profile posted on *The Avro Archive*, October

1998, on the Arrow cancellation: "Governments and torches can destroy an air-craft but they cannot destroy hope and aspiration, and the majesty of the questing spirit. In the hearts of the people the dream lives on" (http://tsw.odyssey.on.ca/~dmackechnie/Welcome.html).

The Internet profile contains important details of Zurakowski's early flight testing career. Author Bialkowski's father worked with Zurakowski at Avro Canada and bought the neighbouring property to Zurakowski's Kartuzy Lodge on the shore of Lake Kaminiskeg, near Barrys Bay, Ontario. Bialkowski himself witnessed Zurakowski's demonstration of the CF-100 at the Farnborough airshow in 1955, and he spent nearly 40 summers at the lake. Zurakowski has fact-checked Bialkowski's account, which contains material to be found nowhere else.

Shutting down the National Dream is, of course, the title of Greig Stewart's award-winning study of Avro Canada from its postwar founding to cancellation of the Avro Arrow (op. cit.). The "Government and torches" quotation above also appears at the end of Zurakowski's foreword to Stewart's book.

[Zurakowski] instructed at Poland's Central Flying School in Deblin: Although not with a squadron when the Germans invaded Poland, Zurakowski flew a combat sortie the second day of the war in a PZL P.7 open-cockpit, gull-wing monoplane with fixed landing gear. The P.7 was the immediate, lower-powered ancestor of the P.11C, which, although itself obsolete, was Poland's first-line fighter in 1939. In the P.7, a world-beater in 1931 with a top speed of 197 mph, Zurakowski simply could not catch Luftwaffe bombers, let alone their 350-mph Messerschmitt Bf 109E escorts.

Bialkowski, op. cit., credits the Polish aviation magazine *Lotnictwo,* May 1993, for this tidbit. The P.7 peaked at 50 mph less than a Jumo-powered Heinkel 111H bomber. It seems reasonable to assume the P.7s were intended to be used as advanced fighter-trainers for pilots almost ready to fly the P.11C and were pressed into front-line service in desperation.

"A cool, clinical approach" to air fighting: Quoted by Bialkowski, op. cit., from Geoffrey Norris, *Jet Adventure* (London: Phoenix House, 1962), chapter entitled "The Impossible Pilot," p. 94. "As a fighter pilot Zurakowski showed the same cool, clinical approach which was to characterize his test flying in later years."

"But," as he later told the story, "they got me instead": The basis of my account of Zu-rakowski's Spitfire bailout is the anecdote as told by Zurakowski to John Melady, author of *Pilots: Canadian Stories from the Cockpit* (Toronto: McClelland & Stew-art, 1989), pp. 106–7. Melady's straightforward account, mostly in Zurakowski's words, is supplemented in my version with information from *Aces High,* op. cit.,

which dates the incident, names the pilot who likely shot Zurakowski down, and identifies Zura's Spitfire. Mayer's victory total, which includes eight in Spain, comes from Col. Raymond F. Tolliver and Trevor J. Constable, *Fighter Aces of the Luftwaffe* (Fallbrook, California: Aero Publishers, 1977), p. 411.

[*The Hornet*] *was all the more sporty when one engine failed on takeoff:* In fact, A&AEE Boscombe Down Report 828 "was concerned with the handling tests of PX211, the second production Hornet F.Mk.1, during September and October, 1945. The machine was found to be deficient in longitudinal stability . . . and to possess dangerous engine failure characteristics. In the case of engine failure, if swift action were not taken by the pilot, the machine quickly entered a vertical dive with the rudder held immovably fully over towards the stopped engine. To cure these defects, a larger horizontal tail was introduced and the F.Mk.3 featured a dorsal fin, which was installed retrospectively on earlier Hornets." Peter Lewis, *The British Fighter since 1912*, op. cit., pp. 305–6.

[*Zurakowski's*] *eye-catching loop of the Hornet:* I am grateful to the Bialkowski Internet profile, op. cit., for linking Zurakowski's flight test exploits in the DH Hornet with the Zurabatic Cartwheel, a link that Zurakowski confirmed to me. The statement beginning "Zura never let an opportunity pass by" is quoted by Bialkowski from Lewis G. Cooper, *The Hornet File* (London: Air Britain Publications, 1992).

"*The only way to do a cartwheel*": Aside from Bialkowski's account, op. cit., my summary of the evolution of the Cartwheel manoeuvre depends on my conversations with Zurakowski at Kartuzy Lodge, op. cit.

The quotes beginning with "Even at stalling speed" and ending with "I could reduce the speed to a lower value. To zero" are taken from Bialkowski, op. cit., who attributes them to an article in the September/October 1986 issue of *Wingspan* without naming the author or listing pages.

"*And,*" *Zurakowski says today, "I forgot about it":* Author interview with Zurakowski, op. cit.

In 1947 Jan Zurakowski joined the Gloster Aircraft Company . . . as a test pilot: This date is contrary to many published accounts but has been confirmed by Zurakowski twice. *Aces High*, op. cit., has Zurakowski leaving the RAF for Gloster's in 1950 (p. 656). Bialkowski's fact-checked biography, op. cit., gives 1947, and Zurakowski prefaced his verbal account of "Test Flying the Arrow and Other High-Speed Jet Aircraft" to the Canadian Aviation Historical Society on March 1, 1978—

since published in the *CAHS Journal* (Winter 1979, pp. 100–13)—by saying on page 101 that after a year at ETPS (March 1944–January 1945) he was posted to the A&AEE, where he tested the DH Hornet in the fall of 1945. "Two years later I left the Royal Air Force and accepted the position of experimental test pilot with Gloster Aircraft Company in England." Where he worked for none other than Bill Waterton.

Exactly how the engine-out controlled spin . . . came to be a much more spectacular vertical pinwheel manoeuvre in the jet-powered Meteor: As we have seen, many of the basic dates of Zurakowski's career have been mis-stated by as many as three years in otherwise impressive reference works. It follows that most of the intermediate dates when Zurakowski was thinking about the Cartwheel and outlining it to others are, at best, speculative. My account is compiled from several sources, very few of them faultless. No one of those involved seems to have kept diary notes. Zurakowski's practice Cartwheels were added to multi-task test flights and therefore not necessarily entered into his logbooks. More than half a century has elapsed since he planned this aerial manoeuvre, and, in fact-checking my draft manuscript, Zurakowski emphasized his doubts about the recollections of others. I have tried to make clear my own circumspection, especially in the matter of dates. These are often estimated from the dates of availability of the equipment needed to perform the manoeuvre.

Middleton's *Test Pilots,* op. cit., gives a capsule summary of Zurakowski's career and the origins of the Zurabatic Cartwheel on p. 134.

"The Meteor had a very bad reputation": Mike Retallack's highly readable memoir of RAF flight training in the late 1950s, entitled "Mastering the Meteor," appeared in *Aeroplane,* November 1993, pp. 52–56. For the record, Zurakowski does not agree that the Meteor had a bad reputation.

The conversation reported . . . by Fred Sanders, who was head of Gloster's flight test department: I am using this account of the origins of the Zurabatic Cartwheel despite inaccuracies in Middleton's treatment of Zurakowski's career. He has Zurakowski joining Gloster Aircraft in 1945 (*Aces High* has it as 1950; the correct date is 1947) and Avro Canada in 1951 (1952 is correct). I have taken the liberty of changing the latter date to 1952 in the passage I quote (op. cit., p. 134) in the text. It seems to me that Middleton's account of the origins of this aviation milestone, attributed as it is to a named first-hand source, rings true.

Larry Milberry dates Zurakowski's performance of the Cartwheel at the Society of British Aircraft Constructors (SBAC) Farnborough airshow, 1951. It was, Milberry says, "an entirely new aerobatic manoeuvre which amazed everyone" (*Avro CF-100,* op. cit., p. 46).

"Rolls-Royce gave [the Meteor's R-R Derwent engines] more thrust": The additional thrust was forthcoming in the form of the completely redesigned Derwent V jet engine, which increased the Meteor F.Mk.IV's thrust to 3,500 pounds per engine (from the 2,000 pounds apiece the wartime Meteor F.Mk.III's Derwent Is produced). These new engines made possible the Meteor's world airspeed records, including the absolute world record Bill Waterton was involved in setting and a city-to-city record set by Zurakowski for the London-Copenhagen-London round trip.

A development of the Meteor F.4 was the F.Mk.8, first flown by Zurakowski October 12, 1948. The F.8 had a Martin-Baker ejection seat, bigger vertical tail (which helped in engine-out situations), and the Mk.4's Derwent V power. Gloster used the F.8 as the basis for a ground-attack fighter, known unofficially as the Reaper, that the company developed as a private venture in the hope it would attract the RAF's interest. The prototype, registered by GAC as G-AMCJ, first flew in the hands of Jim Cooksey, September 4, 1950, from Gloster's Moreton Valance test facility. Among the changes were belly and outboard underwing racks for rockets, as well as wingtip fuel tanks, with the necessary stressing of the wings for these greater loads.

"They accused me of what they call 'shooting a line'": Author interview with Zurakowski, op. cit. Zurakowski was appalled to have been accused of such a transgression. To him, that was the turning point in his plans to perform the Cartwheel. His honour was now at stake.

The immediate impetus was a request from the GAC staff: This information, as well as the number of underwing rockets G-AMCJ carried, is from Bialkowski's Internet profile, op. cit.

Zurakowski would initiate a zoom-climb: This description of the Zurabatic Cartwheel is adapted from Peter Cope's *Flying* article, op. cit.

Normal spins ... in the Meteor were ... often irrecoverable: It is important to record here Zurakowski's objections to using quotes describing the Meteor as being difficult to fly on one engine, to recover from normal or flat spins, or even from inverted spins. In fact, Zurakowski told me, inverted spins, where the aircraft is on its back, are easier to recover from than normal ones because the tail is in undisturbed air!

"The spin characteristics of the Meteor were very good on the Mk.III and Mk.8. I was doing up to ten turns of spin, with easy immediate recovery," he wrote me on August 23, 2001. An inverted spin in a Meteor "was difficult to obtain: recovery was easy."

"Basically, it was a very simple manoeuvre": Author interview with Zurakowski, op. cit. A pattern is evident here. The aviation world marvels at the Cartwheel; Zurakowski claims that any qualified pilot could do it. The case each way:

Peter Cope believes that five Meteors were lost during the week after Zurakowski unveiled the Cartwheel due to RAF pilots attempting the manoeuvre (author interview with Cope, op. cit.). F/L Retallack (*Aeroplane*, op. cit., p. 54), believed the weight of rockets and tip tanks on the Meteor outer wings was essential to perform the Cartwheel but saw F/O Max Bacon do it in a standard Meteor without external ordinance. Retallack tried it that way and wrote: "I do not know whether any other pilots were able to do this without rockets, but many of us tried without success, finishing up in all sorts of positions but never the right one."

Zurakowski, on the other hand, believes that if five Meteors had been lost in the week after Farnborough, he would have heard about it. He says he didn't. One of the Meteor's export successes was Denmark, which bought 20 two-seat NF.Mk.11s; Zurakowski recalls the Gloster service department informing him that the members of one entire Danish squadron were able to perform the Cartwheel. The Israeli Defence Forces used the Cartwheel, Zurakowski says, "as an operational manoeuvre." This, he told me, "is a further indication that there is nothing especially difficult about it" (author interview with Zurakowski, op. cit.). Source for Meteor export data: Tony Buttler, *Gloster Meteor* (Milton Keynes, Buckinghamshire: Hall Park Books Warpaint Series #22, 1999), Production List pp. 7–8.

Often, Zurakowski would spin the Meteor deliberately: "It was simply reaching enough speed going down again, rather than stopping further turning, that's all. Sometimes I was using spin to lose height, because I had to do [the Cartwheel at] 35 [hundred feet] from a safety point of view. But I had to get quickly down. This was nothing to do with the Cartwheel itself. It was simply the problem of losing altitude quickly because I have to present [my entire demonstration] inside three minutes" (author interview with Zurakowski, op. cit.).

[Zurakowski] also performed [the Cartwheel] in a clean F.Mk.8 Meteor: "The rockets," Zurakowski explained to me, "added a bit of [momentum]. On standard aircraft you could stop nose-down, but with rockets there was higher inertia, so it was a longer time before the fin and rudder could overcome the momentum. The nose would overshoot a bit, so with a bit of oscillation, you could get back to the vertical condition" (author interview with Zurakowski, op. cit.).

Buttler, in *Gloster Meteor,* op. cit., p. 36 lower left, shows the Reaper proto-type, civil-registered G-AMCJ (later known as the G-7-1), photographed at Farn-borough in 1950, with what appear to be eight rockets under its port wing panel and a fuel tank at its tip. Assuming Zurakowski flew AMCJ similarly configured on each of the five days of the 1951 Farnborough airshow, it seems reasonable for observers to have concluded, as Cope did in his *Flying* article, op. cit., that the ad-ditional mass represented by the rockets (Cope believes there were 16 per side), which weighed 1,500 pounds apiece, and presumably full wingtip tanks were the key to performing the Cartwheel. Buttler, op. cit., p. 37, writes that Zurakowski did the Cartwheel with "Twenty-four wing-mounted rockets"—12 per side—"and tip tanks . . . with relatively little internal fuel which meant much of the weight was distributed away from the centre of the aircraft to help the spin."

One final irony. AMCJ, the G-7-1 ground attack prototype, attracted no orders despite Zurakowski's historic demonstration that, fully loaded, it was still quite manoeuvrable. As Zurakowski notes ruefully, the powers that be chose de Havil-land's Venom as the RAF's low-level ground-attack jet, despite its being powered by an engine that performed best at higher altitudes.

"Up to the end of 1955 . . . about 3,500 Meteor aircraft were produced": Zurakowski lecture to the CAHS, op. cit., *CAHS Journal,* p. 101.

Jan's older brother Bronislaw . . . is an aerodynamicist: Before the war, Bronislaw worked for RWD, the company that built the airplane Jan soloed in. Postwar, he worked first on gliders, then on a Polish helicopter design that was cancelled at about the same time, 1959, as the CF-105 Arrow. A prototype resides in the science museum at Krakow. After that, his company became a builder of Russian-designed Mil helicopters.

"Five years of experimental testing taught me not to accept much at face value": Zurakowski went on to document his difficulties with the Gloster engineers, who refused to believe him when, at the wind-tunnel stage in Javelin testing, "it became obvious to me, more than two years before the first flight, that longi-tudinal instability was present in the Javelin at lower speeds."

Gloster engineers specified that the Javelin prototypes be flight tested only at those speeds at which they would be stable. Zurakowski's solution, as usual, was to take his doubts to a higher level. "I was faced with a difficult problem. Urgent modifications were required, but control of the flight test program was in the hands of the design office which did not want to face the facts . . . During one of the flights I decided to check the low speed range. It did not look safe, so I climbed to 30,000 feet and slowly started reducing speed. I reached a condition when, with the tailplane setting fully up and elevator fully down (both controls in diving position), the aircraft was still climbing, and finally stalled and went into a spin.

"Spin recovery," he noted dryly, "was satisfactory." Source: Zurakowski lecture to the CAHS, op. cit., *CAHS Journal,* p. 101.

"Sooner or later . . . any Arrow that gets into service will [have its deficiencies] discovered": Author interview with Zurakowski, op. cit.

What if the pilot, flying on instruments . . . was unknowingly . . . in a dive: Larry Milberry's account of Zurakowski's supersonic CF-100 flights in December 1952 (*Avro CF-100,* op. cit., pp. 48–49) squares with the test pilot's recollections in 1979 to the CAHS, op. cit. When Zurakowski says, "I asked the experts what would happen if a pilot accidentally exceeded this speed [.85 Mach]"—as Milberry quotes from Zurakowski's address to the CAHS—the question of who those "experts" were is left unanswered.

This question arises from Zurakowski's contention that the Avro design office was proposing a thinner-airfoil, swept-wing CF-103 "to obtain a maximum diving speed of Mach 0.95." The proposal, of course, became redundant when the prototype of the main service version of the CF-100 was found, on Zurakowski's initiative, to be capable of diving at more than Mach 1.

"After this," Zurakowski told the CAHS, "there was hope in the flight test section that the design office understood that cooperation with the flight test section and pilots was necessary for future development. Unfortunately the design office took a different view. A decision was taken to safeguard the design office from unexpected flight test results by controlling the program of every flight test."

"It was now clear that the CF-100 could handle such performance with no repercussions": But it was not necessarily clear that any pilot in any old CF-100 could bust the sound barrier, even in a vertical dive. "Not all airplanes would do it," CF-100 test flight workhorse Peter Cope wrote in his report "High Mach No. Investigation—1.05," the record of his dive test on January 22, 1953. "The technique was to roll inverted at 45,000 feet and go straight down at full power . . . The CF-100 was so marginal in the sonic breakthrough that it depended a great deal on the aerodynamic cleanliness of the individual airplane." Source: Milberry, *Avro CF-100,* op. cit., p. 46.

Avro flight test engineer Hugh Young often flew back-seat with Zurakowski, but "prudence sometimes dictated a solo test"—as, for instance, during the CF-100 supersonic dives. Young recalls sitting up past midnight with colleague Ralph Waechter after Zurakowski's first "made-in-Malton" supersonic bang, doing the calculations from the auto-observer that filmed in-flight instrumentation to prove Zura had gone "a mere whisker over Mach 1." Hugh Young, "Tales My Logbook Tells," in *Aircrew Memories,* published by the Aircrew Association, Vancouver Island Branch, undated, pp. 380–81.

Zurakowski and flight test observer John Hiebert were testing the belly-pack: My summary of the CF-100 belly rocket pack testing and the aircraft's canopy troubles comes from Stewart, op. cit., pp. 176–77, and two passages in Milberry, op. cit.: pp. 51–53, on the rocket pack installation and test firings, which contains Milberry's summary of the August 23, 1954, crash that killed Hiebert, and pp. 58–60 on the CF-100's canopy problems, which was a factor in Hiebert's death and cost a number of other lives. In addition, Peter Cope addressed the canopy problem in his interview with me, op. cit. Zurakowski corrected my draft account and added details of the crash during our interview, op. cit.

At a time when flight test observers were not eager to fly in CF-100 rear seats because of safety concerns, Hiebert made his first such flight with Zurakowski to test the rocket pack and calmly offered advice when the test pilot found his controls locked.

"He was a very good chap," Zurakowski remembers. "Even in the emergency, his advice and remarks were perfect. He said, 'Try to disengage the boosters [on the controls].'" Zurakowski says this was good advice; it might have given Zurakowski manual control had links to the aircraft's flight surfaces not been locked.

"I'll bet you . . . the rest of us wouldn't have found it": Quotes from Chris Pike in this chapter come from my interview with him, op. cit.

"The Avro Aircraft CF-100 Mk.4B was a welcomed newcomer to Farnborough," The Aeroplane *reported:* Quoted in Milberry, *Avro CF-100,* op. cit., p. 71. And not just Farnborough. On the following page, in the caption accompanying a photo of Zurakowski landing CF-100 18321 at Farnborough, Milberry quotes RCAF Air Vice-Marshall E. D. Crew as saying that, during the RAF evaluation, "a short breather was taken to demonstrate the aircraft at the Paris Aero Show, Le Bourget. Led by Jack Woodman, we made some impressive passes over the admiring crowds."

"The flight of June 2, 1953, was the most strenuous I had during my five years on the CF-100": Hugh Young, op. cit., pp. 378–79.

"In 1958 . . . [the CF-105] . . . was by a wide margin the most advanced fighter in the world": Bill Gunston, *Early Supersonic Fighters of the West* (London: Ian Allen, 1976), p. 120. Chapter on the Arrow, pp. 120–37. No better 17 pages have been writ-

ten about Avro Canada's masterpiece. The sentence following the extended quote in the text is this: "But they [the Arrows] were born at the worst possible time."

Gunston continues, making on p. 123 a point that is often overlooked in the vast Canadian literature about the CF-105: "Time after time the history of military aircraft procurement has recorded a programme that could have delivered 99 percent of the requirement within timescale and budget but which escalated away out of reach in a fruitless chase after the missing 1 percent. In January 1954 I was able to spend six hours discussing [Air 7-3, the then months-old operational requirement that led to the Arrow] with Air Vice-Marshall John L. Plant, RCAF, as we waited for fog to clear at Gros Tenquin in France . . . Plant confided that, deep down, he too had a slightly uneasy feeling that 7-3 might be too much for the nation through trying for the last percentage point."

Zurakowski himself has often pointed out that the key requirement of the Arrow, that it be able to sustain a two-G (60-degree) turn at 50,000 feet and Mach 1.5 without losing speed or altitude, has been met by no combat aircraft since the Arrow (notably in his foreword to *Shutting down the National Dream*, op. cit., pp. xi–xii). He feels that the Mach-3 Russian MiG-31 (which did not fly until December 1976) is "similar," suggesting that the requirement for the Arrow is validated by having been echoed on the Cold War's other side.

The design development of the Avro Arrow has been extensively documented: My summary of that development, absorbed from many sources, is in this case condensed from Zurakowski's article "The Flight of the Arrow," pp. 4–7, in the March/April 1987 issue of *Wingspan.* This is a impressively objective memoir from one who has consistently maintained that the Arrow should have been manufactured and deployed. In it, Zurakowski frankly discusses mistakes, unnecessary intra-departmental secrecy, and sheer ineptitude in design and testing that are absent from some book-length sources. A copy of that article was kindly supplied, among other valuable documents, by Anna Zurakowski.

One book consisting of nothing but declassified . . . memos, and another on how the RCAF planned to operate its new weapon: Respectively, those two books are Peter Zuuring, *The Arrow Scrapbook: Rebuilding a Dream and a Nation* (Dalkeith, Ontario: Arrow Alliance Press, 1999) and Lt. Col. T. F. J. Leversedge, foreword to *The Arrow: Avro CF-105 Mk.1 Pilot's Operating Instructions and RCAF Testing/ Basing Plans* (Erin, Ontario: Boston Mills Press, 1999). More than 40 years after the CF-105's cancellation, the Arrow cult thrives.

Whether the Arrow would be subject to the same instability at supersonic speeds that plagued . . . American breakthrough designs: "Yes," Zurakowski writes, "there was a problem with aircraft directional stability under some flight conditions. Which solution was right? First, to increase stability by aerodynamic changes"— such as additional fin area—"which would involve a weight penalty without guarantee that all flight conditions would be satisfactory. Or, second, introduce reliable electronic stability augmentation needed anyway for the weapons system.

"The latter choice was made, but it involved the risk of developing and proving the system on an aircraft otherwise unsafe under some conditions if the system failed. Loss of an aircraft in early development could be a disaster for the company."

Not to mention the pilot. From *Wingspan,* op. cit., p. 5.

Another cause for worry was the inability of anyone to fly the Arrow's simulator. Neither Zurakowski nor his scheduled first-flight chase pilot, Polish WW2 six-victory ace Wladyslaw (Spud) Potocki, could keep the simulator under control very long. It was an early such contraption with an IBM 704 computer at its heart. Zurakowski, consummate pilot that he was, could keep the simulator flying for three seconds. Potocki, whom Zurakowski credits with having been a better instrument pilot than he, lasted 11 seconds.

"What next?" Zurakowski wondered. "To develop this simulator to flyable condition, or to fly the actual aircraft? I recommended disregarding the simulator for the time being and going ahead with the first flight." Would the first prototype Arrow, RL 201, fly like the simulator? *Wingspan,* op. cit., p. 6.

"My answer was that I did not know": Wingspan, op. cit., p. 5. Zurakowski tells the same story in the Winter 1978 CAHS *Journal* report of his lecture on Arrow flight testing, op. cit., p. 104.

The one aspect of the five CF-105 prototypes that fulfilled all expectations was their performance: For convenience, I have based my account of Arrow flight testing on Zurakowski's article in *Wingspan,* op. cit., supplemented with dates and flight numbers taken from the valuable flight log provided by the Arrowheads, *Avro Arrow,* op. cit., pp. 115–19. Other informative resources in the same volume are the conclusions to Zurakowski's report on the Arrow's flying characteristics, p. 63, and the Arrowheads' extended treatment of Zurakowski's landing accident June 11, 1958, pp. 65–71. Bill Gunston's comments on the Arrow landing gear come from his *Early Supersonic Fighters of the West,* op. cit., p. 130.

"I exceeded 1,000 mph": Although Zurakowski modestly claims in his *Wingspan* article to have gone supersonic on the seventh flight of Arrow 201 April 18, the log in *Avro Arrow* indicates he did Mach 1.1 on 201's third flight, April 3. Then again, April 18's Mach 1.52, a nice round 1,000 mph, achieved "at 49,000 feet . . . on

climb, still accelerating, showing excess of thrust available" (*Avro Arrow,* op. cit., p. 63) even with temporary, stop-gap engines, was an enormously impressive claim to be able to make public, as the RCAF did (*CAHS Journal,* op. cit., p. 106). Zurakowski's peak speed in the CF-105 was Mach 1.89. That information was presumably classified at the time.

RL 201 . . . *ended up on its belly: Avro Arrow,* op. cit., seven-photo sequence showing accident, pp. 67–69.

"I suddenly realized that the aircraft was pulling to the left": Wingspan, op. cit., p. 7; *CAHS Journal,* op. cit., p. 106. Immediate subsequent quotes common to both sources.

Zurakowski made his last flight: Avro Arrow, op. cit., "Chronological Flight Log of the Avro Arrow," pp. 115–18.

CHAPTER 7: DE HAVILLAND CANADA

"We didn't even think of the de Havilland guys as test pilots": I hate to make Stan Haswell the fall guy here. His dig, part of my interview with him June 17, 1999, merely extends a friendly rivalry between A.V. Roe of Canada and de Havilland Canada that existed until DHC took over Avro's facilities at Malton and a contract with Douglas Aircraft to produce DC-9 wingsets after the Avro Arrow was cancelled in 1959.

I repeated Haswell's comment to retired DHC test pilot George Neal, at the end of my interview with him, also June 17, 1999, just to see how Neal would react. Neal is a DHC lifer who does not always see the humour in jibes about his company. But this time he laughed. "Yes," he replied, "but, you know, those graduates of the Empire Test Pilots' School fly only proven airplanes."

Touché. Neal certified the DHC-2 Beaver on floats (its trickiest configuration) and first-flighted and certified the DHC-3 Otter. His experiences with the DHC-4 Caribou, from the first flight on, were harrowing enough to show what unpleasant surprises can await the test pilots of aircraft that push limits other than sheer speed and altitude.

From 1946 to the end of 1998, the company sold 4,271 airplanes of eight different types of its own design: Production figures from Fred Hotson, *De Havilland in Canada* (Toronto: CANAV Books, 1999), p. 363. The total includes only aircraft built at Downsview and therefore does not count the 1,014 DHC-1 Chipmunks built in England or the 66 built in Portugal. Bombardier Regional Aircraft,

Downsview, is currently assembling 8Q-400 twin-turboprop airliners, lengthened developments of the DHC Dash-8.

A modified version of the Twin Otter ... is still being produced in China: The Harbin Y-12 has landing gear suitable for even more primitive airstrips and a different tail group, but it is recognizable as a Twin Otter derivative.

Capt. Geoffrey de Havilland ... was often his own test pilot: Capt. de Havilland co-founded what had become the most prolific combined aero engine-airframe manufacturing concern in the world by WW2. Although the capable Hubert Broad did most of the de Havilland company's first flights—and there were many of those between the wars—Capt. de Havilland made his last first flight, that of the prototype DH.94 Moth Minor monoplane, June 22, 1937. Capt. de Havilland soon turned the Moth Minor's flight testing over to Geoffrey Jr. and John Cunningham, the two of whom parachuted from a DH.94 that did not recover from its aftmost centre-of-gravity spin tests.

Two of de Havilland's three sons were killed flying the company's designs: John in a Mosquito involved in a wartime midair collision and Geoffrey Jr. in the breakup of the experimental tailless DH.108, likely at about the speed of sound, September 27, 1946. Geoffrey Jr. was de Havilland's CTP at the time.

Incidentally, Kurt Tank, chief designer of the German wartime Focke-Wulf Flugzeugbau, performed the first flight of his Ta 154 twin-engine night-fighter on July 1, 1943, nine months after it was ordered. The English test pilot Eric "Winkle" Brown, who interviewed Tank after the war, suggested Tank had misgivings about the bonding agents in his mostly wood Moskito. Indeed, the first two production examples broke up in the air. Tank may have done his own first flight partly for that reason (Capt. Eric Brown, *Testing for Combat* [Shrewsbury: Airlife Publishing, 1994], pp. 79–81). Brown considered the DH.108 "highly dangerous, mainly due to longitudinal instability," op. cit., p. 44.

Another company where test flying was undertaken by the design head was the Sikorsky Division of United Aircraft, where Igor Sikorsky spearheaded his organization's transition from fixed-wing to rotary-wing aviation by flight testing his new helicopter designs himself. In the sense that he was mastering a new form of manned flight, Sikorsky was following directly in the footsteps of the Wright Brothers, who felt that the problem of manned flight was less a matter of hardware than of piloting skill—of learning how to fly. That was also largely the case with the helicopter as it emerged during the Second World War. Very few pilots other than Sikorsky had any idea how to fly a rotary-wing aircraft with few, if any, of the airplane-like flight characteristics of the helicopter's immediate ancestor, the autogiro.

The Moths . . . extended those pleasures to new classes of airmen: And to the most celebrated pilot of all time, Charles Lindberg, who took the future Anne Morrow Lindberg up in a rented Moth for their first date on October 16, 1928, at Roosevelt Field, New York City. From A. Scott Berg, *Lindberg* (New York: G.P. Putnam's Sons, 1998), pp. 194–95.

"As the actual construction advanced day by day": Extended quote from Capt. Geoffrey de Havilland, *Sky Fever* (London: Hamish Hamilton, 1961), pp. 122–24. I have presented the excerpt, with the exception of insertions for clarity, exactly as it appears in the book but re-paragraphed it to break up some very long passages.

The date of the first flight of the DH.60 Moth comes from A. J. Jackson, *De Havilland Aircraft since 1915* (London: Putnam, 1962), p. 194. Information on subsequent Moth types is from the same source.

"Something outstanding in light aeroplanes": De Havilland goes on to write, "The success of the Moth was due very much to its being just the right size and of the simplest possible construction with sufficient reliable power to carry two people and some luggage. It had good cruising speed [70 mph] and range [about 300 miles], low landing speed [40 mph], was easy to handle and could be housed in a small garage by folding the wings. It was low in first cost [£650] and upkeep" (de Havilland, op. cit., p. 124).

Capt.—later, Sir—Geoffrey aptly named his light aircraft series Moths, partly, he explains in *Sky Fever,* pp. 122–23, because his interest as a lepidopterist told him there would be many other kinds of British moths after which he could name airplanes. Later types were called Fox Moth, Hornet Moth, Tiger Moth, and so on. The original Moth was called the Cirrus Moth because of its engine, which consisted of one-half of a 120hp Aircraft Disposal Co. (Airdisco) V/8, mounted on a new crankcase designed by Airdisco's Maj. Frank Halford and named the Cirrus I.

Nowhere were Moths fitted more frequently with floats and skis than in Canada: For a more complete account of the founding of the de Havilland Aircraft of Canada operation and its phenomenal sales successes with the Moth, see Hotson, *DH in Canada,* op. cit., pp. 20–69, and the present author's *Otter & Twin Otter: The Universal Airplanes* (Vancouver: Douglas & McIntyre, 1998), Chapter 4.

"You find a people with a big outlook": Francis St. Barbe, writing in 1927 in the de Havilland *Gazette* company publication after selling Canada's federal government 10 Moths for flying clubs and a further 23 for the Royal Canadian Air Force as trainers, quoted in Fred Hotson, *The de Havilland of Canada Story* (Toronto:

CANAV Books, 1983), p. 15. This book, long out of print, was recently superceded by the same author's updated and more lavishly produced *De Havilland in Canada*, op. cit., in which the equivalent passage is on p. 19. Hotson's account of the early years of DHC in the latter book begins on p. 20 and runs, with much new material and many never-before-published archival photographs, to p. 69.

Fred W. Hotson is another former DHC test and demonstration pilot. He was born in 1913, was hired by DHC directly from high school in 1935, and became a flying instructor with the British Commonwealth Air Training Plan in 1941. He was chosen to join the ferry flight department of the RAF's Transport Command in 1944, completing 20 aircraft delivery round trips to Europe and Africa. After earning his public transport licence and instrument rating after the war, Hotson made aircraft deliveries to South America and then became a bush pilot in northern Ontario and Quebec. In 1948 he began flying a Grumman Mallard for the Ontario Paper Company, eventually becoming the company's chief pilot, a post he held for 18 years. A highlight of his career was his 1966 study of the possibilities of using STOL aircraft to address the aviation needs of Afghanistan. He returned to DHC in 1967 as a test and demonstration pilot, primarily as a DHC-6 Twin Otter flight instructor, in which capacity he returned to Afghanistan with that country's first Twin Otter. He retired as a pilot with 13,000 hours on 25 types.

Hotson assumed the presidency of the Canadian Aviation Historical Society in 1969, serving for 15 years. His beautifully written account of the first east-west air crossing of the Atlantic, *The Bremen* (Toronto: CANAV Books, 1988), won him a nonfiction book award. He was inducted into Canada's Aviation Hall of Fame in 1998. Hotson's two histories of DHC document much that he experienced firsthand or personally gleaned from the individuals involved. Both books are clearly labours of love.

Erskine Leigh Capreol was DHC's first test pilot: Information on Leigh Capreol comes from *They Led the Way*, op. cit., p. 36; and Hotson, *DH in Canada*, op. cit., including a short profile on pp. 22–24 and scattered references to Capreol's contributions from pp. 22–45, covering Capreol's DHC years, 1928–34. *They Led the Way*, which outlines the careers of the outstanding personalities in Canadian aviation history, was published to commemorate the twenty-fifth anniversary of Canada's Aviation Hall of Fame in 1998. Capreol was elected to the hall in 1981.

After leaving Austin Airways in 1935, Capreol joined Noorduyn Aviation of Montreal as CTP. Although he did not make the first flight of the Noorduyn Norseman, Capreol did the subsequent early developmental flight testing on the float-, wheel-, and ski-equipped Norseman, considered the first wholly Canadian designed and built bush plane. John McDonough made the Norseman first flight—the most important between-wars first flight in Canada—November 14, 1935, on behalf of Lloyd's of London and filed a highly laudatory report on the Norseman's flight characteristics (Larry Milberry, *Air Transport in Canada*, Vol. 1 [Toronto: CANAV Books, 1997], p. 95).

McDonough called the Norseman "a distinct advance" in aircraft suited for Canadian geography and climate. Milberry notes that the Norseman prototype CF-AYO first flew on floats as an indication of Noorduyn's commitment to bush flying as its primary use. A great deal of developmental work remained to be done after McDonough's early flights, which focussed upon measuring its performance. Capreol did the development testing.

McDonough came to work at DHC early in 1939 (Hotson, *DH in Canada*, op. cit., p. 81) as managing director Phil Garratt's assistant, overseeing, for example, DHC's early wartime expansion. When the question of specialized engineering projects not directly related to Tiger Moth, Anson, or Mosquito production arose, it was thought best to remove those projects from the Downsview plant to a separate entity. Thus was born Central Aircraft Ltd. of London, Ontario. McDonough became its manager. Central Aircraft became a clearinghouse for Mosquitoes with manufacturing flaws and was the entry point to DHC for Fred Buller, later chief design engineer of the Beaver.

In 1939, Capreol was loaned to National Steel Car, Malton, to perform the first flight of its licence-built Westland Lysander STOL utility aircraft on August 16, and he was involved in early flight testing of North American Yale trainers. Soon afterward, he returned to Noorduyn to supervise what became a staff of seven pilots doing the flight testing of hundreds of Norsemans and the Yale's successor, the Harvard trainer. The Norsemans, in particular, were being adapted to handle much higher gross weights for service with the U.S. Army Air Forces.

For a portrait of Capreol as CTP at Noorduyn, see Duncan McLaren, *Bush to Boardroom: A Personal View of Five Decades of Aviation History* (Winnipeg: Watson & Dwyer, 1992). McLaren had a colourful career with the prewar Canadian Airways and the Hudson's Bay Co., as a test pilot with Noorduyn under Capreol during the war, and with Queen Charlotte Airlines and Pacific Western afterward.

An insight in McLaren's sketch of Capreol, known universally as "Cap," was the fairly loose rein Noorduyn's chief test pilot allowed his staff. The weather around Montreal being what it is, McLaren and the rest enjoyed lengthy periods of inactivity, offset by long days and hectic schedules, including much night flying, when weather permitted. Capreol also tried to maintain his pilots' proficiency in, of all skills, formation flying, in Harvard trainers.

"From time to time Capreol would get some of us together to practise formation flying," McLaren remembered. "Formation flying never did much for me but when the boss said fly, we flew. Cap was the leader and my position was usually immediately on his right. I think Alf Cockle flew on Cap's left side. Two of our other pilots made up the balance of the usual formation. One day after cruising around for a while Cap decided to take us on a dive over the airport.

"To this day I can remember thinking, 'I must be almost out of fuel in the right wing tank. I sure don't want to blow a tank and lose power in this manoeuvre. My wing man might collide with me.' So, as we tipped over into the dive I switched tanks. We were tucked in tight together and picking up speed when I had to pull up and hard right to avoid a collision with Cap. Of course I was having a fit because I wondered what my wing man was doing to avoid colliding with me. In a nutshell: Cap blew his tank, the engine quit, so he slowed down; the rest of us pulled out and up, inadvertently executing what used to be known as a 'Prince of Wales Feather'" (McLaren, op. cit., pp. 124–25).

Capreol may have been the only A Category instructor in Canada: David Fletcher and Doug MacPhail, *Harvard! The North American Trainers in Canada* (Dundas, Ontario: DCF Flying Books, 1990), say he was the only A Category instructor on p. 57, but I have seen that statement nowhere else.

Capreol and the DHC hangar crew also helped prepare the twin-engine DH.84 Dragon, Seafarer II: Special thanks to Blanche E. Warren, the widow of DHC's original Canadian employee Frank Warren, who kindly replied to my request for information about Leigh Capreol by providing copies of newspaper clippings detailing the Mollisons' preparations for what would have been an epic flight, as well as a photocopy of Fred Hotson's account on p. 33 of *The DHC Story*, op. cit.

Phil Garratt first joined the company in 1928 as a volunteer production test pilot: For a more detailed summary of Garratt's pre-DHC flying career, see Sean Rossiter, *Otter & Twin Otter* (Vancouver: Douglas & McIntyre, 1998), p. 44.

Among the pilots at Mount Dennis, in addition to Garratt, was W. F. (Freddie) Shaylor, who, like Garratt, sat on the board of DH England (Hotson, *DH in Canada,* p. 112). Shaylor owned Skyways Ltd., a flying training school that shared space at Mount Dennis with DHC.

The great Eddie Allen: Allen was "the most outstanding American test pilot of his generation" in the estimation of aviation historian Richard Hallion, writing in *Test Pilots: The Frontiersmen of Flight* (Washington, D.C.: Smithsonian Institution Press, 1981), p. 72. Before the Second World War it was unusual for aircraft manufacturers to employ test pilots for very long—if only because, like Boeing's prewar CTP Leslie Tower, they were all too often killed in accidents.

Spradbrow seldom gets credit for his wartime contribution: One outstanding example of an authoritative source that perpetuated this error about de Havilland Jr. making KB300's first flight is the 1974 edition of Peter Lewis' *The British Bomber since 1914* (London: Putnam & Co., 1974), p. 325. This myth was so pervasive that Joe Holliday, photographer/writer with DHC's employee publication *The de Havilland Mosquito,* in his memoir *Mosquito: The Wooden Wonder Aircraft of World War II* (Markham, Ontario: Paperjacks, 1980), p. 76, claimed in his original edition, published in 1970, that "The story of the turn of fate that gave Spradbrow the credit for making the 'unofficial' first flight of . . . KB300 is revealed here for the first time."

Geoffrey de Havilland Jr. did put on a show in KB300 five days after Spradbrow took her up for the first time. In the presence of Canada's munitions minister, the RCAF chief of air staff, flight pioneer J. A. D. McCurdy (who built Canada's first airplane, the Silver Dart, and flew it at Baddeck, Nova Scotia, in 1909), and 4,000 DHC employees, de Havilland took off into a vertical climb, did a wingover into a full-power dive, pulled out at hangar level, and did the first of several low high-speed passes over DHC's Downsview facility. He did climbing rolls and half-rolls, made his last pass with one propeller feathered, and then climbed and slow-rolled on one engine. Production manager R. J. Moffatt was heard to exclaim, "I still don't think it can be done" (Holliday, op. cit., p. 79).

Some credit is also due the 1943 flight test hangar gang who prepared KB300 for these first flights. Superintendent Fred Staines was "a six-foot, two-inch, big-fisted ex-flier and farmer" who had flown over much of northern Canada. His deputy was Don Whitmore, a sports buff. Jack Wilson, Sam Dunn, and George Sparrow prepared aircraft for flight and deliveries. Frank Bailey was manager of flight test administration (Holliday, op. cit., p. 96).

Spradbrow was a compact man . . . [with] "a very pleasant attitude": Frank Warren, the company's original Canadian employee, rose to become DHC's plant one superintendent, 1941–44, and thereafter became superintendent, flight test, Mosquito production, until January 1945. After late-war service at Greenwood, Nova Scotia, and Dorval as senior service engineer on Mosquitoes, he returned to Downsview as superintendent of postwar programs. Letter to the author from Blanche Warren, January 3, 2001.

Spradbrow and his staff . . . were soon climbing into Mosquito models that were different from the British ones: A photo in Hotson, *DH in Canada,* op. cit., p. 78, shows Spradbrow, Follett, Fisher, and de Bliquy beside an Anson, likely during 1941–42, when Anson production was at its height. They were DHC's early-war test pilots.

Frank Fisher, born in England in 1905, came to Canada in 1920 as a shipboard wireless operator, sailing the Great Lakes for three years. He was taking flying lessons in 1924 while working at his trade for the OPAS when he met the legendary bush pilot Harold Anthony "Doc" Oakes, who had himself just left the OPAS. Oakes was involved in pioneering northern mineral exploration from the air, for which he was awarded the first Trans-Canada (McKee) Trophy for service to aviation in 1928. He hired Fisher as a pilot for Northern Aerial Minerals Exploration because of Fisher's enthusiasm. Fisher went on to fly for three other outfits, living while flying for General Airways with his wife in a house at Chapleau owned by the older brother of Austin Airways founders Chuck and Jack. That connection led him to Austin Airways in March 1934, when Fisher became Austin's first full-time pilot. The last reference to Fisher in Larry Milberry's history of Austin Airways, from which the above material is taken, is April 1936, when Fisher flew a *Toronto Star* reporter to the Moose River gold mine in Nova Scotia, where three Toronto men were trapped underground. Larry Milberry, *Austin Airways, Canada's Oldest Airline* (Toronto: CANAV Books, 1985), esp. pp. 12–14. Anecdotes from Fisher's flying career, p. 18. Trip to Moose River, p. 22.

Wooll and his observer Tim Stone would bail out of a Mosquito at 17,000 feet: Hotson, DH *in Canada*, op. cit., pp. 89–90.

The dust-up . . . left the audience "looking on with their mouths agape": Holliday, *Mosquito*, op. cit., p. 122.

DHC's impressive flight test department [*was*] *reduced to the single person of George Turner:* Postwar CTP Russ Bannock (author interview March 5, 2000) recalls Bill Calder, who supervised the production of DHC's postwar Fox Moths, as having done some test flying as well. One of Calder's great contributions to DHC as plant manager was to hand-pick, from the many thousands of wartime employees, the relative few with whom the company thrived when it began building its own designs. This may have been one more instance of management at DHC having flight test savvy.

CHAPTER 8: RUSS BANNOCK

Chronology: I have interviewed Russ Bannock on three occasions, most recently March 5, 2000. I have previously summarized Bannock's wartime career on pp. 73–75 of my *The Immortal Beaver* (Vancouver: Douglas & McIntyre, 1996), the Chapter 8 Notes of which list five sources for that summary, footnotes 3–7, p. 177.

Other brief accounts of his career can be found in *Aces High,* op. cit., pp. 110–11, and in Oswald, ed., *They Led the Way,* op. cit., pp. 18–19, the short biographical citation that accompanied Bannock's induction into Canada's Aviation Hall of Fame in 1983.

"They knew we were there": This quote and the story of Bannock and Bruce's raid on Bourges Avord is from Ted Barris' *Behind the Glory: Training Heroes in Canadian Skies* (Toronto: Macmillan Canada, 1992). The quotes from Winston Churchill (p. 84) and from Bannock re the top 10 graduates of wings classes (p. 214), as well as the basis of the account of his and Bruce's first victory at Bourges Avord (pp. 276–77) are also from Barris. Material from Barris' retelling of the Bourges Avord mission is augmented by details supplied to me by Bannock by phone August 6, 2001.

Barris quotes Bannock in the caption for a photograph of him on the sixth page of the photo island in *Behind the Glory:* "Overseas, a pilot who completed a tour got an immediate Distinguished Flying Cross, but the fellow who slogged through 2,000 hours of instruction in Canada and turned out a lot of first-class pilots didn't automatically get a decoration. Instructors didn't get the recognition they deserved."

One payoff for instructing, though, was the possibility of applying in combat theory learned and taught. Of the pilots with the 418 Squadron Bannock commanded during September 1944, "virtually all," according to Barris, were former flying instructors, all of them with 1,000–2,000 hours in their logbooks. Barris names four: Don McFadyen (first BCATP grad to become an A2 instructor); Charlie Krause, who racked up 1,400 hours in two years at Dunnville, Ontario; Larry Walker, who left Dunnville with 1,650 hours; and John Evans, who had instructed at Calgary and Hagersville, Ontario.

From the time the unit was re-equipped with Mosquitoes between March 1943 and May 1944, 418 Squadron "enjoyed a period of great success," the authors of *Aces High* report: claims of 96¼ aircraft shot down in the air and 73 on the ground, making 418 the fourth-highest-scoring squadron in the RCAF. From June to August of 1944, with the emphasis on intercepting V-1s, 418 Squadron claimed 83 of those.

I am further grateful to Ted Barris for taking me to Russ Bannock's house on January 5, 1995, and introducing me to him.

As impressive as Bannock's war record and experience . . . were: Russ Bannock's wartime score is less subject to debate than those of many aces and is often quoted, as Hotson does (*The DHC Story,* op. cit., p. 117), at 11 aircraft and 19 buzz bombs destroyed—a fair rounded-off total. I have cited Bannock's score as itemized by the authors of *Aces High,* op. cit., pp. 110–11.

"Geoffrey de Havilland Jr. put me in the cockpit of a Vampire": Author interview with Russ Bannock, March 5, 2000.

"If you make a good trainer I'll sell it": Quoted by Hotson, *The DHC Story,* op. cit., pp. 115–16.

From lofting to first flight took seven months, 22 days: Hotson, *The DHC Story,* op. cit., p. 126.

Fillingham flew the Chipmunk, at most, half a dozen times: Author interview with Russ Bannock, March 5, 2000. Bannock's comment indicates how quickly home-grown test pilots took over DHC's postwar work load.

Fillingham did, however, do a good deal of development flying in England on Numbers 10 and 11 Chipmunk prototypes, which were extensively modified to meet the RAF's requirements. There were many changes: new disc brakes capable of differential braking for steering on the ground; a slightly more powerful Gipsy Major engine operating a vacuum pump, a generator, and a metal propeller; landing gear changes to put the point of contact farther forward and counteract the centre-of-gravity change due to installation of a radio; and batteries moved to the rear, eventually requiring a tailplane leading-edge anti-spin strake to aid in spin recovery. All of these and more had to be tested. Fillingham was rewarded for his efforts when he won the 1953 King's Cup at Southend in Number 11 Chipmunk, G-AKDN. From Bill Fisher, R. W. Brown, and T. Rothermel, *Chipmunk—The First Fifty Years* (Tunbridge Wells: Air-Britain Publications, 1996), pp. 3–5.

Bannock regarded the Chipmunk as a strong airplane, stressed to a "pretty high G factor": This quote and the following one regarding Charlie Stockford are from my interview with Bannock, March 5, 2000.

Stockford was flying with CF-DJF-X's centre-of-gravity in its aftmost position: The Stockford crash is described in Hotson, *The DHC Story,* op. cit., pp. 118–20. Hotson notes dryly, "The loss of test aircraft No. 2 was a blow to the program, even though the criteria on spins were firmly established."

So they went back up, spun again, and Bannock recovered: From author interview with Bannock, March 5, 2000.

Test pilot Bannock was happy with the Chipmunk's testing and development, but salesman Bannock was frustrated with the way it was marketed. The Canadian government decreed during the immediate postwar years that exports had to be paid for with hard currency, which at the time meant American dollars or pounds sterling. Many of the countries that wanted to buy Chipmunks didn't have hard currency. The RCAF was a reluctant buyer, taking only three of the initial series. In time, Bannock and Buck Buchanan proposed to the RCAF that it buy 50 for flying clubs and veteran pilot refresher courses. Finally, in 1955, the RCAF ordered 60 more as its primary trainer.

It wasn't that DHC wasn't thinking big. They sent Chipmunk demonstrators to the DH affiliates in Britain, Australia, India, New Zealand, South Africa, and South America, the authors of *Chipmunk,* op. cit., p. 3, note. Most of those examples found their way into private hands. The first major orders came from India, Thailand, and Egypt.

But, according to the authors of *Chipmunk,* it was the RAF Reserve Command's order for 750 that led to production at DH's Hatfield and Chester plants, accounting for 111 and 889 Chipmunks respectively, bringing U.K. production to 1,000. It seems fair to conclude that the RAF requirement for such basics as radios (and therefore electrical systems) made the Chipmunk the success it became. Meanwhile, DHC built 217 (including the Thai and Egyptian ones), and the Portuguese air force's Oficinas Gerais de Material Aeronautico (OGMA) built a further 66. Other air arms that used the Chipmunk include those of Lebanon, Denmark, Sri Lanka, Indonesia, Ghana, Iran, Iraq, Ireland, Kenya, Malaysia, Mozambique, New Zealand, Nigeria, Saudi Arabia, South Africa, Sweden, Switzerland, Syria, Uruguay, Zambia, and Zimbabwe. Many of these nations acquired their Chipmunks secondhand.

The total production of 1,283 wasn't bad for the first original design from a company just finding its postwar feet, although you could hardly blame Bannock for wanting to have built and sold more of them at home. Having a stop-gap replacement for the Tiger Moth stay in service for more than 40 years is impressive, too.

The resulting DHC-2 Beaver made the company: Dick Hiscocks was for the rest of his life bemused at how a hurried makeover of a two-thirds–designed airplane that involved compromise after compromise and turned a greyhound into a bulldog turned out to be the best-selling Canadian aircraft ever. He was the first to credit the flight test staff with developing the Beaver into the best of its kind in the world. By July 1947, the brawnier fuselage Hiscocks put behind the Beaver's big round engine was being tortured in a test rig, and by mid-August the prototype was assembled and ready for its first flight.

"The Beaver was coming along": Author interview with Bannock, March 5, 2000.

"It's a delightful aircraft to fly and I do not think we need to make many changes": Bannock quoted in Rossiter, *Immortal Beaver,* op. cit., p. 72.

[Bannock] took Dick Hiscocks by the elbow "and dragged me to the tail," as Hiscocks remembered it: Hiscocks told this story in a dinner speech to the Canadian Aeronautics and Space Institute, Vancouver branch, April 1993, p. 10 of transcript.

"In the early days of the Beaver, as soon as I'd come down from a flight": Author interview with Bannock, March 5, 2000.

Neal was returning not just to DHC but to his family: DHC Neals, in order of age: father John F. Neal Sr.; sister Kay, the eldest; John, head of the engine shop 1940–41, head of the propeller shop at this time; George; Evelyn Neal LoPatriello; and Doris Neal, who worked there for about a year.

"Eventually . . . I hired George Neal": Bannock makes clear how much he admires George Neal's talent as a pilot, but the two are opposites in personal style. Neal started with DHC in the late 1930s as a mechanic in the engine shop, and he remains a hands-on restorer of old airplanes. He never became an executive type, even as chief test pilot, but he did make certain concessions, which Bannock appreciated. "After George had been a test pilot for a year or so, we moved to our new factory at the south end of Downsview (we had been at the north end). And we built a dining room for sort of the senior people, and we advised George that he was a member of the staff of the company and we would like him to use the staff dining room. And it took about six months to get him to put a suit on. Eventually I persuaded him to have a suit available so he could go in and have a meal." Author interview with Russ Bannock, March 5, 2000.

The most spectacularly successful sales demonstration of any Canadian aircraft: Author interview with Russ Bannock, January 5, 1995. The story is told in greater detail in Rossiter, *Immortal Beaver,* op. cit., pp. 87–91, an account that includes a short biography of Balchen, a native of Norway who was the first U.S. armed forces officer to order the Beaver.

Just as important, the Beaver sale paved the way for continued sales of DHC types to the U.S. Army. The Otter corrected the Beaver's minor flaw of not necessarily being able to get out of any strip it could land on, doing so with twice the payload. The twin-engine Caribou tripled the Otter's payload. And the Twin Otter corrected what some saw as the Otter's niggling little flaws with twin-engine reliability and nose wheel landing gear for better crosswind field performance.

"I just put [Neal] in the airplane," Bannock smiles: Author interview with Bannock, March 5, 2000.

Bannock ... was practically guaranteeing quantity production of the company's designs: His greatest sales coup was the DHC-4 Caribou. Not in terms of numbers alone, of course. The U.S. Army bought 169 Caribous. But that sale led eventually to a production run of 307 of a design priced at several times that of the Otter; a design that was superceded after 1965 by 121 copies of the Caribou's turbine-engine development, the DHC-5 Buffalo; and a design that pointed the company toward DHC's main business of the last quarter of the twentieth century: regional, feeder, and commuter airliners. The Caribou was Bannock's finest moment from a sales point of view because, as a result of his presentation, the Army committed itself within days to buying five test models right from the outset of the program, almost guaranteeing a production run without knowing how the prototypes would behave.

[Neal] was at the controls of third prototype CF-LKI-X with DOT test pilot Walter Gadzos in the right-hand seat: For a more complete account of Neal and Gadzos' mishap, see Chapter 9 of this book, "George Neal: Testing from the Inside Out."

See also "The Summer of a Thousand Stalls," by F. A. (Ted) Johnson, in Burt Ellis, ed., *De Havilland, You STOL My Heart Away* (Toronto: de Havilland Human Resources Department, 1993), pp. 94–98.

What [Bannock] has called DHC's "biggest engineering project": This and the subsequent two quotes are from Bannock's memoir on his return to DHC in 1975, "Marketing the Dash-7," in *STOL My Heart Away,* op. cit., pp. 172–74. Dash-7 and Dash-8 production and sales figures are from Hotson, *The DHC Story,* op. cit., p. 365.

A further footnote to Bannock's return as CEO: Bannock had resigned from DHC in 1968 over the issue of ceasing production of the Beaver and the Otter. In 1977, as CEO, he instructed DHC's engineering staff to design a small single-engine utility aircraft—a PT6 turboprop-powered Beaver-Otter replacement—and got his board's approval. But the project was subsequently dropped by his successors. Bannock ruefully noted in 1993 that the "similar" Cessna Caravan single-engine utility transport, conceived in 1978, had sold 500 copies by then and was still going strong. He rejoined Bannock Aerospace in July 1978, again addressing the demand for DHC airplanes, some of them long out of production.

CHAPTER 9: GEORGE NEAL

Chronology: My sources for this condensed biography of George Neal include the four interviews I have had with him, the first on June 16, 1995 (on Beaver flight testing); May 28, 1997 (Otter); June 17, 1999, and March 12, 2000 (the crash of Caribou

LKI). Neal has told me the story of the crash at least three times. Another worth-while source on his career is the two-page bio that accompanied his induction into the Canadian Aviation Hall of Fame in 1995 and the somewhat different version of the same bio that appears in Oswald, ed., *They Led the Way*, op. cit. Additional de-tails of Neal's career, including such tidbits as the name of his first flying instructor and his first rates of pay, come from an undated tape of a talk by Neal, recorded by the Canadian Aviation Historical Society, in which he describes the Caribou crash.

Among later overhauls and conversions Neal tested: For George Neal, the list of aircraft types repaired and overhauled during the immediate postwar period is a point of personal pride: he had been one of the hand-picked mechanics doing postwar engine and propeller work before he became a test pilot with DHC. He notes that DHC was turning out 50 new aircraft or overhauls per month with a skeleton work force of 2,000.

The de Havilland Canada DHC-4 Caribou is a medium-sized, twin-engine, short takeoff and landing transport: My brief history of the Caribou depends on several sources, among them Chapter 7, "The Caribou," from Fred Hotson's *The DHC Story*, op. cit., pp. 192–221 and appendices; Wayne Mutza's *C-7 Caribou in Action* (Carrollton, Texas: Squadron/Signal Publications, 1993); "Globetrotting Rein-deer" by Ken Ellis, in *Air Enthusiast 74*, March–April 1998, pp. 20–33; and "Aircraft in Detail: DHC-4 Caribou," by Alan W. Hall, in *Scale Aircraft Modelling*, February 1998, pp. 576–91. A previous summary by the present author of the Caribou's difficult gestation can be found in Chapter 12, "DHC Survives the DHC-4," in *Otter & Twin Otter*, op. cit., pp. 123–35.

"We were supposed to demonstrate that maximum dive speed was free of flutter": Author interviews with George Neal June 17, 1999 and March 12, 2000. A tape recorder failure made a repeat interview necessary, although a set of written notes from the earlier one made possible an enriched account. Neal was most gracious about covering the same ground twice.

Flutter is defined . . . as "Rapid and uncontrolled oscillation of a flight control surface": My authority on engineering and aeronautical matters is Dale Crane's *Dictionary of Aeronautical Terms*, 3rd ed. (Newcastle, Washington: Aviation Supplies & Academics, 1997); in this case, p. 223.

"The elevator forces were fairly heavy, and the speed slow to decrease": Neal consulted a copy of his report on the last flight of LKI during our interview of March 12, 2000, and he read this and the following sentence from it.

"You go up and you do a systematic check": Neal has patiently tried to explain test flight and the evolution of its techniques to me each time we have spoken. This paragraph, from June 16, 1995, is fitted into a passage from our conversation of March 12, 2000.

In early 1940, Neal was photographed: That photo appears on p. 24 of the present author's *The Immortal Beaver,* op. cit. Information in the following paragraph comes from my first interview with Neal, on the subject of the Beaver's flight test program, taped June 16, 1995.

"The early test pilots . . . had no instrumentation": Author interview with George Neal, March 12, 2000.

"A stall is where the airflow breaks down all across the wing": Author interview with George Neal, June 16, 1995.

He also flew the Otter's subsequent two-year development and certification programs: The Otter, when re-engined with a turbine, has been called the biggest single-engine transport aircraft in the world. This is an arguable proposition. The claim is made in the sales promotion literature for the Vazar Dash-3 PT6A turbine Otter conversion. It would be easier to justify a claim that the Otter is the world's most efficient single-engine load carrier.

The aircraft most similar to the Otter, the Russian Antonov An-2 "Colt" biplane utility aircraft, is one-third heavier when loaded and more powerful than the stock Otter, but it carries a lighter load. Coincidentally, the first licensed engine conversion for the Otter involves transplanting a derivative of the An-2's 1,000hp Polish PZL radial engine and four-bladed propeller in place of the Otter's 600hp Pratt & Whitney R-1340 radial and shortened Hamilton-Standard DC-3 three-blade prop. This conversion is offered by Airtech Canada Aviation Services. Using the PZL engine increases the Otter's efficiency advantage over the An-2, whereas Vazar's turbine conversion and Viking Air's forthcoming turbine/wing upgrade move the Otter into an entirely new class, lifting the turbo-Otter's disposable load by half, to 1.5 tons.

"The thing that I didn't think could happen": Author interview with George Neal, March 12, 2000.

CHAPTER 10: BOB FOWLER

Chronology: My mini-biography of Bob Fowler has as its sources lengthy interviews with him on May 28 and August 21, 1997, and March 6 and 7, 2000;

subsequent follow-up telephone conversations and written correspondence; his profile in Oswald, ed., *They Led the Way*, op. cit., pp. 53–54; and the many references to him in Fred Hotson's histories of DHC, op. cit.

Worked with National Aeronautics and Space Administration's Ames Flight Research Center, Moffett Field, California, to develop and evaluate Augmentor Wing Jet Research Aircraft: To create the Boeing/de Havilland/NASA Augmentor Wing Jet STOL Research Aircraft, Boeing took a stock Buffalo, removed its engines and nine feet from each wingtip, and installed two Rolls-Royce Spey turbofan jet engines, the hot gases of which exhausted through swivelling nozzles much like those of the Harrier jump-jet. Bypass fan air from the engines was ducted to the oversized flaps, "blowing" them to increase efficiency. The Augmentor Wing, so named for the increased airflow over its flap and aileron span, demonstrated 7½-degree approaches at 63–69 mph and takeoff rolls as short as 300 feet (and 450 feet to clear a 35-foot screen). Fowler flew the Augmentor Wing with project research pilot Dr. Bob Innis shortly after its first flight May 1, 1972.

Information on Augmentor Wing: Hotson, *The DHC Story, op. cit.*, pp. 227–29; Paul F. Borchers, James A. Franklin, and Jay W. Fletcher, *Flight Research at Ames: Fifty-Seven Years of Development and Validation of Aeronautical Technology* (Ames Research Center, California: National Aeronautics and Space Administration, 1998), pp. 50–51, courtesy of NASA Ames test pilot Bill Hindson; and Bowers, *Boeing Aircraft since 1916*, op. cit., p. 549.

[The B-25] was "a peerless aircraft to fly": Author interview with Bob Fowler, May 28, 1997.

[Milstead-Warren] was ... "one peach of a pilot": Author interview with Fowler, March 6 and 7, 2000.

You passed [high school maths and science] ... "or you became a gunner": Author interview with Fowler, March 6 and 7, 2000.

[Pennfield Ridge] was ... "a solid little British enclave": This and the succeeding two quotes are from "Ventura Lost" by Bob Fowler, CAHS *Journal,* Spring 1999, pp. 4–11 and 35.

"Sometimes ... we can embark on what seems a perfectly innocuous event": "Ventura Lost," op. cit., p. 5. Because much of the tension is lost in my condensation of Fowler's account, I commend the original version to the reader's attention. Fowler is a great storyteller and a very graceful writer.

It was mid-afternoon August 6 when Fowler's Mitchell, Orange Four, was hit by flak at 12,000 feet: Fowler has told me this story at least twice. For this occasion, he checked the notes he made at the time it happened, notes he plans to use in his own writing about what he calls the B-25 "prang." He was also kind enough to answer questions, notably during a telephone conversation August 29, 2001.

"Russ and I both stayed at an air officer's club for Canadians": Author interview with Fowler, March 6 and 7, 2000.

"I was very impressed with him," Bannock says of Fowler: This and the following quote come from an interview I had with Russ Bannock, March 5, 2000.

"You had to be a salesman first," Fowler remembers: Author interview with Bob Fowler, March 6 and 7, 2000.

That April, another Otter crashed at Goose Bay: Using evidence common to both crashes, the Royal Aeronautical Establishment's Fred Jones traced the problem to a valve in the flap hydraulic system; prevented from closing by a .02-inch metal particle left during the machining process, it failed to maintain pressure in the system, allowing the flaps to suddenly retract in the slipstream. Their sudden closure compounded the effects of previously set nose-down stabilizer trim.

The Otter crash investigation resulted in the addition of a hydraulic filter and a back-up shuttle valve with a shear edge, and an added interlinked tab between flaps and elevator that re-trims the elevator setting for any flap position. This linkage was fitted to all Otters and Twin Otters.

Fowler and Johnson embarked upon what Johnson later called "The Summer of a Thousand Stalls": Johnson, "The Summer of a Thousand Stalls," op. cit., pp. 94–98.

"I had no such conflict that was not open, healthy, and productive": Fowler's notation on draft chapter manuscript, December 22, 2001.

With its new T64s, the Caribou could exceed its maximum level flight speed on one engine: From Hotson, *The DHC Story*, op. cit. Pages 208–10 offer a good summary of the T64 Caribou program. Fowler calls this assertion a "slight exaggeration."

"At one time in the air we had both of them go into reverse": Bob Fowler telephone interview with the author, August 20, 2001. This account of the T64 Caribou mid-air propeller blade reversal is assembled from several highly technical conversations with Fowler. His logbooks do not yield a date for this otherwise

unforgettable event. Modern constant-speed propeller blades change pitch as the air load in the propeller changes. They do this to keep the speeds at which the governor drives them within pre-set revolutions-per-minute pilot settings. In that way, propeller governors serve as the aerial equivalents of automobile transmissions. If the engine rpm increases beyond the number for which the propeller governor is set by the pilot, the pitch of the propeller's blades will increase, or become more coarse, and the propeller rpm will slow down. When the engine rpm decreases below that for which the governor is set, the propeller blade-angle pitch decreases, becoming finer, decreasing the air load on the propeller, allowing the propeller to speed back up to its governor setting. My explanation here is adapted from Dale Crane's *Dictionary of Aeronautical Terms*, 3rd ed. (Newcastle, Washington: Aviation Supplies & Academics, 1997). In a free turbine such as the T64 (unlike a piston engine), the propellers and engines are separately controlled.

As Fowler recalled their pre-flight briefing, "Georgas said, 'The way the curves are tending to go with what we've done so far, and the way everything on the ground [indicates], in the absence of a fine pitch stop, there's not a thing to prevent the thing going into reverse if we get too close to where the rpm change for a change in blade pitch reverses.'

"This is as a result of a thing called advance ratio. That's the twist on the blade. The blade gets finer toward the tip, and coarser towards the hub. And so the most effective part of the blade is out toward the tip. Well, if more of the blade goes to reverse before the rest of the blade goes to reverse, the propeller responds the wrong way from going to fine, because it's increasing negative pitch on the tip in an effort to slow the propeller down, and what's happening is, the propeller's going faster. And so it keeps trying to do that, and it just drove it right to reverse." Author interview with Bob Fowler, March 6 and 7, 2000.

The Buffalo . . . proved capable of lifting payloads up to five tons from almost any relatively smooth surface three football fields long: Including water. The experimental "Bell-Bottom Buffalo," with its rubberized, inflated Bell Air Cushion Landing System under-fuselage hull, could operate like a flying boat. Fowler did its initial testing in 1975. The last batch of Buffaloes, with more powerful T64s, could take nine tons, at the cost of a longer takeoff run. Information on "Bell-Bottom Buffalo" mainly from Hotson, *The DHC Story*, op. cit., pp. 226–27.

"The Buffalo was a big thing. It had a T-tail": Author interview with Fowler, March 6 and 7, 2000.

"The managing director asked me whether we were going to finish the Buffalo on time": Author interview with Fowler, March 6 and 7, 2000.

[Fowler] had done the first flight tests of the engine that powered the Twin Otter: A light twin-engine airplane had been on the agenda at DHC for as long as anyone could remember—certainly through the 10 years that elapsed between the first flight of the single-engine Otter in 1951 and the first flights of the engine that made a twin Otter possible. All of DHC's 1950s' schemes for a twin-engine Otter were defeated by the weight of cast-iron radial engines like the ones that had powered the Beaver, the Otter, and the Caribou. The Otter's P&W R-1340 radial produces 600hp but weighs 650 pounds. The weight of two cancelled out any worthwhile payload increase from the twin engines, and an engine-out situation would have meant landing was unavoidable and imminent.

Suddenly, in 1961, there appeared the PT6 turboprop, which weighed only 230 pounds and initially produced 400 shaft horsepower. The extra 200hp of two later PT6s over the R-1340 was a useful increase (with more to come from future PT6 development). An appropriately sized aircraft powered by two PT6s could climb on one of them. And each PT6 on the Twin Otter was more reliable than the single-engine Otter's R-1340, by far. So the Twin Otter was a very safe airplane.

Flying the x-Otter with its PT6s was one more way Fowler inadvertently prepared [to fly] the Twin Otter: It was a coincidence that preliminary design of the Twin Otter quickly resolved itself into a layout that looked a lot like the x-Otter 3682. Two programs, one experimental and one the design of a new commercial airplane, produced similar-looking results—with the obvious exception that the jet in the x-Otter's fuselage was replaced with seats in the Twin Otter. For Fowler, though, one important link between the two aircraft was that, after flying the x-Otter for slightly more than two years on twin-PT6 power, he found himself almost immediately doing the first flight of a new commercial airplane powered by two of those same engines.

"It was called the twin-engine Otter": Author interview with Fowler, March 6 and 7, 2000.

Dick Hiscocks . . . pointed out in 1993 that . . . the Twin Otter represented 10 to 20 percent of all scheduled aircraft: "Whither STOL?" by Richard D. Hiscocks, in Ellis, ed., *De Havilland, You STOL My Heart Away,* op. cit., pp. 269–76.

Fowler, with test pilot A. M. "Mick" Saunders and flight test engineer Barry Hubbard, did the Twin Otter's initial flight May 20, 1965: Mick Saunders was another of the DHC flight test engineers who was a very fine pilot himself. From Montreal, fluent in French, a McGill Engineering graduate, Saunders was a 2TAF Typhoon pilot during the war and flew Vampire jets during the 1950s with the RCAF reserve and at DHC.

In my March 6 and 7, 2000, interview with Fowler, he called Saunders "the best flight test engineer and pilot I ever flew with . . . Always the gentleman. Very quiet guy. He wouldn't argue. He'd debate, but he wouldn't argue. Tremendous detail guy. He just thought his job was to make your job as easy as he could possibly make it. He would watch everything. When you're flying a prototype like that you're looking at the flight instruments constantly and you want that thing to be within a knot of the planned speed. You don't have time to be looking at a new engine installation to see if everything's working all right. Mick's watching it like a hawk."

Accordingly, Fowler selected Saunders to fill the right-hand seat on his first flights of the Buffalo, the Twin Otter, and the Dash-7 and Dash-8 regional turboprop airliners. Saunders, having retired from DHC, was killed in England flight testing an overhauled Dash-7 in March 1999.

Barry Hubbard had his own moment of glory at DHC as the flight engineer in a Buffalo crew featuring pilot Tom Appleton and co-pilot Bill Pullen on a flight that took 17 minutes from takeoff to touchdown, reaching 30,000 feet, and setting six world time-to-climb records—beating, among others, a four-engine Lockheed Orion maritime patrol aircraft's time to 29,500 feet by almost two and a half minutes. Hotson, *The DHC Story,* op. cit., pp. 225–26.

Martin Sharp, historian of DH England, was there: Sharp is the author of *DH: An Account of de Havilland History* (London: Faber and Faber, 1960), which Capt. Geoffrey de Havilland recommended in the preface to his autobiography, *Sky Fever,* op. cit. News of Capt. de Havilland's death arrived at Downsview May 21, 1965, the day after the Twin Otter's first flight. Story and subsequent quotes from author interview with Fowler by phone, August 10, 2001.

"I used to kid the engineers . . . about the wheels being not terribly wide-track": My account of Bob Fowler's rock 'n' roll runway tests of the prototype Twin Otter is from a telephone interview I conducted with him on August 20, 2001.

"It's a completely different airplane with those great big 30-foot floats": My account of Bob Fowler's float porpoising tests is from my interview with him March 6 and 7, 2000, as is Fowler's outline of his flight test philosophy.

BIBLIOGRAPHY

A.V. ROE OF CANADA

Brown, Peter Harry, and Pat H. Broeske. *Howard Hughes: The Untold Story*.
New York: Penguin Books, 1996.

Callwood, June. "The Day the Iroquois Flew." *Maclean's,* February 1, 1958,
pp. 11–13, 43–46.

Floyd, Jim. *The Avro Jetliner*. Erin, Ontario: Boston Mills Press, 1986.

Haswell, Stan. "Testing the CF-100." *CAHS* (Canadian Aviation Historical Society)
Journal, Fall 1983, pp. 86–93.

McGregor, Gordon. *The Adolescence of an Airline*. Montreal: Air Canada, 1980.

Mellberg, William. "The World's Second—North America's First." *Air Enthusiast*
46, June–August 1992, pp. 52–59.

Middleton, Don. *Test Pilots: The Story of British Test Flying, 1903–1984*. London:
William Collins Sons, 1985.

Milberry, Larry. *The Avro CF-100*. Toronto: CANAV Books, 1981.

Organ, Richard, Ron Page, Don Watson, and Les Wilkinson. *Avro Arrow*. Erin,
Ontario: Boston Mills Press, 1982.

Page, Ron. *Canuck CF-100 All-Weather Fighter*. Erin, Ontario: Boston Mills Press,
1981.

Peck, Earl G. "B-47 Stratojet." In Robin Higham and Carol Williams, eds., *Flying
Combat Aircraft of the USAAF-USAF*, Vol. 2. Ames, Iowa: Iowa State University
Press, 1978. Pp. 82–88.

Pickler, Ron, and Larry Milberry. *Canadair: The First 50 Years.* Toronto: CANAV Books, 1995.
Stewart, Greig. *Shutting down the National Dream.* Toronto: McGraw-Hill Ryerson, 1991.

JIMMY ORRELL

Holmes, Harry. Obituary, "J. H. 'Jimmy' Orrell." *Aeroplane,* October 1988, p. 611.
Jones, Barry. "Avro's Flying Lab." *Aeroplane,* September 1995, pp. 34–42.
Middleton, Don. "Test Pilot Profile No. 1: J. H. 'Jimmy' Orrell." *Aeroplane,* October 1980, pp. 512–14.

BILL WATERTON

Halliday, Hugh. *242 Squadron: The Canadian Years.* Stittsville, Ontario: Canada's Wings, 1981.
Waterton, W. A. "Bill." *The Quick and the Dead.* London: Frederick Muller, 1956.

JAN ZURAKOWSKI

Bialkowski, W. L. "Janusz Zurakowski: Portrait of a World-Famous Pilot." October 1998. *The Avro Archive.* http://tsw.odyssey.on.ca/~dmackechnie/Welcome.html
Cope, Peter. "The Zurabatic Cartwheel." *Flying,* May 1966, p. 69.
Melady, John. *Pilots: Canadian Stories from the Cockpit.* Toronto: McClelland & Stewart, 1989.
Norris, Geoffrey. *Jet Adventure.* London: Phoenix House, 1962.
Straight Arrow: The Jan Zurakowski Story. 1998. White Pine Pictures.
Zurakowski, Jan. "Flight of the Arrow." *Wingspan,* March–April 1987, pp. 4–7.
Zurakowski, Jan. "Test Flying the Arrow and Other High-Speed Jet Aircraft." *CAHS Journal,* Winter 1979, pp. 100–13.

DE HAVILLAND AIRCRAFT OF CANADA

de Havilland, Capt. Geoffrey. *Sky Fever.* London: Hamish Hamilton, 1961.
Ellis, Ken. "Globetrotting Reindeer." *Air Enthusiast 74,* March–April 1998, pp. 20–33.
Fisher, Bill, R. W. Brown, and T. Rothermel. *Chipmunk: The First Fifty Years.* Tunbridge Wells: Air-Britain Publications, 1996.
Holliday, Joe. *Mosquito: The Wooden Wonder Aircraft of World War II.* Markham, Ontario: Paperjacks, 1980.
Hotson, Fred. *De Havilland in Canada.* Toronto: CANAV Books, 1999.
Hotson, Fred. "Flight Test." *Canadian Aviation,* Special Issue: *De Havilland at 60,* June 1988, pp. 16–20.

Hotson, Fred. *The de Havilland of Canada Story.* Toronto: CANAV Books, 1983.

Jackson, A. J. *De Havilland Aircraft since 1915.* London: Putnam, 1962.

Rossiter, Sean. *Otter & Twin Otter: The Universal Airplanes.* Vancouver: Douglas & McIntyre, 1998.

Sharp, Martin C. *DH: An Account of de Havilland History.* London: Faber and Faber, 1960.

RUSS BANNOCK

Bannock, Russ. "Marketing the Dash-7." In Burt Ellis, ed., *De Havilland, You STOL My Heart Away.* Toronto: de Havilland Human Resources Department, 1993. Pp. 172–74.

Bannock, Russ. "Selling Uncle Sam." *Canadian Aviation,* Special Issue: *De Havilland at 60,* June 1988, pp. 22–25.

Barris, Ted. *Behind the Glory: Training Heroes in Canadian Skies.* Toronto: Macmillan Canada, 1992.

Rossiter, Sean. *The Immortal Beaver.* Vancouver: Douglas & McIntyre, 1996.

BOB FOWLER

Fowler, Bob. "Ventura Lost." *CAHS Journal,* Spring 1999, pp. 4–11 and 35.

Johnson, Ted. "The Summer of a Thousand Stalls." In Bert Ellis, ed., *De Havilland, You STOL My Heart Away.* Toronto: de Havilland Human Resources Department, 1993. Pp. 94–98.

TEST PILOTS AND FLIGHT TESTING

Brown, Eric. *Testing for Combat.* Shrewsbury: Airlife Publishing, 1994.

Hallion, Richard. *Test Pilots: The Frontiersmen of Flight.* Washington, D.C.: Smithsonian Institution Press, 1988.

Johnson, Brian. *Test Pilots.* London: BBC Publications, 1986.

Rawlings, John, and Hilary Sedgewick. *Learn to Test, Test to Learn: The History of the Empire Test Pilots' School.* Shrewsbury: Airlife Publishing, 1991.

Shores, Christopher, and Clive Williams. *Aces High.* London: Grub Street, 1994.

FURTHER RESOURCES

Bowers, Peter M. *Boeing Aircraft since 1916.* Annapolis: Naval Institute Press, 1989.

Crane, Dale. *Dictionary of Aeronautical Terms,* 3rd ed. Newcastle, Washington: Aviation Supplies & Academics, 1997.

Gunston, Bill. *Early Supersonic Fighters of the West.* London: Ian Allen, 1976.

Gunston, Bill. *The Illustrated Encyclopedia of Aircraft Armament.* New York: Orion Books, 1988.

Gunston, Bill. *World Encyclopedia of Aero Engines,* 3rd ed. Yeovil: Patrick
    Stephens, 1996.

Lewis, Peter. *The British Bomber since 1914.* London: Putnam & Co., 1974.

Lewis, Peter. *The British Fighter since 1912.* London: Putnam, 1965.

Milberry, Larry. *Air Transport in Canada,* Vol. 1. Toronto: CANAV Books, 1997.

Oswald, Mary E., ed. *They Led the Way: Members of Canada's Aviation Hall of
    Fame.* Wetaskiwin, Alberta: Canada's Aviation Hall of Fame, 1999.

➤ INDEX

Mk.4 making Cartwheel possible,
232; Zura says spins, Cartwheel, easy
in Meteor, 232–33
Zurakowski, Anna Danielska, 6, 104, 120
Zurakowski, Bronislaw, 114, 234
Zurakowski, s/l Jan, 2, 6, 10, 23–24, 33,
95; chronol., 99–100; awarded McKee
Trophy (1958), 100; youth, 104; dives
CF-100 supersonic, 115–16; on CF-105
performance advance, 121–22; on CF-
105 landing gear specs, 122–23; fine-
tuning CF-105's auto-stabilizer
system, 123; CF-105 landing gear
accident, 123–24; flight test
philosophy, 235–36